On the Muslim Question

The Public Square Book Series
Princeton University Press
Ruth O'Brien, Series Editor

On the Muslim Question

Anne Norton

Princeton University Press
Princeton and Oxford

Copyright © 2013 by Princeton University Press

Published by Princeton University Press,
41 William Street, Princeton, New Jersey 08540
In the United Kingdom: Princeton University Press,
6 Oxford Street, Woodstock, Oxfordshire OX20 1TW
press.princeton.edu

All Rights Reserved

Library of Congress Cataloging-in-Publication Data
Norton, Anne.
On the Muslim question / Anne Norton.
p. cm. — (The public square book series)
Includes bibliographical references and index.
ISBN 978-0-691-15704-7 (alk. paper)
1. Islamic sociology. 2. Islam—Social aspects. 3. Islam—
Economic aspects. 4. Islam—Political aspects. I. Title.
BP173.25.N67 2013
305.6'97—dc23
2012030799

British Library Cataloging-in-Publication Data is available

This book has been composed in Sabon

Printed on acid-free paper. ∞

Printed in the United States of America

10 9 8 7 6 5 4 3 2 1

On the surface, it looks like an embroidered garment, full of colored figures and dyes. Everybody loves it and loves to reside in it, because there is no human wish or desire that this city does not satisfy. The nations emigrate to it, and reside there, and it grows beyond measure. People of every race multiply in it, and this by all kinds of copulation and marriages. . . . Strangers cannot be distinguished from the residents. All kinds of wishes and ways of life are to be found in it. . . . The bigger, the more civilized, the more populated, the more productive, and the more perfect it is, the more prevalent and the greater are the good and the evil it possesses.
— al Farabi on the democratic city

Liberty, Equality, Fraternity.

Contents

Foreword by Ruth O'Brien   ix

Introduction   On the Muslim Question:
 Philosophy, Politics, and the Western Street   1

Part I   Muslim Questions

Chapter 1   Freedom of Speech   15
Chapter 2   Sex and Sexuality   45
Chapter 3   Women and War   67
Chapter 4   Terror   82
Chapter 5   Equality   94
Chapter 6   Democracy   118

Part II   In the Western Street

Chapter 7   Where Is Europe?   141
Chapter 8   "Islamofascism" and the
 Burden of the Holocaust   164
Chapter 9   In the American Desert   176
Chapter 10   There Is No Clash of Civilizations   195

Acknowledgments   229
Notes   233
Index   247

Foreword

Ruth O'Brien

Anne Norton's *On the Muslim Question* upends established political and academic arguments. It is a Public Square book given its many compelling turns of phrase, like "as Jews became American, Americans became more Jewish." Readers will be taken by surprise as Norton's insights are explicated in simple language. The book is free of academic jargon and cultural studies clichés.

Yet *On the Muslim Question* is a Public Square book not just because of its aesthetic construction. It is political theory. It is breathtaking in its vision, its scope, and its ambition. Just as the Jewish question heralded a broadly humane appeal, *On the Muslim Question* calls for the emancipation of Muslims—not for Muslims, not for Muslim societies, and not for Islam, but to ensure nothing less than the survival of Western civilization, by guaranteeing the Enlightenment values and institutions we claim to hold so dear. Assuaging false fears and dispelling unfounded threats about Muslims and Islam is essential for politics and philosophy in Europe and the United States.

Norton shows how opposition to Islam diverts our attention from the questions of our day—"the status of women, sexuality, equality and difference, faith and secularism." Piece by piece, she takes apart the political and philosophical assumptions underlying the clumsy Western condemnation of Islam—false assumptions about freedom of speech and freedoms regarding sex and sexuality. She juxtaposes women and war, unraveling, for instance, the story about Lynndie England, the American soldier "pointing cheerily" at the genitals of male prisoners at Abu Ghraib. Norton demonstrates that such "sexual humiliation" strategies "transformed a common human vulnerability into a vulnerability peculiar to one culture and a site of the power of Western over Arab culture."

What makes this a Public Square book is that Norton unpacks so many complex contemporary events, like the mullahs' outcries against the Danish cartoons of Muhammad, to show that Muslims have been miscast as "enemies of free speech." And while she convincingly criticizes John Rawls's "Kazanistan" and Paul Berman's "Islamofascism," she renders equally devastating critiques of philosophers, such as Slavoj Žižek and Jacques Derrida, whom readers might associate with Norton's oeuvre in political theory. Norton's scholarship, her analysis, and the way she unwinds *On the Muslim Question* are relentless, all while being constructed in artful argument and elegant prose.

Norton renders comprehensive and insightful critiques of how European figures such as Geert Wilders and Joseph Ratzinger attribute the failure of multiculturalism to Islam—and how feminists and feminist theory do the same thing. Norton shows us the dangers associated with false threats in their views about Islam, dangers that affect not just Muslims, but Christians, Jews, and secular humanists. Islam, and its position toward women, she argues, does not present "special, perhaps insurmountable, challenges to the human rights of women." Unlike these feminists, she does not insist that Muslim women must disavow their religion to speak in the West.

Norton also shows that secularism in Europe—France, for instance, with its *laïcité*—has not produced the promised neutrality in the public sphere. Nonetheless, she is subtle in the contrasts she draws between Europe and the United States. "New" nations, like the United States, have different policies privileging civil liberties and civil rights from those of "old" countries; and so it is for different reasons that American citizenship, like *laïcité*, fails to protect Muslim citizens from "surveillance, detention, unlawful searches, and the assaults of discrimination."

Despite this devastating analysis, *On the Muslim Question* surprises the reader one last time as it ends with a chapter imbued with hope. There is no utopia, or even a call to action, other than understanding everyday events that are already occurring among us. To Norton, Muslim, Christian, Jewish, Hindu, atheist, and secular "ordinary" people are already "crafting a common life together"; and for this reason, the book fills the public sphere with a sense of expectation, waiting for us to realize it.

On the Muslim Question

INTRODUCTION

On the Muslim Question: Philosophy, Politics, and the Western Street

The Jewish question was fundamental for politics and philosophy in the Enlightenment. In our time, as the Enlightenment fades, the Muslim question has taken its place.

The emancipation of the Jews was central to Enlightenment philosophy and politics. Enlightened statesmen endeavored to change the laws that had relegated Jews to second-class citizenship, and to end the pogroms that had filled Europe with terror. The freedom of Jews to vote, to participate in politics as equals, and to walk through their cities as equals accompanied the expansion of democracy and marked the achievement of liberal constitutions. As the West became more enlightened, more liberal, more democratic, it left behind the laws and customs that had required discrimination against Jews.

So it was in philosophy. Marx's essay "On the Jewish Question" saw the Jew as the site where post-Enlightenment Europe confronted the specter of theology in citizenship. The Jewish question enfolded questions of citizenship, religion, difference and belonging, integration and the preservation of culture. Jewish emancipation was evidence of both the achievements and the limits of liberal institutions. Long before Marx, Spinoza's political theology made the Jewish question central to determining the place of religion in the state, and to the achievement of enlightenment in politics. Hegel's political theology constructed Abraham as the father of individuality. Whether they praised or blamed liberalism, whether they sought to advance or to forestall democracy, Western philosophers saw the Jewish question as the axis on which these struggles turned. Modern struggles over faith and secularism, progress and loss, alienation and community, equality and difference were fought out on the terrain of the Jewish question. Late modern philosophy has the Holocaust at its heart.[1]

The preoccupations of philosophy fade against the harshness of the problems of politics. There was, in the shadow of the Enlightenment, a second Jewish question bound with the first. As politics and philosophy worked in the world, the question of the place of Jews and the practices of antisemitism presented wrongs to be righted, challenges to the promise and ambitions of the Enlightenment. It was characteristic of the Jewish question in its practical and historical form that Jews were marked out as a political threat even as they were subject to political assaults; marked as evil even as conduct toward them testified to the failure of the ethical systems that had abandoned them. The Jewish question marked the great failures as well as the great achievements of the Enlightenment.

In our time, the figure of the Muslim has become the axis where questions of political philosophy and political theology, politics and ethics meet. Islam is marked as the preeminent danger to politics; to Christians, Jews, and secular humanists; to women, sex, and sexuality; to the values and institutions of the Enlightenment. In relation to Muslims and Islam, liberty, equality, and fraternity become not imperatives but questions: Liberty? Equality? Fraternity? They are asked of Muslims and Islam. They are asked of us all.

The liberal and social democratic states of our time hesitate before Muslims: hesitate to include them, hesitate to extend them the rights and privileges of citizenship. Though we maintain our belief that law is neutral, that the Constitution secures rights, and that America has true freedom of religion, American citizenship has not protected America's Muslim citizens from surveillance, detention, unlawful searches, and the assaults of discrimination. The American confrontation with the Muslim question has exposed non-Muslim Americans to the same threats of discrimination, surveillance, detention, and imprisonment when they act as allies.

Europe has furnished no stronger, surer protection of rights. France's severe republican secularism, *laïcité*, has not produced the promised neutrality of the public sphere. The same places that once heard calls for the expulsion of the Jews now hear demands for an end to Muslim immigration. France burns in the riots of its Muslim suburbs, the *banlieues d'Islam*. French society is torn by controversies over the veil. Norwegian children are massacred by a man who sees himself as the champion of Europe against Islam. Partisan politics in the Netherlands and Denmark centers on the Muslim question. In Germany and the United Kingdom, the prime ministers orate against multiculturalism and the hazards of extremist Islam. The conditions (formal and informal) set for the inclusion of Turkey in the European Union provide an institutional and juridical map of European anxieties: the status of women, the place of religion and the family, the permissibility of ethnic identification, the use and limits of state violence.

The concerns the West directs at Muslims map sites of domestic anxiety. European states—indeed all the states of the liberal and social democratic West—are faced with continuing questions about the status of women, sexuality, equality and difference, faith and secularism. They are fueled by anxieties over the meaning of the past and the direction of the future. The European constitutional crisis is impelled in part by an uncertainty over the status of Christianity in the constitution of Europe. Here, the question is not the inclusion or exclusion of Turkey, a nation predominately Muslim in culture and faith, but the identity of the receiving nations. Europe is asked if it is Christian or secular, and cannot find an answer.

In America, the Muslim question takes a different form. Analysts of American politics from Alexis de Tocqueville to Louis Hartz have observed that America is a liberal nation, born in, from, and to the Enlightenment. American Christians and American secularists alike were able to give the same answer to the Jewish question, the answer of inclusion that turned on partial and reciprocal assimilation. As Jews became American, Americans became more Jewish.

America confronts the Muslim question without the imperative to acceptance. The figure of the Muslim does not bridge the divide between the Christian and the secular, or provide a model for the chosen. For Americans, who see themselves in the place of Isaac and Jacob, as people of the covenant, wrestling with the angel, the figure of the Muslim raises the problem of Ishmael and Esau, of those in the desert, outside the covenant.

The West as a whole is confronted by changes in the practices and understanding of sovereignty, and by challenges to those liberal and neoliberal institutions that have thus far held a potentially rebellious democracy in check. As it was with the Jewish question, so it is with the Muslim question: in the most fundamental sense, what is at stake is the value of Western civilization. The figure of the Muslim stands like a sentinel marking the limits of the West: the state system, human rights, civil freedoms, democracy, sovereignty, even the simple requirements of bare life.

States and Rights

The Muslim question, like the Jewish question before it, is connected to fears for national and international security. In the nineteenth century, the Jewish anarchist was the feared agent of global terrorism, using the weapons of terror, operating across state lines, acknowledging no state. Now it is the Muslim terrorist who presents a threat not only to the security of states, but to the security of the state system. In each case, the Muslim and the Jew are marked as both before and after the state in time. They are tribal, never having achieved the state, a state that Hegel marked as essential to the fullness of civilization. They are after the state, which is to say they are the rootless cosmopolites of a post-Westphalian order. They are said to be after the state in a second, more ordinary sense: pursuing it, opposing it, seeking its end.

The figure of the Muslim also marks the limit of rights. Political philosophers and popular discourse alike, in Europe and the United States, have cast the Muslim as the exemplary case for the violation of human rights. Muslim practice, indeed, Islam itself, is said to pose special challenges to rights. In the controversies surrounding Salman Rushdie, Theo van Gogh, Ayaan Hirsi Ali, and the cartoons published first in the Danish press and later around the world, Muslims are portrayed as presenting special challenges to the exercise of freedom of speech. In the debates over the veil, polygamy, and other issues, Muslims are said to be peculiarly hostile to women. As the West begins, uneasily, to accept a wider range of sexual orientations, Muslims are said to be particularly hostile to gay equality. All the dearest rights—freedom of speech, freedom of the press, equality, even the pursuit of happiness—are said to be endangered by Islam.

Sex and Sexuality

A plethora of Western philosophers and theorists, from all corners of the academy, from the old Left to neoconservatives, have joined in an uneasy alliance to condemn Muslims for the oppression of women. Susan Okin, Jean Elshtain, Elisabeth Badinter, Caroline Fourest, and Oriana Fallacci (among many others) have argued that the veil, female circumcision, polygamy, and arranged marriage present special, perhaps insurmountable, challenges to the human rights of women in Muslim cultures. They argue that Europe and America offer a refuge for Muslim women who must leave their own cultures to find their voices and themselves. For these very curious bedfellows, Islam is a religion hostile to women, a dangerous zone of hypermasculinity.

The construction of the Muslim world as hypermasculine accomplishes several useful objects for the West in general and the United States in particular. Attention to the plight of women in the Muslim world turns the gaze of potential critics away from the continuing inequality of women in the West. The rights of women become the justification for military adventures and foreign occupation. No women in her right mind could defend veiling or polygamy, we are told; thus any woman who does so must be deluded or compelled. Protests from the women who are promised liberation are thus read as signs of their oppression, more evidence that intervention is called for. This logic permits no appeal, least of all from those it silences.

Secularism

Slavoj Žižek, citing the debates over the preamble to the European constitution, made the case for atheism as the apex of the Enlightenment. "Where," he asked, "was modern Europe's most precious legacy, that of atheism? What makes modern Europe unique is that it is the first and only civilization in which atheism is a fully legitimate option." Žižek's endorsement of the Enlightenment exclusion of religion is, however, haunted (like the Enlightenment itself) by the return of the repressed. The proof that "atheism is a European legacy worth fighting for" is that it "creates a safe public space for believers," even Muslims.[2] Žižek identifies Muslims as the proper object of tolerance—a disposition he once subjected to a more searching critique.

Marking Muslims as the target of tolerance marks them as other, and as undesirable. Tolerance is not required toward that which is ordinary, familiar; or toward that which is welcome, desirable or good. The object of tolerance is marked as alien and undesirable. W.E.B. Du

Bois once famously asked of African Americans "How does it feel to be a problem?" The same question can be asked of Muslims—on a global scale. Žižek's formula suggests, however, that more is at stake here than tolerance of Islam. If atheism is one of the triumphs of modernity, then it is not only Islam that is to be tolerated and dismissed, but Christianity.

For many secular philosophers and journalistic literati—Christopher Hitchens, for example—the problem of Islam is the problem of religion writ large. The problem with Muslims is that they are more religious, that their religion dominates their lives, that it cannot be fenced out or fenced in. Many Christians would say the same, proudly, of themselves. They deplore the fencing-out and fencing-in of faith. This might seem to impel an alliance between Judeo-Christian conservatives and Muslims. There have been two obstacles to this. More religious Christians and Jews have been slow to form alliances across religious lines. More importantly, Muslims, like Christians and Jews, are often secular. They share with other secularists a suspicion of religious power. They are in a position to see, with special clarity, the limits and fragility of secularism in the West.

Western secularism is said to have its origins in the separation of church and state. Yet, in many places, the West has not achieved that separation. Blasphemy laws remain. Established churches linger. Secularism is said to create and preserve a neutral public sphere, yet throughout the West the pattern of days and holidays preserves a more Christian past. Christianity dominates the eye and the ear in the sight of cathedrals and the sound of church bells. Ideas of state and sovereignty are informed by a very political theology.

Yet if secularism did not succeed in the vaunted separation of church and state, its partial successes are greater than we acknowledge. The secular settlement ensured that religion would be largely immune from the critiques of philosophers. The rebellious and the skeptical were permitted to leave the churches and live untroubled by them—and the churches in their turn could live untroubled by the skeptical. Churches enjoyed immunity from the critiques of reason. They were sheltered from the rough debates of the public square. Skeptics and philosophers held their tongues, or kept their strictures outside the churches, away from the tender ears of the faithful. This was not the triumph of atheism or enlightenment; this was a settlement between old enemies, each unable to defeat the other, each eager to secure a space free from the other's attacks. Once the presence of the Jews served as an uneasy reminder that things might be otherwise. Now it is the presence of Islam that puts the secular settlement in question.

Secularists who fear Islam fear not only Islam, but the return of religious power. The most honest of these acknowledge, as Ayaan Hirsi Ali has, that they oppose religion in all its forms. Christians may fear another rival in the sphere of religion, Jews a challenge to Zionism. The more knowing and cautious may recognize that the refusal of many secularists to give Islam immunity from question might lead to a new willingness to critique Christianity and Judaism as well.

Philosophers and other academics have their own vulnerabilities to reckon with. The writings of al Farabi, Ibn Rushd, Ibn Sina, Ibn Tufayl, Ibn Khaldun, and other Muslim philosophers are placed outside the canon, exiled scholastically to the provinces of area studies, religious studies, and anthropology. The Western canon of political philosophy is distorted by genealogies that excise Muslim writings and Muslim philosophers. Many years ago, Leo Strauss argued that Western philosophy had maimed itself in its willful forgetting of Islam and Judaism. Strauss wrote with reproachful disdain of Western philosophy's resistance to the Jewish and Muslim philosophy of the Middle Ages. He taught his students the interpretive strategies of the Jewish *shul* and the Muslim *madrasa*, and broached the possibility of a radically different resolution of the relation of politics, philosophy, and theology.[3] Strauss argued for the restoration of Jewish and Muslim philosophy to the canon, most notably in the figures of Maimonides and al Farabi. Strauss's call was all too rare and went unheeded. Only in recent years have theorists and philosophers begun to see their genealogies in a larger and more capacious canon.

Democracy

Near the end of his life, the late French philosopher Jacques Derrida called Islam "the other of democracy."[4] Derrida sealed off "Greco-Christian and globalatinizing" traditions from the Islamic sources with which they were bound, on which they fed, and in which they found shelter in hard times. He linked Islam to fascism and Muslims to excessive procreation, while identifying French *laïcité* with the liberty, equality, and fraternity in which it is (for its Muslim citizens) notably deficient. In these respects, Derrida's construction of the Muslim as the other of democracy would seem to be merely a commonplace, if distressing, instance of the failure of intellect before chauvinism. There is, however, something both correct and profound in Derrida's reading.

Muslims have indeed been shown to be democracy's others. They lack democracy, and it must be supplied to them, albeit by undemocratic means. The advancement of liberal democratic institutions in the political realms inhabited by Muslims, like neoliberal institutions in their economic realms, is sought within a regime of conditionality. Democracy, like economic development, can be aided only under certain conditions. The objects of efforts to "democratize" the Middle East are required not merely to win the consent and satisfy the demands of their own electoral constituencies; they must conform to the will of the European Union and the United States. The elected government of Palestine must recognize Israel, whatever its constituents may say; the elected government of Iraq must forgo its choice of prime minister.

The Muslim question spans continents. It unites politicians, philosophers, the press, pundits, and talk-radio ranters in a common anxiety over the clash of civilizations. Yet there is, in these democracies, a popular response that speaks against this. On the streets of the West ordinary people—Muslim, Christian, Jew, Hindu, Buddhist, pagan, atheist, and the rest—are crafting a common life together. These places are the Andalusias of our time, the ornaments of our world. They are hidden in the everyday. We will arrive at those places soon enough, only to find that we are already at home there. But first, let us hear and answer those who argue for the "clash of civilizations," those who fear Islam and take Muslims as the enemy.

Part I

Muslim Questions

CHAPTER 1

Freedom of Speech

A clash of civilizations that saw the West as the realm of enlightenment, and Muslims in the realm of religion, custom, and tradition, has been part of spectacles in the Western public sphere since Ernst Renan lectured—and Jamal al Din al Afghani challenged him—in nineteenth-century Paris. Ayatollah Khomeini gave new life to these civilizational theatrics when he issued his notorious fatwa calling for the assassination of Salman Rushdie. The clash has continued to be enacted in the production of the film *Submission* (a critique of the treatment of women under Islam), the murder of the film's producer, Theo van Gogh, and the threats to its writer, Ayaan Hirsi Ali, as well as in the Danish cartoons of Muhammad and the riots that followed.

The dramas surrounding Rushdie and van Gogh, the Danish cartoons and the satirical magazine *Charlie Hebdo*'s copycat cartoon provocations mark Muslims—some Muslims, fundamentalist Muslims, extremist Muslims, or, simply, Muslims—as the enemies of free speech. Westerners (Christians, Jews, and secularists) are said to be committed to freedom of speech. Freedom of speech is advanced as one of the pillars of an enlightened, modern, and democratic West. "Over and over," Conservative activist Ken Connor wrote in the *Baptist Press*, "we see a vocal segment of the Muslim population attempting to limit speech and impose religion."[1] An editorial on netanyahu.org writes of "the most illiberal force on the planet, Islamic fundamentalists who destroy free speech."[2] "Most of the objections are coming from Islam," the executive director of the UK's National Secular Society claimed; "the freedom of speech is an enlightenment value that Europe must cling to."[3]

The threats to freedom of speech may come from an unexpected quarter. There is more to be said about these well-known stories. There is more to be seen in the cartoons, more to be learned from Salman Rushdie and Theo van Gogh.

The first of the recent controversies to cast freedom of speech as a Muslim question had Salman Rushdie's *The Satanic Verses* at its center. Rushdie's novel, like *Midnight's Children* and his other work, was at once realistic and magical. There are astonishing flights of butterflies, and a man grows the legs of a goat, but the characters also confront ordinary trials and tragedies. They lose their jobs; they lose their faith in the police, in fairness, in the possibility of assimilation. Rushdie brought the immigrant experience and the cadences of South Asian English into the highest circles of English literature.

The Satanic Verses seemed a curious target to many: it was clearly a work of fiction, marked by elaborate fantasy sequences. The novel's complex structure drew attention to the discrimination against British Muslims, their rough accommodations, their alienation, conflicts, self-betrayals, and redemption, and made all that experience vivid and poignant. The portrait of Muhammad was, if not orthodox, sympathetic. That was what I thought. My students were divided. Most students, Muslim, Christian, Jew, and atheist, agreed. But the more orthodox among them, whatever their religion, made common cause with conservative Muslims in disapproving of the book. Rushdie, they argued, ought to have been more respectful of religious belief.

The Rushdie controversy was initially an internal debate. British Muslims and South Asians confronted white Britons. The grievances were British grievances, cast in British terms. Muslims asked why blasphemy laws protected Christians, but not minority religions. Muslims and South Asians voiced their anger over discriminatory blasphemy laws, making these the sign and symbol for an array of forms of discrimination they experienced in Britain. Muslim South Asians confronted not only British society writ large, but the particular politics and social conflicts of their own communities. Rushdie, after all, was South Asian and Muslim. He had outraged other, more religious, Muslim South Asians.

This was thus, at its outset, a very local fuss. Like all such controversies, it touched on other resentments. Rushdie was a man who had achieved recognition in the highest British (indeed, cosmopolitan) literary circles. *The Satanic Verses* was a finalist for the Booker Prize and won the Whitbread Award. *Midnight's Children*, Rushdie's extraordinarily beautiful novel of the first generation born to an independent India, won the Booker Prize. Rushdie had confronted the world of English letters and, like other revolutionaries, had turned it upside down. He could write the King's English when he chose, but he often wrote the Indian English spoken by small shopkeepers.

Rushdie had confronted Britain on its own terrain, and won the acceptance and acclaim that many fellow immigrants lacked. He was wealthy, educated, and famous—and on his own terms. He criticized British colonialism and won acclaim for it. He had succeeded marvelously at things that were a continual trial to many immigrants: speaking English, earning a living, winning respect. *The Satanic Verses* seemed to mock one of the things immigrants hold on to in the journey to become part of their new country—their faith. The book Rushdie wrote was about discrimination, the limits of assimilation and acceptance. The book many British Muslims read was an insult to their faith. Though they came from the same community, Rushdie and these readers were already worlds apart.

The reaction of those British Muslims who were angered by Rushdie's book was a very British one. They demonstrated. The most dramatic of their demands (that the book be banned or that Rushdie be prosecuted for blasphemy) were often cast as the demands of British subjects: blasphemy laws should protect all British faiths equally. The demonstrators, in short, showed how very British they had already become. They were not, however, wholly accepted by their country.

Talal Asad points out, in an article on the Rushdie Affair, that the British government issued a series of warnings against violence to British Muslims despite the fact that "no arrests or injuries had occurred as a result of the demonstrations."[4] The government's concern was especially remarkable in context. London had seen not only years of IRA bombings, but also the riots of Brixton and Notting Hill Gate in which South Asians had been notable for their absence. Street demonstrations by many groups—"antiracists, fascists, feminists, gays, 'prolife' activists, trade unionists, and students"—had involved scuffles with the police and some had taken a violent turn. Violence against South Asians was, however, well-documented. Experience suggested that demonstrations by South Asian Muslims were unlikely to be violent. Experience was correct. There were no injuries and no arrests. Why, Talal Asad asked, did the liberal middle class repeatedly denounce "Muslim violence," why did the government anticipate it, and, I might add, why are the Rushdie demonstrations remembered as violent when violence was absent?

Salman Rushdie was endangered not by the conduct of Western Muslims, but by the actions of the late Ayatollah Khomeini. Khomeini, who may never have read the book, issued a statement permitting—calling on—Muslims to kill Salman Rushdie. He later put a price on Rushdie's head, offering a bounty to anyone who killed him or his publishers. Rushdie went into hiding. He was protected by the police before and after he went into hiding. But he was also protected by something less visible, deeper, and more effective. He was protected by his fellow citizens of all faiths. The British Muslims who had demonstrated against Rushdie's book did not turn to assassination after Khomeini's edict. They were angry and they did what we're supposed do when we're angry. They complained, they wrote the papers and their representatives, and they demonstrated. There were Muslims (perhaps angry Muslims) in the police forces that protected Rushdie in England and in the United States. They made it possible for Rushdie to write and travel. Rushdie was targeted by a powerful man, a cleric but far more than a cleric: the authoritarian ruler of a large and rather wealthy nation. As a cleric, he had influence beyond the borders of Iran. As Iran's ruler, he commanded a military, spies, all the resources of a state. Yet he died, and Rushdie lives.

The martyr to free speech was not Salman Rushdie but Theo van Gogh. The murderer was not a man acting at the command of a learned and powerful foreign cleric, but a second-generation Dutchman with little knowledge of politics or religion, unemployed and acting on his own. Theo van Gogh was also less suited to the role of martyr than Salman Rushdie had been. Rushdie was a respected author: erudite, witty, complex, and cosmopolitan, and commanding a literate and cosmopolitan audience. Theo van Gogh was unwashed and antisemitic, little known outside the Netherlands, and known there principally as a cultural provocateur of remarkable vulgarity. Blond, chubby, aggressively self-promoting, scatological, and a little indulged, he looked—and acted—like a grown-up, European Cartman of *South Park*. Van Gogh, however, belonged to a wealthier, more privileged, social circle, "brought up in a plush suburb of the Hague."[5] The writer Ian Buruma, who knew him, his place, and his people ("we shared mutual friends"), described him as a spoiled rich boy, "a bored Wassenaar brat."[6]

Van Gogh called himself "the village idiot." His website De Gezonde Roker (the healthy smoker) showed him with a woman's red bra tied around his face like a mask. Starting his film career early, he made a schoolboy film featuring his friends eating excrement. He went on to film more outrageous scenes: a pistol shot in a woman's vagina, cats put in a washing machine.[7] His columns and his radio show were intended to offend, and to offend as widely, exuberantly, and outrageously as possible. Buruma recalls van Gogh referring to Jesus as "that rotten fish from Nazareth" and writing of a Jewish filmmaker and novelist that "he could only satisfy his wife by wrapping barbed wire around his penis and crying 'Auschwitz' when he came." One of his Jewish critics, van Gogh wrote, "gets wet dreams about being fucked by Dr. Mengele."[8] Van Gogh was sued by Christians for his characterization of Jesus, and by the Center for Information and Documentation on Israel for his antisemitic invective. Van Gogh aimed many of his most provocative remarks at Jews, Buruma writes, "until the Muslims attracted his particular scorn and were subjected to a constant barrage of abuse, of which 'goat-fuckers' was the most quoted but by no means the most offensive example."[9]

Van Gogh's speech—and his writing and filmmaking— were wild, ungoverned and ungovernable. He would say anything. He would say everything. He seemed the very incarnation of free speech: spilling out of his T-shirts and pants, his mussed blond hair standing on end, too big to hold, too wild to rule.

His unruliness defied one set of conventions only to affirm another. Van Gogh belonged to the Amsterdam of cannabis and copulation. In this city, the prostitutes sitting in the windows and the marijuana cafés that dot the city are now as important to the tourist industry—and as iconically Dutch—as tulips and Gouda once were. Peter van der Veer called van Gogh "the personification of the Dutch ethos since the 1970s."[10]

Amsterdam since the 1970s is still, as it was in the seventeenth century, a city noted for its embarrassment of riches. If freedom is the freedom to consume what one pleases, to put anything one chooses into one's mouth, to use one's body in any way one pleases, then Amsterdam may be a free city. Theo van Gogh reveled in that freedom, surpassing his fellow citizens. He was the hearty eater, the "healthy smoker." He wore what he pleased and he did as he chose. He celebrated the sexual freedom of Amsterdam, the freedom to consume, to enjoy, to take pleasure wherever and however one desires.

These are the freedoms of the wealthy and the privileged: of people who can buy goods and command pleasures. They are the freedoms of a people whose children still have presents brought to them by a Christian saint and a little black servant, Sinterklaas and Zwarte Piet. Their pleasures are not very different from the pleasures of their forefathers—those strict seventeenth-century Calvinists—except that they have become a little more catholic.

The seventeenth-century Dutch had printed seditious pamphlets for the whole of Europe. At the close of the millennium, freedom of expression concerned more private matters. In the new Netherlands, the website for prospective citizens declares that "people have the freedom of expression to show that they are homosexuals or lesbians."[11] This must be not only accepted, but affirmed. The Netherlands no longer deals significantly in the market for political sedition. The sexually inflected mockery that the seventeenth- and eighteenth-century Dutch used to challenge great powers and attack established hierarchies is now used to reinforce them.

The commemoration of Theo van Gogh's death involved the repeated employment of a sexually explicit ethnic slur for Muslims: "goat-fuckers." The slur was rendered childlike and amiable by the employment of stuffed-toy goats. Who could object to the display of a few charming stuffed animals? "Goat-fucker" is not, I've been told, a special slur for Muslims. It's said about the kind of men Americans call "hillbillies" and "rednecks": those who belong to what Karl Marx called "the idiocy of rural life." "Goat-fuckers" construed Muslims as hypersexual rustics, always masculine, never feminine, outside the order of urbanity and civility.

As is so often the case, it is not Islam but Europe that is the source of the deepest European anxieties. It is not the foreign that fills people with fear, but the familiar; not the future, but the past. Few of the Dutch know much about the rural life of immigrants from Turkey or Morocco. The customs and traditions they fear are not those of the Rif or Anatolia but those that belong to their own memories: to a rural Europe that was not picturesque but primitive. They fear the foreign less than the familiar. They belong to a Europe in which the power of religion to bind and loose, to govern conduct, is radically diminished but easily remembered.

Cosmopolitan, sexually liberated Europeans remember that their appetites were once constrained by poverty, or religion, or convention. They revel in release from all of these. The achievement of pleasure is self-determination in the smallest, most intimate sense: what one wears, whom one has sex with and how. These are, they believe, the pleasures and freedoms of the city. They fear that small towns may shelter smaller minds, and that the past they have escaped is hiding in the countryside.

Islam calls up the specter of the return of religion, the life of the village: the return of the repressed. The immigrants remind their uneasy hosts of an all-too-easily remembered past of war, poverty, religion, and repression. Every day, on every street, in offices and homes, the sight of immigrant laborers recalls a past of hard and futile work, where fears started at the next village and loyalties ended with the family, a past of deep political conflicts. For women, for homosexuals, indeed for many who enjoy the consumer pleasures of postindustrial Europe, that past was a prison. The presence of the immigrants is the presence of the past. Often what is feared in them is not the alien, but the familiar.

The Danish Cartoons

One upon a time, in a warm house in another, colder country, a man began to write a book. He was a very nice man. He had a "cozy kitchen" in a house in a neighborhood full of different kinds of people.[12] Every morning his children would go off to school with all the other children: with little Anders and little Nasser, little Wun and little Carsten. One day the man decided he would write a book.

The demand that set off the cartoon controversy in Denmark seems the most benign, and may be the most interesting, of the free speech controversies. Kåre Bluitgen, a Danish author of children's books, was writing a biography of the prophet Muhammad and found it difficult to find an illustrator.[13] No one wanted to draw Muhammad. This is hardly surprising. Islam, like Judaism, rejects the representation of God. Islam also resists representations of the prophets and, in stricter interpretations, all human forms. The illustrators who declined Bluitgen's invitation must have known this and explained it to him, because they indicated that they feared Muslim reprisals. Bluitgen said he wanted to "explain Islam to Danish children." Including the illustrations was misleading as well as offensive, yet Bluitgen persisted. Bluitgen, as a journalist in *Die Zeit* wrote, "had the best of intentions."[14]

Bluitgen's difficulties were written up in an article in the Danish journal *Politiken*.[15] Two weeks later (and not to be outdone) another paper, *Jyllands-Posten*, published "Muhammad's ansigt" (The face of Muhammad), a collection of twelve cartoons and an essay by the paper's cultural editor, Flemming Rose.[16] Rose and the *Jyllands-Posten* "are not fundamentalists in our support for freedom of expression," as he wrote in an article in the *Washington Post*. They "would not publish pornographic images, or graphic images of dead bodies; swear words rarely make it into our pages." But, as he says, "the cartoon story is different." Rose was driven to publish, he writes, because a Danish stand-up comedian felt he could urinate on the Bible but not on the Koran.[17] The *New York Times* was not impressed with this explanation, which they called "juvenile."[18]

The now-notorious article came and went. There appears to have been no significant reaction at all either within Denmark or in the Middle East. It's not that the cartoons went unnoticed by newspapers in the Middle East: the Egyptian newspaper *El Fagr* had published them with a negative editorial in October, which neither urged nor produced a violent reaction. The *Jyllands-Posten* appears to have been dissatisfied with the lack of reaction to the cartoons, and circulated them, after publication, to prominent imams in Copenhagen, including Ahmad Abu Laban. The imams were disturbed, but again, there was no violent (or even inflammatory) reaction.

Months later, Abu Laban and other Danish imams brought a folio of these and other antisemitic, anti-Muslim cartoons to a meeting of the Organization of the Islamic Conference they were scheduled to attend in Mecca. The imams wished to discuss the rising tide of anti-Muslim sentiment in Europe. They therefore brought not only the cartoons published in *Jyllands-Posten* but other examples of anti-Muslim caricature. Jytte Klausen, author of a book on the controversy, refers to these as "the fake cartoons," though there is no indication that the imams laid them at the door of *Jyllands-Posten* or in any way suggested that they were among the commissioned cartoons. There was nothing fake about them. The additional cartoons the imams brought to Cairo were real: real caricatures, real insults, received by real people. The meeting produced a formal diplomatic expression of "concern at rising hatred against Islam and Muslims" and over "using the freedom of expression as a pretext for defaming religions." It did not call for violent action, and no violence occurred.

One of the Danish imams later said of himself and his colleagues, "We are not professional enough to know what would be the response of media, nor the interest of politicians there."[19] He might have said the same of the Danish journalists.

As the cartoons began to circulate farther afield, the file enlarged. Muslims added other, more offensive, caricatures, and the images moved outside Europe, outside the realm of the diplomatic, and into a rougher politics. Politicians and media figures in the Islamic world did as Flemming Rose and *Jyllands-Posten* editor in chief Carsten Juste had done: circulating and supplementing the images in the hope of kindling a more outraged, more political, more violent, more newsworthy, and more profitable response. They got it—but not at home, not in Europe, not in the West.

Jytte Klausen is a scholar who has produced some of the most reliable and evenhanded work on Muslims in

Europe. Her study of the cartoon controversy is invaluable in many respects, but misleading in others. Most importantly, Klausen exaggerates the violence associated with the cartoons. Table 2 in the book presents the "number of victims associated with demonstrations against the Danish cartoons."[20] The number of deaths and injuries appears large indeed until one reads the table carefully. Klausen counts 241–48+ deaths over a four-month period, of which 205–7 come from a single five-day period in Nigeria. She counts 790–800+ injuries, of which 485+ come from Nigeria.[21] These figures are, unfortunately, not remarkable in the Nigerian context. Comparable clusters of deaths have occurred both before and after the cartoon controversy. The BBC reported over 200 deaths in Nigeria on January 20, 2010, writing that "the area has seen several bouts of deadly violence in recent years. At least 200 people were killed in an outbreak of fighting between Muslims and Christians in 2008, while some 1,000 died in a riot in 2001."[22]

The next largest—but much smaller—group of deaths (11) was of Libyan rioters shot by Libyan police. This group of rioters had split off from a larger peaceful demonstration, and was attacked by the police after it became violent. The link to the Danish cartoons is also tenuous here. The killings were of Muslim Libyans by Muslim Libyans. The protest was directed at the Italian consulate and was prompted by an Italian minister who wore a T-shirt displaying the cartoons during a television appearance. The cartoons became inflammatory in the Libyan context only when they were linked to Libya's former colonizer, Italy.[23] In light of subsequent events, we might now wonder whether the confrontations between Libyan police and Libyan demonstrators were really about the cartoons at all, or whether they were the occasion for the expression of anger at a repressive regime. The 4 deaths in Afghani riots against the cartoons might be compared with 14 deaths in anti-US riots in the same period. Denmark has soldiers serving with US forces in Afghanistan and, cartoons or no cartoons, is a target for Afghans who object to the presence of coalition forces.[24] Only one of the deaths and none of the injuries occurred in the West. The single Western death was the suicide of a Muslim in police custody.

Let us be clear about this. The idea that the cartoon controversy set off violent confrontations between Muslims and non-Muslim Westerners is simply wrong. Violence did occur outside the West. It occurred in places where violence is common, where any number of issues, at home or abroad, actual or rumored, can set it off. People were injured; people died. Those people were Pakistani, Nigerian, Afghani, Libyan, and usually Muslim. They were casualties in continuing violent conflicts. Those conflicts continue today, without reference to the Danish cartoons.

Klausen also accepts the conventional construction of the cartoon controversy as a dispute over freedom of speech that divided Muslims and Westerners. This construction is also misleading. It assumes that Westerners cannot be Muslims, and that Muslims are by definition not Western. There was also—and this is critical—no threat to freedom of speech. No Dane feared the intervention of the state. No Dane feared the reaction of outraged majority sentiment. They did not even fear the "sickly oversensitivity" of the Muslims they sought to offend. They were correct. *Jyllands-Posten* published the cartoons. The newspaper was printed, circulated, and read. Those who objected to the cartoons did so in print and in demonstrations that remained peaceful.

If the object of the publication of the cartoons was to affirm the right to freedom of the press or free speech, or even the "right" to offend, *Jyllands-Posten* should have been delighted with the result. They weren't. Simply proving that Danes could publish what they chose was not enough. They intended to provoke. If one insult wasn't enough, it would have to be repeated.

What Kåre Bluitgen sought was simply a representation of Muhammad according to early twenty-first-century Danish conventions, an illustration like other illustrations. He wanted Muhammad represented, and represented according to Western conventions. In doing so, he insisted on the priority of his preferred artistic conventions over the religious preferences of his Muslim compatriots. "They cannot represent themselves, they must be represented."

Flemming Rose intensified the demand. In sending out his call for editorial cartoons of Muhammad, he called for representations of Muhammad that were at least mundane, and almost certainly comical, mocking, or satiric—for those are the characteristics of the newspaper cartoon. He required that Muhammad be represented in a manner that removed him from all connection to the sacred and the divine, in a form that invited mockery. The author of the children's book might (in principle) have welcomed a portrait of Muhammad as prophet or hero. The cultural editor of *Jyllands-Posten* had more restrictive requirements. He wanted satire.

There is, even in Denmark, no shortage of images of Muhammad. A visit to any library of moderate size turns up many representations of Muhammad, even a few by

Muslims. There are images of Muhammad in paintings, in illustrations to histories and works on religion, culture, and civilization. Some show the face veiled. Others show a face of flame. Western representations of Muhammad usually show a man's face and form, but they are no less fanciful for that. They are all figments of the artists' imaginations. What Bluitgen called for was necessarily a fiction, and it was not a fiction in short supply. The Danes were not in a visual desert, deprived of all access to images of Muhammad, however dreadful that prospect might be.

The demand is not simply that Muhammad be visible—nor even that he be represented as an imagined Westerner (Christian, secular, liberal) would have him, by Western artists and authors, according to Western conventions—but that these representations constantly proliferate, that they are repeated over and over again. It is not enough that artists may draw Muhammad in forms that might be offensive to some Muslims; they *must* do so. It is not enough that they do so once; the images must be endlessly repeated, published and republished. If Muslims do not react, the images are brought to their religious leaders. If the religious leaders do not react, the images are republished, and recirculated. Is this goading? Or is something fragile being shored up here?

I have written here of Western conventions, Western criteria. This is how the controversy presented itself, but the adjective is not correct. The conventions that Kåre Bluitgen used in his children's book were not those of "the West" but those of Denmark, and a particular time and place in Denmark: not only Christian, but Protestant; not only Protestant, but secularized; not only secularized, but secular in the manner of a Jutland Dane.

Flemming Rose was not holding to local conventions, but to a particular political position. Muslims were to be subject to cultural initiation through humiliation: hazed like pledges in a national fraternity. "Humour, even offensive humour, brings people together," Rose told *Die Zeit*, "because by making fun of people we're also including them in our society. It's not always easy for those concerned, but that's the price they've got to pay."[25] Muslims were, however, only the occasion for the dispute: Rose took aim at a much larger target. He defied the conventions that urged respect for religious beliefs in the public sphere in order to advance a narrower political agenda.

In calling for, publishing, and republishing the cartoon images of Muhammad, Rose and Juste advanced a narrow provincial view, and they advanced it not as the view of a local, insular community, nor as Danish, but as the view proper to all Westerners, indeed, to all reasonable people. Westerners might be flattered by the thought that equates the West with the reasonable, but they should balk at a West not big enough to hold Copenhagen, much less Denmark.

And of course they do. The original cartoons testify to that. One cartoonist's work may not show Muhammad at all. Anticipating a reaction to the cartoons, he shows a Muslim, calm and authoritative, faced with another set of Muslims: two armed men apparently leading a violent, barbaric mob. The central figure stops the mob at the door, saying, "Calm down, friends. After all it's just a drawing by an infidel from Southern Jutland."[26] The cartoon mocks both the enraged Muslims and the provincial Danes. The moderate figure is placed under the crescent of Islam, inside the building under attack. The barbaric figures are outside and stopped in their tracks.

This cartoon skewers two provincialisms at once and aligns moderation with civility. The text of the cartoon aligns the moderate Muslim with the enraged mob he calls "friends." The cartoon is also drawn as if we, the readers, stood with the central figure within the building.

One cartoon caricatures Bluitgen rather than Muhammad. Bluitgen is shown as a rather silly-looking schoolboy, bearing a stick figure drawing, presumably of Muhammad, and wearing a turban crowned with an orange, and the (English) words "PR gimmick." (The phrase "an orange in the turban" signifies "a lucky break" in Danish.)[27] This cartoon also attempted to minimize the political significance of the editor's provocation. More importantly, it refused the clash of civilizations, putting Bluitgen in the turban that signifies Islam.

Another of the cartoonists pursued the same strategy, offering a haloed figure (presumably Muhammad) in a lineup of racially diverse men and women, all wearing turbans. The lineup includes the far-right Danish politician Pia Kjærsgaard and Bluitgen himself. Bluitgen, again, is marked as a media hound. He holds a sign reading, "Kåre's Public Relations, call and get an offer." The witness is saying, "I don't know which one he is." The image represents Muhammad but simultaneously appears to mock Danish ignorance—or perhaps conveys the idea that, as there are no contemporary portraits of Muhammad, no image could be other than a fiction.

One cartoonist avoided the representation of the prophet Muhammad altogether, by taking the editor's request literally. His cartoon of Muhammad shows "Mohammed, Valbyskole 7A," a Danish schoolboy, wearing Western clothes, pointing to a text on a blackboard. The text is written in Farsi, in Arabic characters, and reads,

"*Jyllands-Posten*'s journalists are right-wing instigators."[28] The caricature has a certain ambivalence. Mohammed's shirt reads, "*frem-tiden,*" meaning "in times to come" or, simply, "the future." An anxious Dane might read it as a representation of a future in which schools are given over to Danish Muslim critics of the press. A less anxious reader might see the schoolboy Mohammed as speaking for the cartoonist and read the cartoon (quite literally) as a cosmopolitan critique of the *Jyllandes-Posten* by a writer who sees Danish Muslims in Denmark's future. In any case, this is one smart cartoon. The cartoonist has refused the command to caricature the prophet Muhammad, avoided offense to the pious, unsettled the usual equation of Muslim and Arab, and drawn attention to the presence—and Danishness—of Danish Mohammeds.

Objections to the publication and republication of the Muhammad cartoons came from a variety of Westerners, as well as the belatedly outraged in the East. Some were Christian, some Muslim, some secular, some religious, some liberal, some conservative, some thoughtful, some bigoted. Tariq Ramadan wrote that "Muslims must understand that laughing at religion is a part of the broader culture in which they live in Europe, going back to Voltaire." He endorsed the principle of freedom of speech, and affirmed the legality of the cartoons, though he condemned their publication. "In any society," he wrote, "there is a civic understanding that free speech should be used wisely so not as to provoke sensitivities, particularly in hybrid, multicultural societies we see in the world today. It is a matter of civic responsibility and wisdom, not a question of legality or rights."[29]

Emran Qureishi concurred, arguing that the controversy obscured not only Muslim traditions of free expression, but also those Muslims who had paid a heavy price for freedom of speech. He recalled that my own teacher, "Fazlur Rahman, a brilliant and deeply religious Pakistani scholar of Islam, had to flee his native land for the University of Chicago." Qureishi affirmed the principle of freedom of speech. "The answer," he wrote, "is not more censorship. But it would be nice if Western champions of freedom of speech didn't trivialize it by deriving pleasure from their ability to gratuitously offend Muslims. They view freedom of speech much as Islamic fundamentalists do—simply as the ability to offend—rather than as the cornerstone of a liberal democratic polity."[30] As Qureishi observed, the freedom of speech defended owed less to liberal traditions of democratic debate than to Jerry Springer.

Most newspapers in the United States and Britain chose not to publish the cartoons, citing editorial policies of respect for religious belief. The *Wall Street Journal*'s editorial read, "The right to mock a religion may be absolute, but so is the right to publish most forms of pornography: Neither is appropriate in a serious publication," adding, "That applies whether the religion is Islam, Christianity or any other, and whether the cartoons are being published for the first time or reprinted elsewhere as acts of solidarity in the face of an implied threat." Anders Gyllenhaal, editor of the Minneapolis *Star-Tribune*, citing the "purposely sacrilegious" character of the cartoons, wrote that the *Star-Tribune* doesn't publish something offensive "simply to prove we can."[31] The *New York Times* lead editorial read, "The New York Times and much of the rest of the nation's news media have reported on the cartoons but refrained from showing them. That seems a reasonable choice for news organizations that usually refrain from gratuitous assaults on religious symbols."

Support for the cartoons crossed the same lines. Most European newspapers published the cartoons, presenting their action as a courageous defense of free speech. Praising one's own courage is always suspect, but in this case it seems more than usually disingenuous. Insulting a minority religion is a poor test of both freedom of speech and civil courage. If offending Muslims is an act of courage, then the right-wing Parisian Odile Bonnivard, ladling out her "pig soup," should be in the running for the Legion of Honor. If freedom of speech is at issue, a defiance of majority opinion would have provided a more effective test. Had *Jyllands-Posten* called for the public sounding of the Muslim call to prayer, or defended the wearing of headscarves, we might praise its civil courage. European journalists, however, preened themselves on their courage in attacking a minority population with little political power, subject to discrimination and continuing slights.

A more complex endorsement of the reprinting of the cartoons came from diverse elements of the European Right. Dyab Abou Jahjah of the Arab European League agreed with the position taken by the European press, writing that he too believed "that one must be able of publishing and saying anything. I do not believe in red lines, and I do not believe that anything should be above the freedom of human expression." He added, "I know that most Arabs and Muslims would disagree with me on this point, but this is not what bothers me, what bothers me is that most Europeans don't realize that they also disagree with me."

> Europeans think that freedom of speech is guaranteed in Europe, and that they are defending it against Islamic pressure. This is a view that is widely propagated and

defended by groups from across the political spectrum. Reality, however, presents us Muslims living in Europe with another experience. Muslims and others in Europe cannot say everything they often want to say and they risk being arrested and prosecuted if they do.

They could not, for example, express "disgust" with homosexuality, or call it "a sickness and a deviation."[32] Abou Jahjah was immediately endorsed by Paul Belien, the editor of the *Brussels Journal*, "The Voice of Conservatism in Europe."

"Mr. Jahjah certainly has a point here," Belien wrote. "Not only Muslims are not allowed to voice all their opinions. Only last week the French parliamentarian Christian Vanneste was sentenced in court to a heavy fine because he had stated that 'homosexual behaviour endangers the survival of humanity' and that 'heterosexuality is morally superior to homosexuality.'" Belien also noted that Ayaan Hirsi Ali, commonly seen as an advocate of freedom of expression, "wants all religious schools abolished" and had demanded the defunding of a Calvinist party that had not fielded women candidates for office.[33]

The conservative Flemish nationalist Belien and Abou Jahjah both endorse the principle of freedom of speech. Both regard Europe as a place where speech is not free. Both condemn European hypocrisy, and both call for greater freedom of expression. Neither is powerful or influential. Both endorse the expression of opinions that are unpopular, shocking to many, and in some cases illegal. Both hope to use freedom of expression to create a different Europe. Abou Jahjah and Belien—despite their other differences—both want a Europe in which homosexuality is illegal, homosexuals are hounded, and the family is sacred.

This is not pretty, but it is what the Enlightenment aimed to protect. Speech of this kind—politically unpopular speech; speech that would outrage the powerful or the many; speech that extends the range of political debate; speech that addresses questions of immediate political moment—is what freedom of speech was meant to secure. Shock jocks, whether they speak on American radio, post cartoons on the front page, or urinate on the Bible or the Koran, may be protected—I believe they are—by provisions securing freedom of speech, but they are parasites on a right that has far more profound commitments. They diminish a right meant to secure speech that is more political, more important, and far more dangerous than theirs.

The toleration of shock-jockery, of speech that is intended to entertain—and entertain profitably—is an easy business, and a corrupt one. Shock-jockery first appears as a supplement to politics, a little activity on the fringe, a little "Bam!" as Emeril might say, something to spice up politics. Rush Limbaugh, Michael Savage, Al Franken, and Ann Coulter liven up politics, and in the case of Ann Coulter lend a little aging T&A to a venue usually short on spandex. But as these voices become more popular (because they are horrifying or amusing), more profitable (because they are more popular), and more pervasive (because they are more profitable), they come to replace politics: on the airwaves, on television, and, finally, in the minds of the people.

The shock jocks of the United States and the political spectacles of Europe provide the comforting illusion that the West is the realm of freedom of speech. They enable us Westerners to pride ourselves on the places where speech is free and to forget those places where it is not. They enable us to congratulate ourselves on principles the West continues to compromise.

Speech in Europe and the United States is less free than we like to think, and many—Christians, Jews, and secularists; Americans and Europeans; liberals and conservatives—are pleased to have it so. In the United States, often presented as a bastion of freedom of expression, free speech gives way to property rights. The right to free speech dies on the shop floor, whether that shop is a factory or a store in a shopping mall. In Europe, laws and regulations govern the content as well as the sites of speech. The United Kingdom has laws against the incitement of religious and racial hatred and strict laws against libel and defamation. Sweden, Norway, Denmark, Finland, and Iceland all prohibit speech inciting racial and religious hatred. Blasphemy laws are common, with most protecting the established religion.[34]

Other restrictions on freedoms of speech and expression see more use. Laws in Germany and other European countries govern—quite strictly—speech and writing on the Holocaust and Nazism. Speakers and authors are forbidden to deny or diminish the Holocaust. Antisemitic speech is forbidden. The presence of antisemitism, white supremacy, Nazi memorabilia, Holocaust denial, and other illegal or offensive material on American websites has been of great concern to Europeans. These opinions are expressed and these items sold in the United States. Nazis have marched in Skokie, and other places, organized in Idaho and Pennsylvania, sold their books and tracts and videos, and yet there is good reason to believe that they are held in more contempt here than in Europe.

European officials have called for additional restrictions on the Internet. British home secretary Jacqui Smith drew attention to the breadth and depth of expanding governance of the Internet, arguing for the development of filters to remove militant material from the Web, like those commonly used to limit children's access to pornographic material. "If we are ready and willing to take action to stop the grooming of the vulnerable young on social networking sites, then I believe we should also take action against those who groom vulnerable people for the purposes of violent extremism."[35] It is not entirely clear how Smith proposed to identify "vulnerable people" unless all Muslims were to be put in the category, once again to be placed, like children, under a benign and paternal British rule. Internet service providers resisted, with an industry blog arguing that "what the U.K. wants to do sounds like a scaled-down version of the so-called Great Firewall of China, in which Internet users in China cannot access a wide variety of material that government doesn't want them to see."[36] The controversy over WikiLeaks in the West made visible the strict regulation of several forms and categories of political speech—in the United States as well as in Europe.

Casting the debate over the threats to Rushdie and the murder of Theo van Gogh as moments when the friends of free speech confront its enemies conceals the many compromises—some principled, some self-serving—that have accompanied the politics of free expression in the West. It may be that the West's restrictions on speech are all defensible (I would argue against that), but their presence and significance must be acknowledged.

Casting the debate over the Danish cartoons and *Charia Hebdo* as moments in a clash of civilizations presents a false West, and a false Islam. Muslim secularists and free speech fundamentalists disappear. Western cosmopolitans and cultural conservatives disappear as well. Each civilization is reduced to something more parochial: more narrow, less thoughtful; more uniform, less contentious; more dogmatic, less political—in short, less civilized.

Casting the controversy over the cartoons, *Submission*, or Geert Wilders's film *Fitna* as a debate over free speech conceals the strategies that most endanger free speech in the West. We of the West are encouraged to think that we are free to speak freely when we are most constrained; to exchange the hazardous practice of speaking truth to power for the less risky business of mocking minorities; to forget that the right to remain silent is at the heart of freedom of speech; and to believe that—as far as our conduct, and our theories of justice, are concerned—nothing more needs to be said.

Things That Still Need to Be Said: The Right to Remain Silent

Theo van Gogh and many others in the West have championed a position holding not only that "anything could be said" but that "everything must be said." Perhaps this is an effort to make freedom of speech real: putting it in action, testing it, giving it form and content in the world. Perhaps it is a clumsy and misguided effort against restrictions on freedom of speech: constantly trying to extend, if not what *can* be said, at least what *is* said. Perhaps it serves as a distraction. If so much is said, then it appears that every view has a voice, and everyone is heard. If such outrageous things can be said, well, then: nothing more needs to be said.

In parts of the Netherlands, of Europe and America, of the West, where "everything must be said" there are still things that must be said quietly or not at all. There are still hazards to our freedom of speech.

In the period of the Enlightenment—in the past—threats to freedom of speech came from those who tried to silence speakers. Political expression, self-determination, the organization of those forces of resistance and solidarity necessary to democracy (and to reason) depended on the freedom of people to speak their minds. They still do. There is, however, more than one way to take away freedom of speech. People can be silenced, of course, but they can also be made to speak. Struggles for religious and political freedom in the United States and Europe were marked by resistance to loyalty oaths and Test Acts. The Twelve Articles of a rebellious German peasantry and the "Remonstrance" of the Levellers both objected to coerced testimony and self-incrimination. The Fifth Amendment of the Constitution of the United States testifies to the importance of ensuring that no one is made to speak against his or her will, recognizing that silence is essential to citizenship. These struggles acknowledged that true freedom of speech required not only the freedom to speak, but also the freedom to keep silent, particularly about matters of conscience and where confession would place a person in danger. Silence secured not only safety, but a space that might be given to faith or doubt, certainty or questioning.

Freedom of speech also requires that when people speak, they speak as they choose, according to their own will. We know people can be made to say things they do not wish to say. The Inquisition, and other inquisitorial institutions, past and present, have developed a number of techniques for making people speak against their will. "We have ways of making you talk" is what we have the most abhorrent villains say.

There are more subtle and sophisticated ways of making people talk. Anyone who has read Michel Foucault or watched daytime television knows the power of the confessional impulse. Late moderns in Europe and America are taught to reveal themselves whether they want to or not. We are expected to speak, and speak endlessly, of matters once thought wholly private.

The Muslim question shows us people who are not permitted to speak freely, who are obliged instead to say what others would like them to say, to speak scripts dictated to them by others. These compulsory speech acts are a prominent part of contemporary political discourse. They include the demand that "moderate Muslims," "more Muslims," or "Muslims" denounce the 9/11 attacks, accept or even engage in the mockery of their religion; the demand that Palestinian politicians, Palestinian academics, the Palestinian Authority, or "Palestinians" recognize Israel or denounce terrorism. These people can speak—they are required to speak—but they cannot speak freely.

That these demands are asymmetrical indicates the presence of prejudice. That the demands proliferate testifies to the radical narrowing of the right to free speech. The emergence of new—and the revival of old—strategies to constrain speech extends beyond the initial Muslim targets to Christians, Jews, and secularists, to anyone who wants to dissent from or go beyond the prescribed speech.

The vision that shows Muslims opposed to freedom of speech also makes Muslims the compulsory targets of that speech. It is not enough that one speak of Muslims. It is not even enough that one speak ill of them. One is required to speak ill of Muslims—and to do it in prescribed ways. Freedom of speech is not secured in the study of Islam, in writing or speaking of Muslims. Freedom of speech is not secured by those who call, however controversially, for the conversion of Christians to Islam. Freedom of speech is not advanced by the call to prayer. Speech is said to be "free speech" when—and only when—it is used to attack Muslims, Islam, or the Koran. When free speech becomes a Muslim question, its principle fails and its practice narrows. In this account, freedom of speech is no longer a matter of supporting the expression of unpopular opinions, defending the rights of minorities to a place in the public square, or speaking truth to power.

Political expression, self-determination, the organization of those forces of resistance and solidarity necessary to democracy and to reason depend on the freedom of people to speak their minds. There are still too many things that have to be whispered. There are still things that need to be said. There are still things we hope to hear. I have heard an American congressman take the oath of office on Jefferson's copy of the Koran. One day I may hear the call to prayer, the one that comes in the dark hours before the dawn, in Amsterdam or Chicago and in a woman's voice. One day I may see the European press defend a woman for wearing the hijab or a religious Muslim for critiquing the pretended neutrality of *laïcité*.

Early modern liberalism recognized the hazards of denying silence, and of compelling speech. Early liberals protested against compulsory speech acts in resistance to loyalty oaths and compulsory professions of faith, and enshrined the right to remain silent. Late modern thought recognized that the demand for self-disclosure made possible greater surveillance, repression, and control. We must recognize that the compulsory speech acts required of Muslims and in regard to Muslims follow the same logic. Political correctness is not a phenomenon of the Left; it lives and prospers on the right as well. If we are to protect freedom of speech and expression effectively, we must recognize that the greatest threats now come not from those who would silence speech, but from those who would dictate just what it is we have to say.

CHAPTER 2

Sex and Sexuality

Condemnation of Islam's treatment of women has united conservative Catholics and nostalgic Stalinists, neoliberals and social democrats. This rare point of unity among philosophers and politicians more often found at each other's throats does not, however, grow from a profound moment of Western cultural consensus. On the contrary, sex and sexuality in the West remain sites of enduring inequalities and fundamental disagreements. This is the terrain of the cultural wars, and underneath the seeming agreement on Islam, debates over sex and sexuality, equality and the sanctity of the family, the role of women, culture and rights, continue unabated.

For both Žižek and Okin, the case of Islam decisively indicts multiculturalism. Okin titled her book *Is Multiculturalism Bad for Women?* The title was doubly misleading. There was only one culture that concerned Okin: Islam. Okin had already decided that the answer to her question was "Yes, Islam is bad for women."[1]

Žižek, whose philosophic position differs radically from that of Susan Okin, shares her antipathy to Islam. He argues that Islam "is grounded on a disavowed femininity," on "the inexistence of the feminine." "And this brings us back to the function of the veil in Islam: what if the true scandal this veil endeavors to obfuscate is not the feminine body hidden by it, but the INEXISTENCE of the feminine?"[2] For Žižek, no less than his colleagues on the right, Islam is a man's world.

Okin's and Žižek's condemnations of "multiculturalism" anticipated the view, later embraced by politicians on the European right (from British prime minister David Cameron to Dutch politician Geert Wilders), that multiculturalism has failed. For the politicians, as for the philosophers, "multiculturalism" means "Islam." Cameron's speech opened as a speech on terror, but he moved rapidly to what he called "the root of the problem . . . Islamic extremism." Cameron insisted that he was distinguishing between Islam and "Islamic extremism" but described both as existing on a single continuum. Acceptable Muslims were to be distinguished by how closely they approached Cameron's own values.

Cameron made the status of women the criterion by which Muslim organizations were to be judged. "Let's properly judge these organisations: Do they believe in universal human rights—including for women?"[3] The implication was that Muslim organizations were in particular danger of falling short of this "universal" measure. German chancellor Angela Merkel and French president Sarkozy echoed Cameron. Wilders could claim to have advanced this view in the Netherlands and in Europe before it was respectable, but he was delighted to see them join his chorus: "Better late than never," he declared. In an address to the Magna Carta Foundation in Rome, Wilders joined in making women's rights a shibboleth. He declared, "Europe is Islamizing at a rapid pace. . . . Women's rights are being trampled. We are confronted with headscarves and burqas, polygamy, female genital mutilation, honour-killings." Women's rights, he insisted, were incompatible with Islam. "An International Women's Day is useless in the Arab world if there is no International Leave Islam Day."[4] Women, Wilders believes, must leave Islam to find themselves.

Ayaan Hirsi Ali is the woman who left. Her case testifies to the possibilities and limits for women in the West.

Theo van Gogh and Ayaan Hirsi Ali presented their film *Submission* as a defense of women against assaults mandated by the Koran. Islam, the film affirmed, was the enemy of women. Hirsi Ali underlined the message with the title of her book *Infidel*. Van Gogh and Hirsi Ali shared a passionate opposition to religion and religious authority and a dedication to shock as a political and artistic strategy. *Submission* is, however, less interesting for its shock value than for its timidity. What it says is less interesting than what it cannot bring itself to say.[5]

Submission begins with a brief shot of a man and woman at a table. They are posed like participants in a news show and dressed in Western clothes. The woman is black, the man white. They are looking off to one side. Behind them is a backlit Orientalist motif, with a veiled woman standing before it. The Western figures are immediately cast into the darkest shadow. The camera focuses on the woman, whose veil appears entirely opaque. She is scanned from head to (hidden) foot. As she spreads a prayer rug, we see her naked feet. As she walks, we see her body beneath the now-transparent burka. As she prays, another woman appears behind her, an older woman whose burka is opaque. The camera follows the contours of the younger woman's body beneath the veil. She is inscribed with Koranic verses. The woman then addresses God, declaring that she is wounded, and her spirit broken. The camera alternates between images of the woman speaking to God and her body, now nearly naked, covered only in part by a sheet and marked by whiplashes. The sound of the lash cuts through her speech to God. She recites portions of the verses concerning the penalty for men and women convicted of adultery and fornication. The short film then recounts the young woman's adulterous affair and abusive marriage, her rape by an uncle, and her pregnancy as the camera follows her naked body and the sound of the lash is heard against Arabic music. The older woman stands tall and authoritative in the background.

The script of *Submission* is Ayaan Hirsi Ali's, the direction van Gogh's. Hirsi Ali's experiences as a Muslim woman underwrite the film. In that sense, the film is about her, but it is not Hirsi Ali who is shown. Most importantly, it is not Ayaan Hirsi Ali's body that is filmed. That failure of nerve is more to be praised than blamed.

For all their willingness to provoke, even to outrage, that was a step too far for Hirsi Ali and van Gogh. Their decision recognized that there would be something intrusive, something demeaning, in stripping away the garments Hirsi Ali chooses to wear in the world. She stands instead in the position of the older woman the film condemns. She stands in the background. She has authority. She wrote the script. She inscribes her words on another woman's body. She tells the barely veiled woman what she should do. But Ayaan Hirsi Ali is not this dark and threatening figure. Ayaan Hirsi Ali is beautiful.

Remembering Ayaan Hirsi Ali's authority alters the message of the film. The young woman who is both veiled and stripped is caught between conflicting demands. The (truly) veiled woman insists that she submit to a harsh and primitive conception of Islam. Ayaan Hirsi Ali offers her salvation through sex. The men in the film do the same. They beat or rape her, or they offer her escape through sexual transgression. There is no moment of real freedom for this woman. She is offered a choice that is no choice at all: submission to a puritan Islam or submission to secular licentiousness. The camera work casts her as a body available to every man's gaze.

There is both an abstract and a profound personal cruelty in the series of imperatives *Submission* issues to women. You must want sex; you must want sex with men. Adultery is sex, sex is love, and love is good. You must want to open your body to men. Muslim women are victims and prisoners. You can have freedom and power only by refusing the Koran.[6]

These are the open, public cruelties. The private cruelties are more profound.

In her memoir *Infidel*, Ayaan Hirsi Ali records the damage done to her body by her traditional and conservative grandmother. Her father had attempted to protect her from the genital cutting that has been endemic in Somali tribal society. He had forbidden it. The local imam had forbidden it as well. Islam and patriarchal authority, in this instance, spoke for the girl. The grandmother, bound within the imperatives of another, more pagan Islam, an Islam disavowed by both the father and the religious authority, waited for an opportunity and had Ayaan Hirsi Ali and her sister subjected to an exceptionally harsh form of cutting.[7]

In *Submission*, sex is pleasure and freedom. This text stands in sharp contrast to the meaning of sex and violence in the life of Ayaan Hirsi Ali. For the wounded bodies of those who have been forced to undergo cutting, sex is unlikely to be simply pleasurable. The harsher the cutting, the greater the enduring pain. Sex may be difficult, painful, and dangerous. The consequences of genital cutting are concealed here. The complexities of this episode in Hirsi Ali's autobiography are ignored as well. In their place, we have the simple lessons of *Submission*: the Koran is bad; adultery is good; Islam harms women; sex is pleasure and freedom.

The concealment of the wounds on Ayaan Hirsi Ali's body might be commended as an act of kindness if it did not so cruelly present sexual pleasure as secular redemption. Hirsi Ali's memoir is more frank, more courageous, and (for those of us trying to find our way) more complex and demanding. Hirsi Ali did not hesitate to make her own wounds visible in the memoir. She tells us that the wounds of her own genital cutting were severe, and that her sister's suffering was worse. Though her father had opposed the cutting, she does not present men as the saviors of women. Nor does she present sexuality as the only or even the primary way for women to find pleasure or freedom. On the contrary, the world of her memoir is one in which men and women are redeemed not by sex, but by politics.

In Hirsi Ali's Somalia, both men and women are damaged. Her brother is held down and cut as she was: at the same time, by the same people. She sees a young boy beaten to death by a mob. Her father is continually on the run, a political exile in danger of assassination. In the Kenyan refugee camp, she sees an armed man sit down on the sand and cry, his head in hands. No one is free: not her father, with his high clan status (a pride she clings to); not her brother; not her husband; not her lover; not armed men. No one is free. All are bound by the demands of clan loyalty, the seductions of clan status, religious imperatives, and familial duty. All are subject to the burdens of a violent and dictatorial politics.

The Netherlands opens the possibility of freedom for Hirsi Ali. She is able to craft her life as an independent, autonomous individual. She can get an education. She was born to a clan and a nation. She chooses to be a citizen.

Hirsi Ali is presented—sometimes she presents herself—as an opponent of Islam. Her writings and her political positions are, however, strikingly ecumenical. She has a catholic disregard for religion in public life. As a member of Parliament in the Netherlands, she opposed funding for Christian schools, to the horror of Christian conservatives who had previously praised her as an apostate heroine.

What made the Netherlands a place of freedom was not the absence of Islam, but the presence of democratic politics, respect for law, and institutions free from corruption. Hirsi Ali concludes *Infidel* with a set of acknowledgments. "I was born," she writes, "in a country torn apart by war and grew up in a continent mostly known for what goes wrong rather than right." It is not surprising, then, that her acknowledgments include expressions of gratitude to people most Westerners regard as problems: "The INS officials, the police . . . the landlords."[8] Hirsi Ali recognized that the absence of corruption among immigration officials, the possibility of going to the police without the need for a bribe or fear of abuse, and of dealing with landlords without fear of fraud or exploitation, are remarkable things. There are few places in the world where one can move freely, confident that officials will deal honestly with you and that the laws protect you. Hirsi Ali's work is, at its core, a celebration of this confident pleasure that is so ordinary, so taken for granted, that it has become invisible to her Dutch compatriots. She sounds like a child in her love of her new country, in her belief that by voting she could change the world. She knows what women want.

When she became a citizen, she writes, "it was the least momentous occasion in the world" for the bureaucrat who gave her a Dutch passport, for the Dutch friends she invited to celebrate with her. "Nobody seemed *proud* of being Dutch." For Hirsi Ali, it was the most momentous occasion in the world. She recounts her intense pleasure in voting: "I gave it a lot of thought. Actually to have the ability to choose the government of Holland—."[9] She would become part of that government.

Hirsi Ali's champions cast her memoir as the story of a woman seeking sexual freedom: "a young girl born to be forced into marriage" (*Elle*, France); "a young girl's first kiss" (*San Francisco Chronicle*); "her desperate flight to the Netherlands to escape an arranged marriage" (*New York Times*). She is "a woman whom radical Muslims have marked for death," with "an unrelenting critique of Islam"; "a crusader . . . an Infidel indeed" (*The Age*). She is "a charismatic figure . . . of arresting and hypnotizing beauty" (Christopher Hitchens, *Slate*), "Intelligent, passionate, beautiful. And living in fear of her life" (*Observer Review*).[10] The story of the "hypnotizing beauty" fleeing the violence of the desert, pursued by fanatical sheikhs, to find love and refuge in the West is clearly entrancing, but it does not do justice to Hirsi Ali.

Perhaps the press and publishers think that no one would be much moved by a woman who fled a violent, corrupt, and dictatorial politics to find helpful bureaucrats, trustworthy police, and honest landlords. Perhaps it is more exciting to imagine her finding sexual freedom than to see her seizing the chance to go to "Holland's oldest university" with "rigorous standards," become a citizen, vote, run for office, or win a seat in Parliament.[11] Perhaps it is safer to show the Muslim woman as a victim, trapped in a loveless marriage and confined to the household, than to show a Muslim woman free to reject her faith and write openly against it. Perhaps it is safer to show a Muslim refugee still in hiding than to show a Dutch woman of African origin with power in the world.

Perhaps we should not be surprised that Theo van Gogh thought it would be more effective (or at least more erotic) to show a woman fleeing Islam to have sex. Naked breasts and a lashed back excite sexual desire as well as sympathy. Wounded genitals might repulse—or, worse, they might reveal a more troubled and troubling form of Western sexuality. If the camera had not moved away in that opening shot, the film might have suggested that a black woman can hold authority with a white man, that pleasure is not a matter for the body alone, that freedom follows not from sexual pleasure but from political power and the possibility of individual autonomy.

Theo van Gogh's website, De Gezonde Roker, provides an ironic commentary on the metaphoric use of sexual for political power. Van Gogh gave himself a heraldic crest emblazoned with a flaccid phallus and the motto *Luctor et emergo* (I will struggle and rise up).[12] Van Gogh's adopted crest can be seen as a gesture of charmingly self-deprecating sexuality. The sign mocks many pretensions at once: the aristocratic pretensions of the crest, motto, and van Gogh's own social milieu;

the pretensions of an arrogant masculinity; the pretensions of the preachy political—those who might inscribe their websites with *Veritas, La lutta continua,* "We shall overcome," and the like. It is also a rather astute, though possible unwitting, cultural commentary.

For van Gogh, as for so many, sexual freedom figured as the sign, perhaps even the substance, of freedom. Sexual power—power over sexuality, power charged with sexuality—is central to politics. The governance of sexuality (who can marry, which forms of sexuality will be permitted or forbidden, encouraging births or limiting population growth) is profoundly political. Conflicts over the governance of sexuality, central to all politics, take a striking form in the Netherlands. Citizens are expected, instructed, even required, to have correct views on sexuality. Not tolerance, but the affectionate recognition of homosexuality becomes the litmus text of belonging. Sexual freedom becomes the form of freedom that comes to stand for all. At some moments, in some contexts, sexual freedom replaces all other freedoms. Thus Dutch political leader Pim Fortuyn could say, in an oft-quoted remark, that he was not a racist, since he had sex with Moroccan boys.

Not all Dutch welcome this sexual economy. Conservative and Calvinist parties protest against state funding (even the legality) of abortion; they deprecate the legality of prostitution and the presence of homosexuality in the public sphere. This has not, however, led them to make common cause with conservative Muslims. On the contrary, conservative efforts at sexual governance point to "the demographic problem." Their vision for the governance of sexuality—opposed to abortion and homosexuality—wants to produce a fertile heterosexual

Netherlands, where immigrants (especially Muslims) need not apply.

The global presentation of the clash of sexual civilizations casts European sexuality as open, unregulated, individually determined, and irreligious. The debate casts all Muslims as culturally and religiously conservative in sexual matters, concealing a wide range of religious, cultural, and personal variation. This clash of sexual civilizations conceals the contours of European sexual politics. The sexual conservatism of much of European society is cast into deep shadow. The presence of sexually conservative Europeans is denied and diminished. Their political power is concealed even as it expands. They are even occasionally presented to liberal observers as liberal and progressive.

Pim Fortuyn's rise to political and cultural power was intimately tied to this sexual economy. Fortuyn's theatrical homosexuality was a spectacular performance of personal freedom. He spoke freely of his desire for unlimited, unrestrained sexual pleasure. He was the man of free appetites in the free market, reveling in consumer indulgences, large and small: the grand Daimler, the little dogs, the fur collars. He became, for many, the symbol of economic success, political independence, and personal freedom. Men like Pim Fortuyn had overcome exclusion. Fortuyn had seen the acceptance of homosexuality in his own lifetime. When he was young, gay men had been forced, like Anne Frank, into hiding. He belonged to the first generation to come out of the closet and into power: gay men who were not simply tolerated, but accepted, even welcomed.

Fortuyn, as several Dutch commentators noted, seemed less a political figure than a cultural figure, less a statesman than an entertainer. Dutch anthropologist Peter van der Veer writes that "campy, extroverted gay entertainers have become hugely popular in the Netherlands. 'They say what everyone thinks' is how such entertainers are usually described, and Fortuyn precisely fitted that image."[13] Fortuyn's performances were witty and entertaining—and they were also politically charged. His coy insistence that he could not be prejudiced since he liked to make love to Moroccan boys was not a simple witticism. Moroccans, it implied, could be used for pleasure and for profit, but they would remain subordinate and exploited. Those who had nodded their heads at Ayaan Hirsi Ali's ahistorical characterization of Muhammad as a pedophile found it possible to overlook Fortuyn's account of his own predilection for Moroccan boys. The question was not what was done, but who did it.

Fortuyn's gayness gave him a license for frankness. He was out of the closet: no longer subject to repression, no longer forced to hide away, Anne Frank out of the attic. Support for his lack of reticence, tact, and discretion was support for frankness in both senses: for unrestrained, honest, uncensored speech; and for the social acceptance of formerly persecuted groups. Pim Fortuyn's flamboyantly gay persona, and its symbolic associations, enabled his supporters (and later his party, the List Pim Fortuyn) to see themselves as supporters rather than persecutors of minorities. Fortuyn's flamboyant homosexuality worked as a kind of secular exculpation. He enabled his supporters to affirm their tolerance even as they manifested their intolerance. Their acceptance of his theatrical homosexuality licensed their refusal of tolerance to Muslims. Sexual freedom became not a metonym for political freedom, but a substitute.

Gay male sexuality became the shibboleth of freedom and modernity for the immigration authorities in the Netherlands. It has been similarly deployed in more cosmopolitan circles. This did not, however, indicate acceptance of queer sexuality, or even the abandonment of slurs. At the same time Islam was castigated for a supposedly distinctive hostility to queer sexuality, Muslims (especially Muslim fundamentalists) were mocked as gay. The now familiar reading of Sodom into Saddam Hussein became a staple of *South Park*. The portrait of Saddam Hussein as the tormentor of a lovelorn Satan had a critical edge: it was the Great Satan, after all, who appeared as both queer and queerly sympathetic.

There were, however, simpler deployments of antigay rhetoric. French (and Francophile Maghrebi) critics of Islam have long argued that Islamic fundamentalists are closeted homosexuals, whose fondness for robes and kohl-lined eyes betrays their sexual repression. Bad politics is analogous to queer sex. Author and critic Bruce Bawer wrote, "European culture leaders should smack down fanatical Islamists. Instead, they're bending over for them."[14] Bawer's emphasis on his own gay identity licenses the sexual economy the metaphor endorses. Proper men use violence; they "smack down." Queer men bend over. Queer sex is bad politics: but only if the wrong men are bending over.

Bawer has lived for many years in Europe and is in full accord with those Europeans who praise the openness of their societies to gay men as they seek to close the gates to Muslims. Like Fortuyn, Bawer deploys his gay identity as a license for intolerance of Islam. There is something perverse in Bawer, the gay proponent of he-man politics, as there was in Fortuyn's camp Islamophobia. They use the former exclusion of gays to license the present and future exclusion of Muslims. They take their experiences of intolerance as furnishing an exculpation for their own intolerant acts and dictats. A deeper perversity rests in their endorsement of sexual norms that are both violent and hierarchical: where Europeans "smack down" Muslims they disagree with, "bending over" is something only the exploited do. Bawer insists, as Fortuyn did, on maintaining a sexual and political economy in which white men are on top and coercion (by the proper party) is the proper order of the world.

If this is to be the future of an enlightened West, embracing the gay with the straight, it isn't nearly queer enough. There is little space here for men who prefer their sex without coercion and between equals. There is no space for men who might regard sex as an act rather than an identity. There is no space for an erotic imaginary in which a dark Muslim might be something other than a sheikh or a slave. There is no space for women at all.

West and East, the world is queerer than they imagine. Muslim men walk the streets of Cairo, and sometimes Paris, hand in hand. They embrace when they meet. No one—no Muslim—bats an eyelid. They are not challenged about their sexuality, or required to give an account of their sexual histories or their desires. They are not obliged to confess. A colleague of mine noted that though homosexuality was illegal in the Gulf states, "I could walk down the street hand in hand with my partner. We can't do that in Philadelphia."

Queerness goes deeper. In *Women with Mustaches and Men without Beards* Afsaneh Najmabadi presents an account of male and female beauty that turns Western aesthetics upside down.[15] In the Iranian world she opens, women are more beautiful with mustaches; men lose their looks quickly, while women's beauty lasts. One sees beauty and age, masculine and feminine differently after reading Najmabadi's book. She enables us to see that the erotic is various and changeable, and that in each place and time only a small part of it is understood. Desire is more complex still. For Richard Burton, for André Gide, for Gustave Flaubert, for Ingres and Géricault, the world of Islam was a place of desire: desire provoked, desire satisfied, desire denied and so all the stronger. In much of Western painting and literature the world of Islam is a safe haven for practices condemned in the West. This travels from high literature to popular culture as *A Thousand and One Nights* gives way to children's versions and then to *Aladdin*. *The Sheikh* (1921) reshaped the performance of masculinity through Valentino's performance, making the veiled man with kohl-lined eyes the object of feminine desire, the representation of a powerful, violent, and seductive masculine power. The 1960s TV series *I Dream of Jeannie* domesticated an erotics of feminine power, making the alien blond and giving a sunny and submissive face to a woman whose power far outstripped a man's. Little is stable here. The veil may be worn by a man or a woman; to repel the gaze or to attract it; to forestall or to provoke desire. The Arabian desert of the Western imagination has held the tents of puritanical fundamentalists and the harems of hedonists. Westerners have come to the Muslim world to free gay men from the shackles of Islam, to save a Cairo gay nightclub, the Queen Boat, and they have come (as Gide did) to practice freely what they could not safely do at home.

When I was in Denmark, Danes would often say to me (in English, and in exactly these words): "We do this very well here. Immigrants should do it our way." "This" applied to everything from day care to manners. I was surprised, not at their claim to do things well (they do), but at their conviction that there was only one way to do something well and that they had a firm grasp on it. The efforts of the Gay International have a similar self-confidence with far less merit.

Political scientist Joseph Massad coined the term the "Gay International" to describe a modern missionary effort. As Massad writes, the activists of the Gay International seek to "liberate Arab and Muslim 'gays and lesbians' from the oppression under which they allegedly live by transforming them from practitioners of same-sex contact into subjects who identify as homosexual and gay."[16] These names, "gay" and "homosexual," have had a short life even in the West, yet they are read as representing identities that are the same in all times and places. They are cast as universal identities, though many even in the West continue to doubt their stability. They run counter to the scholarship on sex and sexuality that recognizes how little we knew of these things, how unsettled our practices and identities are. This missionary position insists that we in the West (or at least those in the Gay International who speak for us) know sex and sexual orientation, and that "we do it very well." We are confident that we can explain to others in less enlightened places what they desire, what they should call themselves, who they are. We are confident that sexual orientation decisively divides the world, that those divisions are always and everywhere the same, that those divisions must be made visible to all, and that those divisions must be ruthlessly policed and maintained. The categories of the Gay International operate according to a kind of one-drop or one-act rule of sexuality. Any same-sex conduct makes one gay or lesbian. This, according to the logic of the Gay International, is freedom and equality. It is nothing of the sort.

Studies of sexuality and discussions of sexuality in Western media and Western scholarship have exploded for the good Socratic reason that we know that we don't know. We are learning and trying to learn. This is yet another argument for a little more modesty in our treatment of sex and sexuality.

What We Veil

The veil is a concealment and a revelation, puritanical and erotic, the work of men and the choice of women. The woman who wears a veil reveals something and conceals more. She reveals herself as a woman, and as one whose practice of the faith is relatively conservative. She conceals not only (and not most importantly) those "hidden treasures" that the Koran suggests women conceal, but a number of other things. A mind as well as a body dwells beneath the veil. We do not know what moved her to veil herself, what part of that veiling is prompted by others, what part is her own choice. We can read her veil, as we might read any choice of garments, but these (like any speech) may be deceptive. Whatever her intention, the veil will draw the gaze. For Muslims, the veil is more legible, more visible as a text. It draws the eye as any text does: because there is much to read in it. The eye may slide easily over a conventional veil worn in Saudi Arabia or Malaysia but an unconventional veil—whether more or less than the mind expects—will hold the eye. Even the expected, conventional veil will be read in passing.

The wearer's politics, understanding of religion, region, age, urbanity, all may be visible in the veil. In the West, the veil draws the eye because it provokes fear and anxiety. The question of what is carried under the veil acquires a new importance in this context: both literal and metaphoric. The veil now prompts fears that weapons might be concealed beneath it, and if not weapons, dangerous sentiments and beliefs. Joan Scott tells the story of a veiled woman at a French bank: the teller "refused to wait on her because her veil might be the disguise for a hold-up." French feminist opponents of the veil, like Caroline Fourest and Fiammetta Venner, cast hijabs as "enemy flags in a war to the death."[17] The war is not against Islam, however, but within the West.

In her brilliant study *The Politics of the Veil*, Joan Scott pulled the veil aside to show us what it concealed in French politics. The veil conceals the presence and durability of racial hierarchies the French insist are absent. The veil conceals the haunting resemblance of the treatment of French Muslims to the treatment of French Jews. The veil shrouds a colonial past the French insist is dead and gone. Scott spreads out that much-vexed piece of cloth and uses it to map the anxieties haunting French politics and society. Liberty, equality, and fraternity are not only the core values of France—they also are demands that the French (like other Westerners) find difficult to satisfy. Liberty becomes more manageable when it is reduced to sexual freedom. The persistence of colonial hierarchies abroad and racism at home haunts the aspiration to Equality. Fraternity is lost in the conflicts over the veil and in those suburbs called the *banlieues d'Islam*. Once again, a seemingly Muslim question reveals itself as a series of questions the West obliquely asks itself.

The philosopher Alain Badiou's look at the veil shows that, as is so often the case with sex in the West, the question is not love but money; not romance but good business; not human rights but the norms of capitalism. Badiou trenchantly observes that it may be not only sex but capitalism which is at stake in the outlawing of the veil. Perhaps, Badiou ventures, there is "a simple explanation: a girl must show what she has to sell." Women's bodies are treated like any other good offered on the open market. "Whoever keeps covered what she has on the market is not a loyal businesswoman."[18] Badiou rejects the idea that veils must be stripped off because any woman wearing a veil must be a fool or a hostage, tyrannized or deluded. The veil, Badiou argues, is neither a sign of submission nor armor against the male gaze. By hiding the woman's body, veiling challenges capitalism and the commodification of female sexuality.

Badiou's critique directs our attention to the intersection and overlap of sexual and economic exploitation. It is not only, as a former member of the Taliban told the *New York Times*, that Westerners would use a woman's naked body to sell a cigarette, that sexual harassment and pay inequities continue to trouble the Western workplace. The critics of finance capital in the streets of Athens, Reykjavik, and New York would do well to examine the economic order's continued dependence on women's unpaid labor.

Badiou's critique of the challenge to the veil might also prompt us to look with a more critical eye on official valorizations of gay male sexuality. These are constructed as the freedom to pursue pleasure, to consume, and hence give as much support to the imperatives of capitalism as they do to sexual equality.

In the West, marriage (gay or straight) is supposed to follow romance. People marry for love; they marry for happiness. When the conservative Theodore Olson and the liberal David Boies argued that same-sex marriage was a constitutionally guaranteed right, they based their argument on the clause in the preamble of the Constitution that secured "the pursuit of happiness."

But marriage, like so much sexual policing, is not just about love; it's about money. Marriage determines rights to property. Marriage is a contract. Like other contracts, it is governed by the state. Laws tell us whom we can marry and whom we can't. They tell us when we can marry (not, say, before the age of sixteen). The laws don't care much about happiness. They do care about sex (if it's useful to the state). Laws in Europe, if not in the United States, reward people who have children. Marriage, in all cases, directs the flow of money. Property flows as marriage directs: to a spouse or a partner, to children. Domestic partnerships and civil unions have the same ties to money. When American corporations began offering benefits to same-sex partners, they required people to establish that they really were partners. This was not a matter of sex or love or romance. It was a matter of money. Partners had to demonstrate not that they had romantic or sexual ties but that they had financial ones. They had to show that they owned property together, that they were named in each other's wills or shared a bank account.

Badiou has sharp eyes. He sees beyond the veil to things we normally keep hidden in the West. Sex and sexuality, like marriage and romance, are closely tied, in the West, to questions of capital and property. The subjection of women is not, as conservatives might like to believe, the work of nature. Nor, as liberals would like to believe, is it the work of archaic customs and religious beliefs. Both conservatives and liberals present feminine subjection as traditional. Badiou recognizes its modernity. Conservatives and liberals place women's protected and subjected status in an ancient past. They may wish to alter those traditions or preserve them, but they concur in seeing them as made, in no small part, by religions. Badiou recognizes that the liberal secular state is no less responsible.

The veil marks the woman beneath it as dangerous. She draws the eye because she is feared. That might be enough to persuade more Western women to turn to the veil, but there is more. The veil is also profoundly erotic. The veil draws the Western eye because it marks the wearer as sexual. If the box says "chocolate," one does not need to see the contents to think of chocolate, to want chocolate, to imagine opening the box. The veil says "sexuality": one need not see what lies beneath. It is ironic that Western women who adopt the veil as a gesture of modesty are marking themselves, every day, to Muslims and non-Muslims, with a sign of that which they wish to conceal.

Because the veil, like all garments, acts as a text, it also obeys the laws of the text. It does not mean only what the wearer wishes it to mean. Its meaning may change. It may lie, and it may be misinterpreted. The woman who wears the most modest clothing may be an adulteress. The woman whom watchers see as the slave of her husband or father may have chosen to wear the veil against his will. The veil is not transparent (even when it is).

Perhaps that is why the veil troubles and fascinates the Enlightenment. In an age, to a philosophy, that insists on transparency, the veil suggests that transparency is not a virtue. The veil argues that there are some things that are better hidden. Nietzsche made this critique explicit (after his fashion) and with reference to veiling: "what if Truth has reasons for not letting us see her reasons?" The veil protests against transparency. In an age that insists on transparency, the veil refuses it. In doing so, the veil refuses the imperative to confess all (especially regarding sex and sexuality). The veil forestalls the confessional imperative, the demand to speak and speak endlessly, that Foucault marked as one of the most imperative and inevitable of the demands of modern life.

CHAPTER 3

Women and War

The construction of the Muslim world as hostile to women accomplishes several useful objects for the West, particularly the United States. Attention to the plight of women in the Muslim world turns the gaze of feminists and other potential critics away from the continuing oppression of women in the West. Western women are told how very fortunate they are. They may still be subject to domestic violence, rape, and sexual assault (even by Western politicians), but these assaults pale before the horrors of polygamy and forced marriage. They may still make only a fraction of what men make, but they should be grateful for it.

Western women are enlisted, with Western men, in the tired project of saving brown women from brown men. In participating in this campaign, they learn to look upon Western models of sex and sexuality as liberating, universally valid, and exempt from criticism. They are turned away from the advancement of women's position at home and enlisted in projects of imperial domination. Discourses of human rights become the justification for military adventures and imperial rule. The advancement of women's rights becomes the justification for invasion and nation building.

Muslim women, and critics, male and female, of Western models of sex and sexuality, are silenced. The price of speech for a Muslim woman in the West is the disavowal of Islam. Books condemning Islam are picked up by publishers and featured on talk shows. Their authors are commended for their courage. Speech in defense of Islam is read as the speech of subjection. Islam oppresses women. Any woman speaking in its favor must be deluded or forced to speak against her will. If she defends the hijab or speaks in defense of polygamy, she cannot be believed. No woman in her right mind could defend these. Any woman who does must be deluded or coerced. The more Muslim women object to Western efforts to "help" them, the more need there is to liberate them.

Western feminists became prisoners of the same logic. The account of the West as the land of free women and the Muslim world as the place of their imprisonment made intervention not only a feminist project, but a shibboleth and a litmus test. A feminist who defended the choice of Islam could not be a true feminist. A feminist who objected to the invasion of Afghanistan must be callously indifferent to the rights of other women.

The Egyptian revolution challenged this picture of Muslim women as victims. The public roles of women like Bothaina Kamel (Egyptian activist and politician), Iman Mohammed (a veiled feminist member of the Muslim Brotherhood), and Tahani el Gebali (vice president of Egypt's Constitutional Court) made it harder to present the Muslim world as a place of "the INEXISTENCE of the feminine." The women whose voices are heard on Leila Zahra's *Words of Women from the Egyptian Revolution* are old and young, veiled and unveiled, frank, fearless and often loud.[1] These women were not the silent victims of Muslim misogyny; they were leading revolutions.

This made it all the more necessary for the most vociferous critics of Islam both to shore up the portrayal of Muslim women as victims, and to insist that Western feminists commit themselves to the "war on Islam." The syndicated columnist Debbie Schlussel, who would later distinguish herself by writing, in response to Osama bin Laden's death, "One down, 1.8 billion to go," seized on Lara Logan. Logan, a CBS reporter covering the Egyptian revolution, was sexually assaulted when she was separated from her crew. Schlussel's response was "So sad, too bad, Lara. No one told her to go there. She knew the risks. And she should have known what Islam is all about. Now she knows."[2] Schlussel's was a double condemnation: Muslims are "animals" and Logan wasn't tough enough.

Or perhaps she had tried to be too tough. Perhaps fear was a public duty. That was the argument made by another right-wing columnist, Michelle Malkin. In a 2004 column, Malkin wrote, "Nothing matters to me more right now than the safety of my home and the survival of my homeland." Both were under threat. Malkin told how she lived in a constant state of alert anxiety. "I have studied the faces on the FBI's most-wanted-terrorists list. When I ride the train, I watch for suspicious packages in empty seats. When I am on the highways, I pay attention to larger trucks and tankers." She wanted to be in constant touch with her husband. She taught her four-year-old child about Saddam Hussein and Osama bin Laden. "This isn't living in fear," Malkin insisted. "This is living with reality." For Malkin, and for many others (even after the death of Osama bin Laden), living in fear was living in reality. As she wrote, "We must live defensively."[3]

Malkin called herself a "security mom," a term coined to describe hawkish suburban women in the 2004 elections: women who, like Malkin, divided their fear between "Islamic terrorists" and illegal immigrants, or, as Malkin termed them, "criminal aliens." "Living defensively" meant living in the protection of a gated community, shopping in malls policed by private security forces, and driving a Hummer or an SUV. Women like Malkin didn't need to fear higher gas prices for their guzzlers. They didn't need to wonder whether they'd make the mortgage on the house. They could drive to the shopping mall anchored by Saks rather than Walmart without worrying about what they could afford. The fears Malkin expressed were fears about luxuries masquerading as necessities.

The women who spoke so readily of their fears were not only Republicans and conservatives. Liberal democrats seized on the same model of womanly fear. Ellen Goodman wrote, "Whether it's domestic violence or crime in the streets or terrorism after 9/11, women are more likely to worry that they or theirs are vulnerable."[4] Women like Goodman found security in Medicare and Social Security. Women like Malkin found it in the police and the military. What remained constant was the conviction that women were afraid. Joe Klein wrote in *Time* magazine, "The war on terrorism is two wars, one for men and one for women." Men saw it as a "video game," Klein wrote; it was "exciting." Women felt "helpless."[5] The idea of the security mom as an important voting bloc evaporated, but the icon and what it represented remained. A good woman feared for her home—and, now, for her homeland.

Before September 11th, Americans called the United States "my country" or "our nation." Shortly after the attack, government and the media began referring to "the homeland" and "homeland security." "Homeland" had once been an alien turn of phrase, one used by nationalists, especially *völkisch* nationalists. It belonged to the Old World, to the Europe Americans had left behind. It was used in films and novels to mark a form of patriotism we had rejected. Now it was to be ours.

Michelle Malkin's coupling of immigration and terror might seemed forced to people who see the man cutting the lawn or washing dishes in the back of the restaurant as posing very little danger. Such immigrants might "take American jobs," but they were often the hardest jobs with the lowest pay. The idea of a border open to the drug wars of Mexico was terrifying, but the illegal immigrant who watched the babies or cleaned the house was clearly more a victim than a threat. Malkin's fears depended on an older history and unspeakable fears.

The phenomenon of the security mom was white flight on a global scale. The security mom feared the arrival of the darker other, whether terrorist or immigrant. The home was no longer a place of safety because the world surrounding the home had changed. Some who fled believed the unwelcome arrivals brought crime and terror with them. Others saw them as a threat in themselves, evidence that the world was changing, or had changed already. The certainties of the world—of the neighborhood—had passed away. There was "a threat to our way of life." But globalization made the threat more difficult to evade. It was no longer enough to move to the suburbs. There was no place to go.

Living defensively was not adequate. The threat might materialize at any time. The fears that prompted white flight began not with the arrival of the first black neighbors, but with the first rumors of their arrival. So it was with terrorism. Terrorism didn't need a moving van. The fear that terrorists might arrive at any time, in any place, made flight impossible. The fear and anger that fueled white flight now sent troops abroad. The home could be made safe only through the power of the homeland. The comforts of domesticity were dependent on dominion.

For the first time, women took part in these military operations on the front lines and—as was slowly acknowledged—in combat roles. Some of the women who went to war were enlisted in projects very much at odds with their oath to defend the Constitution.

Weaponized Sex

Western women, enlisted in the project of liberating—or simply defeating—the Muslim world became tangled in a particularly perverse enterprise in which a project of universal liberation was used to support two systems of subordination. Consider the case of Lynndie England. England's smiling face figures in a number of the photographs from Abu Ghraib. We know her from the photograph of the man on a leash. We recognize her giving a cheerful thumbs-up over the dog pile, and pointing cheerily at the genitals of various prisoners.

Susan Sontag observed that "most of the pictures seem part of a larger confluence of torture and pornography: a young woman leading a naked man around on a leash is classic dominatrix imagery. And you wonder how much of the sexual tortures inflicted on the inmates of Abu Ghraib was inspired by the vast repertory of pornographic imagery available on the Internet—and which ordinary people, by sending out Webcasts of themselves, try to emulate."[6]

The pornographic aspect of the photographs was also recognized and deployed by fundamentalist clerics who had been reproached for their reluctance to condemn torture at Abu Ghraib. Concerned Women for America issued two articles on the abuse that, a critical Christian noted, "both blame American pornography for the soldiers' actions." Robert Knight, of CWA's Culture & Family Institute, blamed homosexuals, feminists, and liberals for "systematically aiding and abetting the cultural depravity that produced the Abu Ghraib scandal." The head of the Southern Baptist Convention's Ethics & Religious Liberty Commission, Richard Land, refusing to fix responsibility in the chain of command, declared, "These people's moral compass didn't work for some reason. My guess is because they've been infected with relativism."[7]

The construction of the photographs as pornographic enabled fundamentalists to condemn Abu Ghraib without condemning torture and without raising questions about the conduct and discipline of the army of occupation and the mercenary forces. They were able to blame Abu Ghraib on groups whose culpability would otherwise seem most improbable: liberals, feminists, and homosexuals.

Characterizing the photographs as pornographic was also used to diminish the gravity of the damage done, the pain endured. The "classic dominatrix pose" of Lynndie England and the "dog piles" of naked men drew the gaze inexorably—drawing it away from photographs of the dead, the bleeding, and the maimed. Eyes slid over the damaged body lying on ice and other photos of the dead, and fixed on the photographs that conformed to the conventions of pornography. Questions about who had been killed unjustly, who had been tortured, and how such things were possible in our military, gave way to questions about relativism. Moral failure referred not to war crimes but to pornography.

Defenders of the Bush administration deployed tropes of pornography and pleasure to render torture benign and defensible.

Sontag recognized this effect:

> To "stack naked men" is like a college fraternity prank, said a caller to Rush Limbaugh and the many millions of Americans who listen to his radio show. Had the caller, one wonders, seen the photographs? No matter. The observation—or is it the fantasy?—was on the mark. What may still be capable of shocking some Americans was Limbaugh's response: "Exactly!" he exclaimed. "Exactly my point. This is no different than what happens at the Skull and Bones initiation, and we're going to ruin people's lives over it."[8]

The comparison to Skull and Bones was a telling one. Skull and Bones is, after all, not quite a fraternity. (It does not seem to be about fraternity—much less liberty and equality—at all.) Skull and Bones is a secret society, and George Bush is a member. Limbaugh's movement from the caller's "fraternity prank" to "the Skull and Bones initiation" was a shift that places Abu Ghraib where it belongs, with George Bush and the politics of secrecy. Limbaugh's revision of his caller's remark moved the comparison from the familiar if reprehensible practices of fraternity hazing to the concealed acts of a secret and secretive elite. In doing so, Limbaugh acknowledged, perhaps unconsciously, the force of the old feminist recognition that pornography is less about pleasure than about power.

England became an icon for abuse: the abuse she perpetrated and the abuse she endured. The ambivalence of her role, abuser and abused, captures a familiar strategy for keeping women down in the West. The strategy is altered, subtly and effectively, in response to globalization.

The logic of lynching once supported white supremacy and male power. White women were instructed to fear black men and to stay far away from them. Rape was the most feared crime, but fears of robbery and assault filled everyday life. White women were taught to avoid any place where black men were, to see them as signs of lawless places, where robbery and assault were common. White men were said to offer safety and protection. Black men were taught to fear white women, who could make false charges against them and see them lynched. They too were taught to seek safety and security from white men. At Abu Ghraib women were once again made the lynchpin of a system of oppression, once again enrolled in a strategy of collaboration. This time, however, the strategy turned not on the fiction of women's weakness, but on the fiction of women's strength.

The presence of women soldiers in Iraq and Afghanistan was advanced by the military and, more importantly, by the media as evidence for the equality of women in the West. The women were seen to serve with men as equals. The photographs seem to record Lynndie England's power. She is a soldier. She has weapons. She commands. She is obeyed. She wears the uniform of her country's military. She serves with men. Her presence at Abu Ghraib testifies to the inclusion of women in the American military, to the equality of men and women.

Her presence testifies that women have access to military power.

The camera lies—or, more precisely, it speaks with a forked tongue. Lynndie England's claims to power could not survive knowledge of her rank, her class, her relations with a man who was both an exploitative superior and an exploitative lover. The photographs portray England as a woman with power over a man; but we know men had power over her. Lynndie England presented herself as a woman with power, but she is formally and informally, publically and privately, subordinated to Corporal Charles Graner. She is free to exhibit her own sexuality, her sexual power, and her power over the sexuality of men, yet the use of her sexuality as a tool of state, by her superior officers, testifies to her subjection.

Structures meant to emancipate can be diverted and transformed to serve as supports for old, established structures of hierarchy and abjection. In the dark moments of unnecessary war and shameful torture, affirmations of the equality of women were diverted into supports for a system that rendered Arabs and Muslims abject; and in this transformation women were rendered abject as well.

Critical readings of the photographs from Abu Ghraib made Lynndie England's subjection visible, but they did little to undo this architecture of abjection, or to disable the narrative that set white women against brown men. They tended, on the contrary, to affirm narratives of female weakness, and to conceal the political processes that so elegantly served several chauvinisms simultaneously. England "came from a poor town in the hollows of West Virginia and lived for a time in a trailer." ABC News asked, "Is Lynndie England Victim or Victimizer?"

quoting her defense psychologist on her failure to speak before she was eight and her special education classes.[9]

ABC's account made England's story a tragedy of failed romance, noting her early unsuccessful marriage and foregrounding her slavish devotion to Corporal Graner. Xavier Amador, a psychologist for England's defense team, testified to England's victimization, in and out of court. "Graner took pictures of her—not only nude pictures of her—he took pictures of her having sex with him," Amador told ABC. "He had another soldier who was older and outranked her take a camera and they had sex together while this soldier took a picture. She felt humiliated. She thought it was perverted. She felt it was wrong. So I asked her why she did it, and she said, 'I didn't want to lose him.'" Amador's account places England in the position of the prisoner, posed in humiliating and perverted settings and photographed. The force of Amador's narrative depends on undermining England's consent, casting her in the role of a woman powerless before an exploitative lover. Casting Graner as England's lover rather than her supervisor placed inquiry into the chain of command outside the narrative. The narrative of women betrayed was echoed in the self-exculpating literary effort of General Janis Karpinski. Karpinski, however, cast the betrayal as a political rather than a personal one.[10]

Amador's narrative also required the absence of the Arab. The psychologist shifted the scene from the photographs of the Arab prisoners to those of Lynndie England. His narrative drew a veil over their presence, and so over the acts that made England notorious. Amador's narrative thus concealed the way in which invidious constructions of the Arab and the Muslim, and narratives of the power of women in the West, were used to conceal the mutual reinforcement of sexual and civilizational hierarchies. Karpinski similarly erases the Arab, especially Arab women, in presenting herself as the victim of male deceit and exploitation.

It was not only Arab men but Arab women who were tortured at Abu Ghraib. The abuse of Iraqi women at Abu Ghraib was hidden in the United States and made visible abroad. The visibility of the abuse abroad redoubled the harm done to these women. They were humiliated, and in some cases further endangered, by the circulation of their photographs in newspapers and on the Internet. The concealment of the abuse in the United States preserved the fiction of Americans as the liberators of Arab and Muslim women.

The defenses made by England and Karpinski may not be adequate to absolve them, but they should make us question the story of the progressive empowerment of women in the Western state. Has the long struggle for women's rights brought us to this? Is this what feminist power looks like?

Americans were forced, in Abu Ghraib and in Guantánamo, to confront the use of women soldiers as agents of sexual humiliation. Female interrogators at Guantánamo threatened prisoners with menstrual blood, performed lap dances, and otherwise sought to use sexuality as a weapon of war. These acts were premised on a view not far from Žižek's. If Islam was "grounded on a disavowed femininity," then menstrual blood might serve as a kind of antimatter, a peerless weapon in the struggle against Islam. "The notion that Arabs are particularly vulnerable to sexual humiliation became a talking point among pro-war Washington conservatives in the months before the

March, 2003, invasion of Iraq," Seymour Hersh wrote in the *New Yorker*.[11] Hersh continued, "One book that was frequently cited was 'The Arab Mind,' a study of Arab culture and psychology, first published in 1973, by Raphael Patai. . . . The book includes a 25-page chapter on Arabs and sex, depicting sex as a taboo vested with shame and repression."[12]

The use of female soldiers and interrogators was said to strike at Arab and Muslim vulnerability to sexual humiliation. It also carried within it a claim of Western superiority. Arab and Muslim vulnerability to sexual humiliation was a consequence of sexism and sexual repression. Yet who would not be humiliated by being forced to strip naked before strangers and enemies? Who (man or woman) would not cringe at being asked to simulate sexual acts, or find the idea of being smeared with menstrual blood repugnant? The strategies of sexual humiliation transformed a common human vulnerability into a vulnerability peculiar to one culture and a site of the power of Western over Arab culture. This discursive sleight of hand is the dark reversal of cultural sensitivity.

The employment of these techniques of torture depends upon the use of American women not as intelligence officers, but as women paid for the performance of specific sexual acts. As a *New York Times* editorial argued, rather plaintively, "Surely no one can approve turning an American soldier into a pseudo-lap-dancer or having another smear fake menstrual blood on an Arab man. These practices are as degrading to the women as they are to the prisoners." Yet those procedures had been not only approved, but officially employed. Unlike the abuses at Abu Ghraib, the weaponized sex at Guantánamo was government procedure: "Women in uniform had been turned into sex workers at Guantánamo."[13] The question at issue in these tactics is not only the treatment of the enemy, but the treatment of one's own. This strategy turns on—and overturns—the inclusion, equality, and freedom of the woman soldier. She is marked out by her sexuality and reduced to it. It is both revealing and tragic that a scene staged to affirm the power of women's equality in the West should speak so tellingly of their subordination. The differences of sex supposedly overcome by the uniform were reaffirmed, and equality vanished. Women's supposed sexual freedom was deployed by the military as a weapon of war. Women soldiers, supposedly the equals of their male colleagues, were reduced to sex workers.

There is another set of pictures from Abu Ghraib, less commonly shown, that shed light on the common subjection of Western and Iraqi women. In these photographs Lynndie England is shown with an Arab woman identified as a prostitute. The photographs present them as equals. They are about the same height and weight; they stand with their arms around each other. Both wear Western clothes. These photographs put the opposition of the West and Islam, American and Arab, in question. The identification of the Arab woman as a prostitute, or (still more tellingly) as "prostituted by her husband," speaks against the claims to equality and power staged in the photographs of England abusing male prisoners. These photographs stage England as one prostitute, or one victim, or one woman, with another. They cast her simultaneously as victim and transgressor, and they point to the presence—outside the space of the photograph—of men more powerful than she who are responsible for her degradation. They suggest the tragedy of the presence of women at Guantánamo and Abu Ghraib. Rather than liberating women, Arab or Western, the American invasion and occupation reduced the status of women and increased their peril—at home and abroad.

CHAPTER 4

Terror

There are two fears in the fear of terrorism: fear of the many and fear of the one. The fear of the many sees the West (or the Western) besieged by an Islam that, this time, breaks through the gates of Vienna to occupy the heart of Europe. The fear of the many encompasses both "the demographic problem" and the arrival of boatloads of economic and political refugees. The fear of the one is a fear of the damage that can be wrought by a single man or woman: the terrorist or the suicide bomber. The battle is fought not only for the cities of the European heartland but for the hearts and minds of East and West. Those who fear terror see that threat as overshadowing foreign wars.

Paul Berman may be one of the most powerful witnesses to the dissolution of the boundaries between Islam and the West. He condemns Islam. He casts himself as a defender of the liberal West. Berman is filled with terror and anger at the thought that the walls dividing Islam and the West might crumble, that we might find ourselves in the company of the Muslim. I think he should set his fears aside. Those walls have already fallen and he is richer for it.

Those Berman places at the heart of his defense and holds closest to his own heart belong to both Islam and the West. Salman Rushdie, Ibn Warraq (the pen name of a prominent critic of Islam), and Ayaan Hirsi Ali are, by their accounts and his, people of two worlds. They are not a beleaguered few, for Berman writes that "Rushdie has metastasized into an entire social class." They live in the West and speak for it. Their enemies, those Berman despises, belong to the West as well. Tariq Ramadan is "the philosopher from Switzerland" (apparently displacing Rousseau, the Citizen of Geneva, in that role). Along with him stand those who have defended Ramadan, or "sneered at" Ayaan Hirsi Ali: Ian Buruma, Timothy Garton Ash, and all those "progressive intellectuals" who took flight into the philosophic territory of Ramadan and al Ghazali.[1] Berman fixes the cosmic conflict as a war in the land of the West and the intellectual terrain of medieval Islam. Berman, Hirsi Ali, and the rest are latter-day Mutazalites, the forces of reason and enlightenment. Ramadan and the intellectuals who have taken flight are disciples of al Ghazali. It is a sorting that would astonish al Ghazali and Ibn Rushd, but it testifies to Berman's recognition that the world is not divided between "Islam and the West." The conflict he writes of is a conflict in the West.

What of the terrorists? Do they belong, as Berman suggests, to another time? Are they enemies not only of liberalism but of modernity? We have become accustomed to seeing terror as the antithesis of modernity, and terrorists as those who refuse to accept the modern order. Faisal Devji suggests another possibility. What if the terrorist organizations feared in the West are the sign and consequence of something many Western critics of Islam have long called for? What if they mark not only the possibility but the emergence of an Islamic reform movement? What if al Qaeda and the like are the Protestant ethic in the spirit of Islam?[2]

There are spectacular reasons for thinking so. When Sadat is shot at a military review, his assassin turns to the camera and says, "I am Khaled Islambouli. I have just killed Pharaoh and I am not afraid to die." His words echo Oliver Cromwell's ownership of regicide: "It was not a thing done in a corner." Another Puritan, Thomas Harrison, declared his fidelity as he went to his death by torture. A passerby called out, "Where is your Good Old Cause now?" and Harrison shot back, "Here in my bosom and I will seal it with my blood." The language of martyrdom and tyrannicide is central to Protestant reform, and central too to the liberal revolutions in the West. Saint-Just's declaration "the revolution begins when the tyrant ends" might (as Thomas Paine thought) have been mistaken, but it drove the French as it had driven the English Revolution. The language of martyrs and martyrdom, the commitment to bearing witness with one's body, in one's blood, the passion of a faith in arms belong to Cromwell and Khomeini, to Crusaders, Roundheads, and *mujahideen*. Cromwell's New Model Army was a modernizing force. His army, like contemporary *mujahideen*, cast themselves, for the most part, as biblical literalists but were more noteworthy for the wild imagination of their interpretations. They were fundamentalists. They condemned monarchy and authoritarianism and yielded to it themselves. By their own accounts, they put the weapons of modern technology at the service of a faith modeled on an earlier austerity.

Time and the work of veneration have worn the sharper edges from Oliver Cromwell, Thomas Cromwell, Cotton Mather, and John Knox. It is easy to forget that the Protestant forces of "the rule of laws, not men" had their enemies burned at the stake.

They beheaded their opponents and owned it proudly. As Cromwell said of the beheading of Charles Stuart, "I think the sound of it has been in most countries." Yet these harsh and (even in their own time) barbarous acts belonged to people we recognize not only as a modernizing force, but as those who impelled England toward the rule of law, constitutional government, and parliamentarianism.

The terrorist is a familiar figure to historians. The anarchists of the nineteenth century were feared as terrorists are feared today. No place was safe from them. They might strike at any time. British suffragettes did more than chain themselves to fences and get themselves trampled by horses. They broke windows, planted bombs, and hurled Molotov cocktails through the windows of politicians' homes, public buildings, and shops. The suffragette we see is the pretty, ineffectual mother in *Mary Poppins* or the stern visage of Susan B. Anthony. The impassioned terrorists of the nineteenth century are hidden from us, but they were part of the making of modernity. The constitutions of the United Kingdom, France, and the United States were, as Nietzsche said of all great things, "soaked in blood thoroughly, and for a long time."

We might have good reasons for forgetting that past. Perhaps Europe has tired of shedding blood. Perhaps, mindful of Gandhi, Mandela, and de Klerk, we have come to suspect that all people need not make liberal constitutions as we in the West made ours. Perhaps the

West forgets its past to secure its future. Perhaps the constitutions won by force are to be secured by other means. Nevertheless, states still rely on armies at the border and police in the interior of the homeland.

Modern states deploy powerful armies at home and abroad. They have sophisticated technologies for policing the population. They can see and hear much that people seek to hide. They have succeeded, too, in persuading people to submit to surveillance. Yet they are not safe from terror.

Liberal and democratic orders are secured by constitutions, by law, by the workings of justice, and by the actions of the people. In a democracy it falls to the people to choose what they will be. They will choose to fence some out, to invite others in. In making those decisions, they are obliged to consider who and what they want to be. They may decide that they want to keep the monarchy they have, the established church they have. They may decide to strip the public square of any sign of faith. They may decide that they want all newcomers to speak as they speak, to wear what they wear, to act as they act. They may make laws and policies to secure these things. They may act privately as well as publicly to secure them. Yet they will not be safe from change.

Change may come like a thief in the night or a bomb in a crowded subway. We fear that 9/11 or the Madrid subway bombings might happen again, that terror will strike unexpectedly in a crowded place, that our world hides monsters, that death strikes randomly, that things are not as they have been. These are familiar fears. They have haunted modernity since the anarchists and masses of the nineteenth century.

These fears are real. The feared threats are true threats. Terror, horror, a sense of randomness and vertigo, and the feeling that the world is out of order, are reasonable passions before the monstrous, the irrational, the random, and the unsettled. The scholar Lorraine Daston calls them "cognitive passions." They belong not to the ignorant and the unthinking but to the thoughtful. Daston writes of the natural world, not the world of politics. We expect certain things of the natural world, she has said. That world is orderly, and whether we think the design is God's or Nature's (or Nature's god's) we know it is orderly, regular, and predictable. The idea (or as they thought centuries ago, the reality) of a pig with the head of man, or a two-headed dog, was monstrous. The world followed universal laws. These governed the great and the small, the universe and the neighborhood. If snow were to come in summer in Alabama, that would be a marvel and a wonder. If it stayed, if it happened without warning on this day or that, it would be unsettling. If we traveled and found cold places warm and warm places cold, rain forests in a drought and deserts flooded, we would be troubled and unsure of our ground.

When the world becomes uncertain, people feel that a once-orderly place has become random. Randomness, when it concerns matters of life and death, of change and an uncertain future, is terrifying. These are not irrational emotions; on the contrary, they are eminently rational. We know that pigs have one sort of head and men another and that a change in the form of man or pig would carry tragic and horrible consequences with it.

Not all sudden changes in the natural order are occasions for fear. When Moses strikes the rock and water flows, people greet it as a miracle. When thirsty people find water in a dry place, they see it as luck (and perhaps as another miracle).

When a magician makes a man float in midair, people wonder at it. When the surrounding world changes—ice melts, and the hunting changes; or droughts come not one year in a hundred, but every year—people fear. We know that even a small change in the natural world that surrounds us might signal a great change, the operation of forces too strong for us to oppose. Even the uncertainty is cause for fear.

These fears are not limited to the natural world. In the political as in the natural world, death strikes randomly; things are not as they have been; the once predictable seems random and uncertain. The once familiar is strangely changed. There are monsters. Terror alters the world of our expectations. The street, the rail station, the city are no longer familiar moments in an urban neighborhood. They are sites of potential danger. One moves watchfully. One watches for something out of place, for that unfamiliar thing (the abandoned bag, the nervous passenger) that will signal the presence of a hidden weapon. The passengers on the train or plane, people on the street are no longer benign. Each is a possible threat. Each might conceal an enemy in the guise of a neighbor.

The person who is not what he or she appears to be is a familiar figure in horror films and fairy tales. Seeing the once familiar and benign reveal itself as alien and hostile calls forth horror. This horror is not irrational, not unthinking, not the product of fear alone. It follows from the recognition that the once familiar has changed, and still greater changes may be hidden. It is a rational response to what may be a dangerous transformation. Terror transforms the social and political world. Public spaces become hiding places.

The reaction to terror is more rational than it might seem. People are right to recognize that familiar places are now dangerous. They see small changes and interpret these as signaling larger changes, and all changes as signaling a threat to themselves or their way of life. Their terror and horror are the product of reason rather than mere reaction. So too with terrorists.

No one should have to argue any longer that terrorism can be a rational and reasonable strategy. The memoirs of Menachem Begin, the frank professions of Ehud Barak, the scholarship of Robert Pape and Alan Krueger all recognize that terrorism can be a rational choice. This recognition diminishes the distance between the terrorist and the one who fears. If the hopes and fears on each side shade over into paranoia and fanaticism, they have their roots in reasoned approaches to history and politics. "If I'd been born a Palestinian," Ehud Barak declared in the course of an Israeli election campaign, "I would have been a terrorist."[3] For Barak, terrorism is not alien, but familiar; not irrational, but rational; not a nihilistic choice, but a political one.

Perhaps it is not the fate of the state but that of individuals that troubles us in terrorism. Perhaps it is not a political but a personal fear that grips us as we watch.

The suicide bomber is a figure of terror in the most literal sense. Reason seems to stop here. No rational person could do such a thing. An enemy soldier is a threat to one's life, to the existence of one's nation or country or people. Yet despite (or perhaps because of) this, the enemy soldier is intelligible. The suicide bomber is far more alien. The suicide bomber is unintelligible, unimaginable: no one can understand the thinking of the suicide bomber. The suicide bomber is uncanny. The German word we translate as uncanny, *unheimlich*, which literally means "unhomelike," captures something of the unsettling, alien character of the suicide bomber.

Like the most uncanny, *unheimlich* things, the suicide bomber is also familiar. No one can tell who might be a suicide bomber. The bomb might be in a boy's backpack; the pregnant woman might be bearing not life but death in the folds of her dress. The suicide bomber can be next to you on a bus, beside you in the line at the train station. The suicide bomber is a threat enclosed in the unthreatening, the alien in the familiar.

Objections to the *burka* or the *niqab*, to Islamic enclaves and the intrusion of other ways of life, are objections to difference, to the alien, to the erosion of a familiar way of life. The figure of the suicide bomber expresses a different set of anxieties. The suicide bomber is an image of what is feared in Muslim immigrants who assimilate.

The suicide bomber is the presence of invisible difference, the threat that cannot be seen. Suicide bombers may appear to be at home. They may seem familiar. They may carry Tintin schoolbags or JanSport backpacks, but the backpack or the schoolbag may hold a bomb. We do not know what is inside them. The more familiar they appear, the more integrated they seem, the greater the threat they pose.

The figure of the suicide bomber presents the possibility that assimilation is not enough, that it will fail, that however well integrated Muslim immigrants, or their children or grandchildren, appear, they will always carry something alien within them. Sheltered in some small corner of the mind are ideas different from those which surround them. These people from another place are in that place no longer but something of the place is in them. They have other ideas, and those may prove explosive.

What happens when the bomb goes off? Pieces of the bomber and the bombed, the alien and familiar, are intermingled. They cannot be sorted out. Any death is the ending of a world. The figure of the suicide bomber captures the fears of those who believe their world is coming to an end. The immigrant who hides the alien threat in familiar clothing will blow the world apart. Afterwards it will be impossible to sort out what was once Muslim from what was once Christian. The pieces of what was truly French or German or British will be scattered, impossible to reassemble. A world will have come to an end.

There is something profoundly correct in these fears. There are those among the immigrants who will blow worlds apart. They carry alien values. They speak in other tongues. They have read other books. Even when they speak without an accent, dress in Western clothes, they carry elements of another culture, another religion, other ways of life within them. They have other ideas. When those ideas are loosed upon the world, the world will cease to be the world it was. No one will be able to reassemble the fragments of the old world. Some will be lost. Some will remain. Some will be propelled far from where they once were and appear in unexpected places. In those times and those places we may be unable to distinguish what was once Christian from what was once Muslim. This prospect fills some with terror. It fills others with hope and wonder.

The figure of the suicide bomber speaks to these fears and to the ever-present problem—and promise—of the individual. The figure of the suicide bomber is a figure not of the many, but of the one. The fear expressed here is not the fear of being demographically overwhelmed. It is not the fear that the public world will become unrecognizable, that one's children will eat couscous instead of coq au vin or hear the call to prayer rather than church bells. The figure of the suicide bomber captures a particular fear: a fear of the individuals that surround us.

That is a familiar fear in Western thought. The great philosopher of the social contract, Thomas Hobbes, thought that our natural condition is one in which every man fears every other. Fear is our natural condition; fear grounds our equality. Though we make contracts, covenants, peoples, nations, and states, we are always vulnerable to one another. That first fear lingers in us. Hobbes saw it drive us to state and Sovereign.

Early fears vacillated between the threats posed by the monarch and those posed by the mob; between the fearsome figure of the anarchist and that of the masses; between the madman and the automaton. Contemporary fears couple the figure of the suicide bomber and the Muslim masses. The figure of the suicide bomber (in scholarship as in popular discourse) is isolated, alienated, and alone; often educated, always at odds with the surrounding world. Like the anarchist, the suicide bomber may be educated or not, may come from a privileged background or not, may be part of a network or not; but always acts alone. Fear of the suicide bomber expresses the fear of the individual who cannot be wholly known; of ideas held in the individual mind, ideas that might not be (cannot be) erased by acculturation.

Living with other people, in a city, a suburb, or a village, requires courage, trust, or forgetfulness. We know (though we forget) that as Hobbes famously observed, anyone can kill anyone else. We know (though we trust it will not happen here) that one person can shoot x in a school, or x on a military base, or x in a shopping center parking lot. We know that, but we forget it. We forget because we trust our neighbors, or, more often, because we accept the risk of living how and where we do: because we want the things that other people bring us. We forget it because if we are to have democratic politics, we must have courage, and courage requires us to forget our fears.

The terrorist preys on our fears, but not only on the simple fear of death. The suicide bomber reminds us that we are always a mystery to one another. The suicide bomber holds the terror and the promise that the world could be blown asunder in a moment, and that this could be the work of one alone. The terrorist is the dark side of individualism. We fear terror because we know that power always lies within our reach.

CHAPTER 5

Equality

The writings of the late philosopher John Rawls capture both the common sense and the aspirations of much of the modern, liberal, secular West. Rawls belongs in an Anglo-American cultural context. His work is most at home in the United States, Canada, Australia, and the United Kingdom, but has a significant following throughout the European West. He had, however, universal ambitions. In *The Law of Peoples*, Rawls laid out a plan for justice among peoples. "The Law of Peoples," Rawls wrote, "extends the idea of the social contract to the Society of Peoples, and lays out the general principles that can and should be accepted by both liberal and nonliberal (but decent) societies as the standard for regulating their behavior toward one another."[1] The forest of Victorian capitals expresses the evangelical imperatives of a Gladstonian liberalism. The imperative tone marks the imperial presumption characteristic of liberalism's later adherents. Liberals, according to this view, can and should offer, unilaterally and without consultation, a set of principles to govern the behavior of all. Liberal principles are the universal standard of the good, though they are not universally accepted. Decent societies are those that can be accommodated within the liberal principles they do not accept.

Throughout the work, Rawls shows the quality that liberals call balance or pragmatism and critics of liberalism see as liberalism's "forked tongue."[2] Liberalism affirms freedom but denies free choice. Liberalism affirms equality but creates and maintains hierarchies. Liberalism praises reciprocity but acts unilaterally. Liberalism affirms its universality but reveals itself as parochial. Amid the abstract affirmations of principles embedded in the Law of Peoples, Rawls gives that Law a place, a history, a genealogy. The Law of Peoples is no more than the expression of a particular people in a particular time and place. Indeed, it may be less, for there are those of us, living in liberal states and committed to freedom, equality, and reciprocity, who have a more capacious sense of humanity and a more demanding sense of what these principles require.

Just peoples, Rawls writes, insist on their own right to recognition and respect, and "are fully prepared to grant the very same proper recognition and respect to other peoples as equals."[3] The world of states may be a world of inequality, but that of peoples can and should be one of equality. That equality falls before the clash of civilizations.

Recognizing that the world does not comprise only liberal peoples, Rawls undertakes to show how the Society of Peoples could also accommodate "decent hierarchical peoples." At this point, Rawls's principled abstraction lapses. "To this end I give an imagined example of a non-liberal Muslim people I call Kazanistan."[4] Those familiar with Rawls's intellectual commitment to neutrality, the philosophic, the principled, and, above all, the abstract, will be startled to see him give an abstract construction an implicit geography and religion. Kazanistan is imagined as one of the "stans," and so it must be rather near Afghanistan, Pakistan, Baluchistan.⁵ It may have some relation to Khazaria, the ancient Jewish kingdom that that served Michael Chabon as the setting for his *Gentlemen of the Road*, or to the Khakis and Kharkeez of Maira Kalman and Rick Meyerowitz's 2001 *New Yorker* cover map.

Rawls's initial introduction of Kazanistan would seem to open the possibility that "liberal peoples" could also be Muslim. After all, he identified Kazanistan as a *nonliberal* Muslim people, implying that there might be a liberal Muslim people. But as he fleshes out the portrait of Kazanistan, that possibility is closed. Muslims, in Rawls's account, are the antithesis of liberalism. They are violent, warlike, imperialistic. Violence is a tenet of orthodox Islam. Muslims discriminate against those who belong to other religions, and exclude them from the central institutions of the state. Muslims do not rule themselves; they have rulers. They subject women. Kazanistan's decency is secured by its departure from what Rawls presents as the Muslim norm. "Unlike most Muslim rulers, the rulers of Kazanistan have not sought empire and territory," Rawls writes. This is because their theologians interpret "*jihad* in a spiritual and moral sense, and not in military terms"—an interpretation that Rawls, following Bernard Lewis, identifies as antique and heterodox. Unlike other Muslims, Kazanistanis take an "enlightened" view of minorities and permit them to serve in the military. Minorities in Kazanistan are not "subjected to arbitrary discrimination, or treated as inferior by Muslims." Women are subjected in Kazanistan, but "dissent has led to important reforms in the rights and role of women." Kazanistan, Rawls tells us, is an "idealized Islamic people."[6] Commentators and reviewers of Rawls's book have not hesitated to elaborate the "Muslim" features of Kazanistan. Rawls did not specify the particular forms of discrimination experienced by women in Kazanistan, but others readily filled the void. David Reidy identified Kazanistan with Oman.[7] John Tasioulas wrote, "If they are female, they may be required to wear hejab (the dress code that requires covering the body from head to toe) in public, and denied access to tertiary education, and, in consequence, to professional occupations."[8] The mere identification of Kazanistan as "Muslim" identified it with a set of discriminatory practices far more burdensome than those found in most Muslim countries.

Other commentators gave more elaborate accounts of the Kazanistanis. One made them Shi'a and imagined them requiring mandatory public fasting. "There seems to be no reason why Kazanistan could not have a custom similar to Muharram and require all members to cooperate in the event."[9] Using the same logic, Michael Gross argued that one "could not preclude" Kazanistani use of amputations as punishment. He then proceeded to offer graphic accounts of the procedure for amputation. Arif Jamal noted that although "for the Rawlsian argument Kazanistan did not necessary need to be a place of Muslims, it is perhaps not surprising" that Rawls made it so. "It is possible that Kazanistan is in fact modeled on present day Pakistan which exhibits the same Kazanistani-type legal conditions in its constitution."[10] Making Kazanistan Muslim was unfortunate, Jamal observed, because it might seem to some that "there was something inevitable about the relation of religious conviction and public policy," or, more precisely, "something inimical about Islam to liberalism (or liberalism to Islam)."[11] Gross's account put this more emphatically, arguing that liberalism and Islamic law are fundamentally at odds. Where they agree, the agreement must be the work of Western liberal influences.[12]

All these accounts (and there are others) owe more to the authors' imaginations than to Islam. Rawls was more laconic in creating his imagined state. His construction of Kazanistan raises a number of questions made unanswerable by the limits of his invention. What is the history of Kazanistan? Was Kazanistan colonized? What about its economy? The excision of history contributes not only to the indictment of Islam but to the exculpation of the West.

Rawls's imaginary Muslim country tells us more about the West than it does about Islam. The problems he sees in his invented Kazanistan reflect defects and injustices in the liberal order that have only become more evident and more evidently dangerous in the years since he wrote. The legacy of colonialism pales before economic and social inequalities of the present in the purportedly nonhierarchical liberal order.

Consider the phrases Rawls uses to indict Islam. Muslim states are characteristically violent and imperialistic, seeking "expansion and territory." This characterization, predicated on an empire whose zenith was well in the past, calmly elides the imperial expansions of the centuries since. The establishment of empire and the extension of territorial dominion belong, in the long epoch before our own, to liberal peoples, among them Britain, France, and the United States. Liberals and liberal theorists (James and John Stuart Mill, Michael Walzer, and

Michael Ignatieff) have urged them on.[13] There is no small historical irony in identifying Muslim peoples with imperial war against the liberal West.

The excision of history becomes still more important when one considers the economic dimensions of the Law of Peoples. A "duty of assistance" Rawls writes, obliges well-off societies to aid burdened societies, but "such societies are neither liberal nor decent." Once formerly burdened societies have been brought into the company of the liberal and decent, they "may still be relatively poor." Rawls does not permit them to resent the economic effects of past injustice. Once "each people has its own liberal or decent government, these feelings are unjustified." The still-burdened peoples are free to decide "the significance and importance" of wealth for themselves. If they are unsatisfied, they can "increase savings" or "borrow from other members of the Society of Peoples." Rawls does not indicate what they should do if they are hungry.

The recent history of Europe testifies to the inadequacy of these measures. Saving, and what neoliberal economists refer to as "austerity measures," increase misery. Borrowing, if it is possible at all, increases dependency. The answers Rawls offers to histories of inequality sound plausible in an imaginary Kazanistan. They are less persuasive in the streets of Athens or Rio, Lisbon, Rome, or Barcelona.

The same ironies echo in the discussion of the treatment of women and minorities. Rawls's assertion that "dissent has led to important reforms in the rights and role of women" applies as readily to the liberal democratic states of the West as it does to Rawls's "idealized Muslim people." One could not credit liberal democratic regimes with much more. Here in the West, women still earn less money than men; still labor under the demands of traditional roles and expectations; are still subjected to a wide range of slights and humiliations; and still lack the full range of rights, privileges, and duties that belong to men. As I write, a Tunisian Islamist, Ali Larayedh, argues that there should be quotas to guarantee women's representation in Parliament, "until they find their voice"—a proposal that would amount to electoral suicide in the United States.[14] With regard to women, liberal democratic regimes cannot honestly claim more than Rawls claims for Kazanistan: that dissent has led to important reforms.

Rawls knows that women in the West, in the liberal order, "have borne and continue to bear, an unjust share of the task of raising, nurturing, and caring for their children." He knows that this injustice is exacerbated by "the laws regulating divorce" (he is less ready to acknowledge injustices beyond the family, in the public realms of liberal democratic states). He does not, however, permit this knowledge of Western failure to correct his identification of Islam with the subjection of women or to question the identification of liberal democratic states with the West. The disparity between the Muslim world and the West arises in no small part because Rawls contrasts an ideal and ideally liberal West with an actual Muslim world (and not the best of it); and because he sets Muslim virtues where he sets Western failings: in the past.

So it is with the case of minorities. Rawls recognizes, albeit in a footnote, that Muslim countries have tolerated religious minorities. That toleration, however, is placed firmly in the past, in the Ottoman Empire. The persecution of religious minorities in the West is placed firmly in the past as well, though the Holocaust remains in living memory. The liberal regimes of the West would be even less well served by a consideration of the relative tolerance of ethnic and racial difference. Here, it would be difficult for the most starry-eyed apostle of the West to count it as the site of freedom and equality. Structures of racial and ethnic inequality are not only part of the liberal past; they are part of the liberal present. The question of religious toleration should be a particular embarrassment, for liberal states continue to discriminate against their Muslim citizens. Mindful of their history, few liberal democratic regimes could claim that they have treated religious, ethnic, or racial minorities as equals. Mindful of the present, they should be honest enough to claim that they too are no more than "decent hierarchical regimes." (The more demanding might ask whether hierarchical states can be said to be decent at all.)

The *Law of Peoples*, like Samuel Huntington's *Clash of Civilizations*, enumerates several civilizational categories, but focuses primarily on one difference and division, that between Islam and the West. Though they are both "well-ordered," though they occupy the first two rungs of Rawls's civilizational ladder, though they together comprise what Rawls calls "well-ordered peoples," Muslim Kazanistan and the secular West, "decent hierarchical peoples" and "liberal peoples," are fundamentally opposed in Rawls's account. They have conceptions of justice that "stand at opposite poles."[15]

The difficulty here is not that Rawls recognized differences in the ability of different peoples, or civilizations, to recognize freedom, secure equality, or do justice. One would have to be willfully blind to ignore the failure of civilizations to attain these admirable ends. There are many civilizations in which people are neither free nor equal. There are many places, at home as well as abroad, where injustice prevails. The problem is not whom Rawls faults, but whom he praises.

Rawls's account arranges peoples in a hierarchy in which liberal peoples are followed by "decent hierarchical peoples," with others still more unfortunate bringing up the rear. Each people has a uniform character. Rawls's division of the world implies that the liberal states govern "well-ordered peoples" and that these adhere, with only anomalous exceptions, to the principles he advances. He refers to these as "familiar principles" for "liberal democratic societies."

Rawls fails to recognize that all civilizations and peoples contain conflicting ideas, concepts, parties, interests, ideals, and aims within themselves. Each has internal failings it must overcome. Rawls was my countryman, my fellow citizen, yet we seem to have looked out on different worlds. Years after his death our people are still fighting the culture wars, still struggling to achieve virtues they conceive in radically different forms.

Rawls is willing to make concessions to reality, but these increase rather than diminish the problems in his account. He argues that liberals can and should accept departures from the ideals he has laid out. If minorities are still discriminated against, but permitted to serve in the military, that should be accepted. If a long struggle has led to reforms in the "rights and role of women," their subject status should be accepted. If people have rulers rather than ruling themselves, yet their governments show a degree of consultation and respect for law, they should be accepted.

There are thus two kinds of reasons for rejecting *The Law of Peoples*. If we accept Rawls's argument that people whose social forms we deprecate still have a place in the world and command some measure of regard and respect, we can and should reject the promulgation of a single uniform standard for all. This imperative is stronger if we admire social forms we find alien or prefer not to practice; and stronger still if we believe in "the equality of peoples." If, on the other hand, we reject Rawls's account on the basis of the false history it smuggles in and the liberal failings it conceals, we can and should reject an idealization of liberal regimes that encourages continuing blindness to their faults.

In Rawls's vision of a "realistic utopia," "liberal democratic peoples" occupy the position of primacy in "well-ordered societies." Their values and practices are made the standard. The question is not whether the standard is adequate, but how much deviation from it should be licensed. The form of the work thus exempts liberal regimes from any scrutiny Muslims, Islam, or consideration of the Muslim question might make necessary.

The Kazanistanis might raise their own queries about the Law of Peoples. They might ask whether they are vested with the right to create a culture as they choose, build an economy, or craft a polity. They might ask whether the global economic order in which they are embedded is subject to standards of justice. They might ask whether the distribution of wealth between nations is just. They might argue that a liberal democratic nation cannot meet even the barest claim to decency if its people starve or lack shelter. They might say that universal standards of decency require that disparities in wealth be limited to a narrow range. They might suggest that the institution of the *zakat*[16] (cast, of course, in different cultural forms) is necessary to secure that human dignity which is itself a human right.

The identification of Islam with hierarchy (albeit "decent" hierarchy) in Rawls's Kazanistan forecloses one of the most powerful critical challenges raised by the Muslim question: the question of equality. There are many dimensions to that question of equality. There is the question of the equality of Muslims citizens in the liberal democratic regimes on which Rawls hoped to build his realistic utopia. There is the demand for equality, national and individual, raised by Muslims against colonial and postcolonial powers. There is the question, raised by Malcolm X and the conversion to Islam of many African Americans, of which religion is most committed to equality or most able to effectively advance it. There is the question of the place of equality in Muslim thought and practice.

Those philosophic and political works that have addressed the relation of Islam to liberalism have tended to assume that liberalism furnished an array of rights not all of which could be found in Islam. The standard might be the Universal Code of Human Rights or John Rawls's theory of justice or some less fully articulated Western common sense, but in all cases the assessment presumed that the West held an exhaustive list of the rights of man; that the rights were fully and correctly understood, and that no more were to be found.

This certainty sits uneasily with the shape of politics in the West in our time. New demands, once thought absurd, emerge as struggles for rights. The right to love whom one chooses, to decide where to confide decisions over one's life and death, are still disputed, still the occasion for struggle in the West. We of the West still struggle—often in the streets—about the justice of our economic systems. Perhaps when we confront another people, the question should not be "Do they have all our rights?" but "Do we have all of theirs?"

As John Rawls marked hierarchy as alien to liberal peoples, the distance between rich and poor grew in the nation where he wrote. Practical equality became more distant. Equality was abandoned as an ideal. There were many defenders of liberty, but few spoke of equality. No one in American politics dared to argue that they might be connected. Equality, if it was regarded at all, was regarded as a formal political matter, entirely separate from economic concerns.

Franklin Roosevelt thought otherwise. He had declared on the eve of World War II, "I would ask no one to defend a democracy which in turn would not defend everyone in the nation against want and privation."[17] For Roosevelt, as for many in America, democracy required attention not only to the welfare of "the economy" but to the welfare of each household economy. A working democracy depended on citizens who were not only formally but practically equal, who had enough not only for life, but for dignity.

Sayyid Qutb is known in the West primarily as the inspiration of terrorists, as an important member of the Muslim Brotherhood, as an archetypal extremist, bent on holy war. This is true, but it is not the whole truth. Reading only a portion of his work, we fail to grapple with the critiques Qutb leveled against inequality, and with his concern for human dignity. There are many defenders of human dignity in modern Arab and Muslim thought. I put Qutb before you because we need to learn modesty. Even this intolerant, fanatic man has something to teach us about human rights, human dignity, and equality.

Qutb's concern is most evident in *Social Justice and Islam*, originally published in 1949. The title will sound odd to early twenty-first-century ears, for "social justice" is a phrase more resonant of the Society of Friends than of the Muslim Brotherhood. The work will sound odd to those who have read Paul Berman's accounts of Sayyid Qutb as the intellectual inspiration for jihad, or who see the Muslim Brotherhood as opposed to modernity and all its works. Qutb did not attempt to restore the culture of the Muslim community of the time of the Prophet. He did not paint his eyes with kohl; he wore a dark suit and a tie. *Social Justice and Islam* is not concerned with the proper punishment for theft, the reinstitution of stoning, or how women cover their hair. It is concerned with equality.

Qutb wrote that women have "a complete equality with men," and that the education of women is not merely possible; it is obligatory. He takes the presence of women in the workplace for granted. He recognized, long before the idea was common among Western feminists, that the workplace should be a place in which women are as comfortable as men and no one need face sexual harassment.[18] The recognition of this issue gives the book a contemporary sound, though it was written before Friedan's *The Feminine Mystique*. So does Qutb's interest in environmental stewardship. Like a number of religious thinkers, Qutb regarded care for the earth as reverence for God. The Koran requires that part of the profits from mining and other activities be paid into a common fund. Qutb read this as the Koran's recognition of the need to repair the damaging effects of these activities and to acknowledge that the earth belongs in the first instance not to men but to God.

That care extends to animals. Qutb recalls the stories of Muhammad in which he praises a man for giving water to a thirsty dog and condemns a woman who failed to feed a cat. The Muslims ask, "Is there a reward for us in the case of animals?" and Muhammad answers, "There is such a reward in the case of every living creature."[19]

Primarily, however, *Social Justice and Islam* is concerned with economics. Qutb's economic recommendations are simple. He was writing at the height of the Cold War, and, like so many of his contemporaries, had the Communist alternative in mind. He lived, moreover, under Nasser's Arab Socialism. Qutb endorsed private property and the free market. (Muslim thinkers almost invariably do.) He gave the usual example of Muhammad, whose career as a merchant made it clear that trade was an honorable way of life, but he gives other reasons as well. "Islam," he wrote "does not demand a compulsory economic equality in the narrow sense of the term." People have different talents and capacities: the best should be encouraged. Some people work harder: they should be rewarded. Compulsory equality would, he argued (in very familiar phrases) stifle creativity and economic growth. Communists call for "equality of wages," but, he argued, "Communism has found itself unable to achieve this equality." In the last analysis, Qutb argued, money is not that important. True equality, human equality, is not a question of money.[20]

In this view, as in others, Qutb expressed a view that is part of American common sense. Political, not economic, equality is the ideal. Socially, too, people should regard each other as equals, possessors of a common, natural humanity. "All men are created equal." They remain equal, we believe, though one might be wealthier, more famous, more athletic, or more educated. They should treat one another as equals despite these differences.

This seems simple to us, but once it altered the face of the political world. It could do so again. The French, and, above all, the American, revolutions changed more than governments. They changed the people. People no longer thought that a man called a lord or a count or a king had any claims on them. In America, rights had taken hold, rooted, and grown, in (and perhaps well before) the time of the revolution. Thomas Paine writes, "If I ask any man in America if he wants a king he retorts and asks me if I take him for an idiot."[21] He goes on to say that Americans are wiser than others only in one respect: they know their rights. The French learned theirs, and lost them: they saw the monarchy restored; they saw the empire of Napoléon. Americans remained democrats and republicans. It is the French, however, who gave voice to the rights of man and citizen for the world, affirming, in the first article of their 1789 declaration of those rights, not only that men are born free and equal, but that they remain so. The liberal revolutions recognized the "sacred and inviolable" right to property. Fearing the power of the state, they strictly limit the state's ability to seize private property. If Qutb is the antithesis of liberalism, it is not on these points.[22]

Qutb affirms human equality. He defends the right to private property and protests against state seizures of property. They lead, he argues, only to corruption and the aggrandizement of the state. If one has a larger income or a few more possessions, that is not a problem, Qutb writes, as long as these differences do not damage political and social equality. These disparities are fine "so long as they did not exceed a reasonable limit."

Qutb gives a practical account of what a reasonable limit might be. "When the American workingman, for example, has his house with hot running water, electricity and gas, his radio set and his private automobile . . . it is not luxury that the White House should be the home of the President." But, he writes, when millions do not have clean running water, it is "undeniably luxury" for a few to drink imported Evian water.[23]

Qutb's practicality extends to his account of the ordinary requirements of justice in economics. The worker is entitled to his wage. But "it is not enough" that wages be paid in full, Qutb writes; "they must also be paid on time." He quotes a direct and earthy saying of the Prophet: "Pay your hired man his wages before the sweat is dry on him."[24] The worker, for his part, must do the work required of him and do it to the best of his ability.

The person who works hard and honestly, the small business owner who runs a useful and honest shop, the farmer, the miner—anyone engaged in business—may work hard and well and still end in poverty. Crops can fail; commodity prices can fall precipitously; goods can fall out of fashion. We are all at the mercy of impersonal economic forces. Poverty may be the result of an individual failing, but, as Qutb observes, poverty would be with us if men were angels. Changes in nature and the market can impoverish the hardworking as well as the lazy, and bring down the wise as well as the foolish.

Qutb recognizes that poverty damages not only the body but the soul. "He is in need of food and so he is humiliated; for there is no need which is more humiliating." If he is forced to ask for charity for himself or his family, "all his self-esteem leaves him, lost forever." Things are little better for the giver of charity. Charity may be a virtue and a blessing, but it feels like a vice. Charity shames the givers of charity, who see the poverty the poor would like to conceal. Charity shames the givers who know that what they have came not only from work and skill, but from the same arbitrary luck that brings poverty. Charity follows pity, and pity is an exchange in which both parties are diminished.

George Kateb, like Rawls, is a Western philosopher suspicious of organized religion (in Kateb's case, suspicious of religion altogether) and committed to the freedom of the individual. He offers a defense of human dignity in a book that bears that phrase as its title.[25] Kateb sees human dignity as threatened by those who acknowledge the dignity of animals. He also sees dignity threatened by calls for redistribution. Kateb recognizes that poverty is destructive and demeaning. He recognizes that differences in wealth are not always (or even often) the result of skill or merit. Often such differences are neither more nor less than a matter of luck. Yet he insists that property rights are "sacred and inviolable," and that even calls for greater charity are out of line: Peter Singer, who has argued that poverty could be eradicated if the wealthy chose to give more, is represented as a greater threat to human dignity than poverty. The practicalities of food and shelter fall before the demands of principle. Kateb has plenty of company. The idea that property rights are "sacred and inviolable" has a large following.

The sanctity of property rights can be defended in only two ways. The first is to make a god of the market. The invisible hand becomes the Invisible Hand of a deity who is, if not all-good, at least all-powerful and deserving of all our love and worship. This belief, which is not often aired openly, seems nevertheless to command most conceptions of the market. The second reason for regarding property rights as inviolable turns on an old sleight of hand. Long ago, Locke argued that you could kill a thief, who had not in any way threatened you, because in taking your money he had shown his willingness to take your life. There are many perversities in this pronouncement. The thief, who threatened no one, is killed; the killer, who struck first and without being threatened, is absolved, and absolved beforehand. The perversity that concerns us here is that which has us take money as currency for the individual. In Locke's accounting, even a small bit of money is worth a human life. Money is no longer a tool for human beings, something they use. Nor is money simply a sign, even a sign for human possessions. Money is the sign for the whole of the human. Money no longer represents a certain value—this much bread or that many bytes—it represents the incalculable value of the human.

Locke had a defense contemporary liberals lack. He could say property rights were sacred and inviolable because his idea of property included rights, and the person's living body. We do not think of property in this way. For us, property means goods or wealth or possessions: exactly those things which are not part of the body. "My property" does not mean "my right to free speech" or "freedom of assembly" or any other right. It means "my stuff." The idea of "my sacred and inviolable right to my stuff" seems, at best, a bit overstated: perhaps undignified. My inviolable Louboutins? My sacred right to Botox? It is odd that someone so concerned about human dignity would be bent on protecting the things that too few human beings own.

There is certainly a connection between people's possessions and their dignity. That relation is an interesting one: it becomes stronger as the number of possessions diminishes. Christian teaching recognized that "the widow's mite" surpasses the lavish contributions of the wealthy. People are more shocked by thefts from the poor than by thefts from the wealthy. They should be. Theft is a crime in both cases, but thefts from the poor are likely to do more harm. The lives of the poor are precarious. A theft can mean the difference between eating and starving, getting to the hospital or not, having shelter or not. Even less burdensome threats do more harm to the poor. The poor have less to lose, so each loss weighs more heavily. Dignity depends (though it should not) on maintaining appearances, on the ability to appear as one among equals, without making vulnerability or misfortune visible to any passerby. A rich person can replace a shirt or a tie or pair of shoes (or, for that matter, an insured Lear jet or a yacht). Human dignity is never in question. The poor may struggle to replace a stolen jacket.

Regarding property as sacred and inviolable does not protect human dignity; it diminishes it. It elevates material things above human dignity, above individual rights. Once slaveholders insisted on their sacred and inviolable right to their human "property." That is now regarded as shocking and perverse, but it is no more perverse, and no more shocking, than a defense of property that tolerates putting human dignity—and human lives—in danger. In altering the classical liberal understanding of property to elevate possessions above persons, we have distorted the meaning of liberalism.

Classical liberals recognized that poverty is not primarily a moral problem; it is an economic and political problem. Poverty is not primarily a private problem; it is a public one. The presence of the poor is a shame to the nation.

Qutb, like many before him, feared the effects of great distances between the rich and the poor. Benjamin Disraeli, the great British conservative, wrote of two nations "between whom there is no intercourse and no sympathy . . . ordered by different manners, and . . . not governed by the same laws . . . the rich and the poor." Long before him, Machiavelli had argued that the poor want only to avoid oppression, while the wealthy and powerful want only to oppress.

The response of many has been that the poor are always with you and charity is a way to win salvation. Charity may be the high road to personal redemption, but it damages politics. Charity is not a relation between equals. It is a relation between the haves and the have-nots. Charity is the sign that equality is absent.

There are those in the West who have recognized that poverty—or, if you prefer, "income inequality"—is not an ethical but a political question. The great free market economist Milton Friedman argued that it was absurd to require poor people to prove they were deserving, and to waste public money by scrutinizing the grocery lists, the kitchens, the budgets, and the eating habits of those on welfare. Friedman didn't believe in welfare as charity at all. He argued that the decision to provide a decent life was a choice made by rational individuals in their own interest. Those interests can be wide-ranging: the desire to diminish crime associated with poverty, to educate more people, or to eliminate homelessness because it is ugly. These interests are not necessarily good or honorable or ethical, but they are rational. Rational individuals have rational reasons for wanting to eliminate the problem of poverty. They should do so without imposing their moral views on others or acting as if their wealth gives them the license to control the decisions of others. If the poor need money, Friedman argued, then just give it to them, no strings attached.

Friedman and Qutb are poles apart. One is a free market economist, arguing for the individual and for individual choice. The other is the founder of a religious association, concerned with what God has laid down for men. Both, however, recognize that private, personal, and ethical responses will not answer the problem of poverty. Poverty should be treated not as an ethical issue, but as an economic one; not as a personal failing, but as a political problem. Both recognize that impersonal economic forces have human consequences. Honorable, hardworking, and intelligent economic actors can be impoverished by unforeseeable acts of God and man: an electrical failure, a computer glitch, a sudden storm, a drought, or a change of taste. Both distrust the state and governmental power, but both recognize that the state can play a valuable role in addressing the problem of poverty, and that it should do so in the simplest and most direct way possible.

Qutb's discussions of economics are clearly directed to the conditions of the modern world. He takes his bearings from the Koran, but he accepts and responds to modern technology. When he discusses the Koranic ban on interest, he notes that "in this present age, there is apparent another reason for prohibiting usury."[26] The ability of some to profit from the money they hold widens the gap between rich and poor. As the money grows without effort, the rich, already far from the desperate needs of the poor and the struggles of the middle class, become more distant still.

Qutb's account of economics contains an implicit critique of the Western view of welfare. Providing enough for any citizen to live a decent life is not charity; it simply provides what is necessary for political equality. Ensuring political equality is a political obligation. To ensure that everyone who dies in the country is buried decently (even if he dies among strangers in a strange land) is not charity; it is an acknowledgment of the dignity that belongs to every human being: a last acknowledgment of the vessel that holds the soul.

There is no question that Qutb has political and theological positions that a democrat or a secularist will find objectionable. That is true, however, of many people whose work we read and use and even canonize. Why shouldn't we make use of what is valuable in Qutb and discard the rest—as we do with Plato and Hegel, Aristotle and Locke? There are, I think, two possible reasons. The first reason is a weak one, but it is surprisingly common. Many people seem to think that there are good political thinkers and bad ones; that the good are always good and the bad invariably bad. Condemning Heidegger or Carl Schmitt may seem quite straightforward: how can one trust the political thinking of men who worked with the Nazis? But if finding bad philosophers is easy, finding the unremittingly good ones is surprisingly difficult. Plato's condemnations of democracy and Aristotle's service to tyrants may seem to belong to a distant (and hence more easily forgiven) time, but Hannah Arendt's condemnations of black students and the civil rights movement cannot be so easily placed in an unenlightened past. A little reading forces one to recognize that Locke, the great republican, was imperfect enough to defend slavery and condemn Catholics. Mill, the defender of liberty, was not so ready to defend the liberty of colonized Indians or less-educated workers.

There is no profit in reading philosophy, especially canonical philosophy, with the naive and erring piety of the fundamentalist. While theorists are alive, they argue and readers argue with them. After death has rendered them unable to change their minds, readers are obliged to read critically: dismissing or condemning some of what they wrote, accepting other works and passages as useful or brilliant. Perhaps the inability to see what is useful and valuable in Qutb is just another instance of a rather commonplace failing, the perverse desire for purity of thought.

There may be more to it than misguided purity. An honest reading of Qutb would raise difficult questions for people in the West—especially for Americans and for the French who still claim allegiance to liberty, equality, and fraternity. They would be obliged to recognize their abandonment of the ideal of equality. They would be obliged to listen to Muslim critics like Qutb—and to Western critics like Alain Badiou, Peter Singer, and Stéphane Hessel. They would be obliged to admit that the man without money is something less than a brother. They would be obliged to recognize that inequality is the enemy of liberty.

Qutb's arguments about welfare, property, and the demands of equality also raise particularly difficult questions for the secular Left. Secularism has become a faith with its own fundamentalisms. The mockery of Christopher Hitchens or Bill Maher fails against the faith of those who feed the poor, who comfort addicts, who shelter the homeless. John DiIulio reminds us that the religious have often done what the state and most citizens would not: they have served the most diminished, the hopeless, and the unworthy.[27] Those the welfare office turns away as undeserving are still fed at the church door.

For citizens as well as believers the question should not be the moral status of the individual—deserving or undeserving. Rather, it should be the character of our political order. Does it honor the dignity of the living? Does it honor its commitments to liberty, equality, and fraternity? Do we live in a country of equals? Or is it merely, as John Rawls might ask, a decent hierarchical society?

CHAPTER 6

Democracy

In the dark of December, as 2010 turned to 2011, the people of Tunisia rose against their authoritarian regime. As winter turned to spring, the Egyptian people flowed into the streets chanting. They faced down water cannons on the bridges of the Nile and built the heart of the nation in Tahrir Square. As I write this, people are battling authoritarian governments in Syria, Yemen, and Bahrain. They chant, "*shaab hurri, shaab hurri,*" calling themselves into being as a *shaab hurri*, a free people. Each of these revolutions has called for democracy. In Tunisia, Egypt, and Libya democratic institutions are taking shape. Those that formed secretly, hidden from the eyes of the government, have come forward. Building democracy is hard work, always opposed and often defeated, but the people who have stood steadfast in Tahrir Square, Manama, Misrata, and Dara'a have already accomplished a great work. They have revealed a falsehood.

Not long before he died, Jacques Derrida wrote a book entitled *Voyous*, translated as *Rogues*. The name referred to those that Derrida saw as the enemies of democracy: the United States and Islam. Derrida's reproach to the United States was the "critique of the nymph Echo": it echoed condemnations of "rogue states" from successive American administrations committed to military adventurism and conquest in the name of democracy. In Derrida's account, the accusation "*voyou*" hit hard rock and echoed back as an accusation: "you, you." "You are the rogue state. Yours are the foreign fighters." There was justice in the charge.

Little of the book, however, was directed at the United States. Instead, Derrida turned to democracy and Islam, which he called "the other of democracy." He seemed to hesitate in this naming, but the boundary was firm. Whether it was "a certain Islam" or "the Arabic and Islamic," it was "the other of democracy." Forgetting perhaps, that the world contains Hindus and Buddhists, followers of Confucius, animists, and others, Derrida had, in a strange reprise of the Cold War, divided the world in two. All those within Judeo-Christian civilization claim their states are democratic, and whether those claims are true or false, they mark them out from Islam. The nonaligned fade into the background or are absorbed into the orbit of one side or the other.

Only Islam, Derrida insisted, refuses democracy.[1]

Derrida was hardly the only scholar to have made that claim. His account echoes Samuel Huntington. John Rawls thought Islam so alien that he was obliged to treat it separately. There are countless scholars, left and right, Anglo-American and Continental, who have insisted that Islam is the other of democracy. For many of these, the insistence seems to come from narrowness of vision, a parochialism learning has not succeeded in dispelling. Derrida should have known better. Perhaps he did.

Derrida knew that Islamist parties had been in the forefront of the campaign for democracy in his native

Algeria. In late 1991 the Islamic Salvation Front (Front Islamique du Salut, the FIS) won the first round of parliamentary elections. The army canceled the second round of elections to forestall the victory of the FIS. In his account of these events, Derrida veils the military intervention, calling it an "interruption" by "the state and the leading party."[2] He argues, moreover, that it was an intervention to save democracy. They thought, he writes, that democratic victory for the FIS would "lead democratically to the end of democracy," so "they decided to put an end to it themselves." They decided "to suspend, at least provisionally, democracy *for its own good*, so as to take care of it, so as to immunize it against a much worse and very likely assault." They were not democrats themselves, these friends; they preferred military rule. Derrida calls this a decision made "in a sovereign fashion." This was no democratic sovereign, for those who decided were not the Algerian people, not even their elected representatives. Some of them were Algerian, Derrida writes, "although not a majority of the Algerian people," and they were joined by "people outside Algeria" who thought it best to put an end to Algerian democracy. The decision to forestall democracy was, in short, a decision made by the Algerian military with the backing and support of "people outside Algeria": Western governments and intellectuals like Derrida. With friends like these, democracy has enemies enough.

Derrida draws three lessons from the ending of the Algerian elections: first, the resistance of Islam to secularism (understood as the French would have it); second, democracy's drive to suicide; and third, that democracy belongs not to the present but perhaps (and only perhaps) to the future and to the past. Each of these ideas holds a meaning different from the lesson Derrida teaches.

The first lesson is the resistance of Islam to a "European" process "of secularization, and so of democratization."³ This is European indeed, for there are many outside Europe who would object to the idea that democracy is identical to secularization. The New World is not persuaded that people need to be stripped of their faith before they can govern themselves. Even those sympathetic to secularism should recognize that it can be found in dictatorships as well as democracies, and in its most severe forms (French *laïcité* or Turkish *laiklik*) has an authoritarian aspect.

Derrrida bases his affirmation of the hostility of Islam to democracy on what he calls "the little I know." He confirms this assessment by arguing the "fact" that Aristotle's *Politics* was "absent in the Islamic importation" and that al Farabi had incorporated "only the theme of the philosopher king." Derrida managed three errors in one sentence: Aristotle was imported not to Islam from Europe, but to Europe from Islam in the period he cites; references to the *Politics* are present in Islamic philosophy of the period; and al Farabi not only takes more than the philosopher king from Plato, he moves Plato in a democratic direction. The substance of the errors here is less interesting than Derrida's willingness to construct Islam as antidemocratic based on what he himself calls his own ignorance.

The first lesson, founded in ignorance, is the hostility of Islam to democracy. Yet if we examine Derrida's lesson carefully, we find another lesson—that the argument that Islam is hostile to democracy is dependent on two things we might choose against: willful ignorance and taking secularism as a substitute for democracy.

Derrida's second lesson is democracy's tendency to suicide. Democracy's enemies, Derrida argued, are those who claim to be "staunch democrats," who work for, call for, and participate in popular elections. They may destroy democracy, and they must be stopped, by any means necessary. Democracy must be killed, as Derrida wrote, "*for its own good*, so as to take care of it." This is not suicide; this is murder.[4]

Wendy Brown has noted "the odd way in which Derrida parses 'democracy.'" "We know," Brown writes, that "the term issues from the Greek *demos* and *cracy*: the people rule. Yet repeatedly in *Rogues*, Derrida substitutes the cognate term *kratos* (strength, force) for *cracy*."[5] It is odd for Derrida to rest so much on the etymology of a word, as if one could not have the thing without the name. Democracy does not require the use of the Greek term, whatever it might mean. When I asked Norwegians what word the ancient Norse used for democracy, they told me easily enough. It translates as "the people steering." Derrida's insistence on the Greek and his delving after the root of the word anchor democracy in Europe and in the past.

The claim of democracy in the West is often, as Derrida recognized, a travesty. They "*present themselves* as democracies."[6] Recall, as Derrida's work does not, the regimes that made "democratic republic" a sign of authoritarianism: the European satellites of the former Soviet Union. Much of Europe came late to democracy—not only Eastern Europe, but Germany, Spain, and Portugal. Democratic challenges to Western authorities, in Greece, Iceland, the United Kingdom, and the United States suggest that in the streets of the liberal West there is still anger at the absence of democracy. The Occupy Wall Street Movement took its bearings from Tahrir Square.

Mindful that the Greeks were read by the children of Ishmael as well as those of Isaac, and that Rome's was an eastern as well as a western empire, we might (taking liberties with the text lest it take liberties from us) argue against restricting the heritage of democracy to the "merely European." These adjectives—Greco-Christian, Greco-Roman, globalatinizing—which would seem to send the descendants of Ishmael into the desert as exiles from democracy, might serve instead to remind us that there is a "Greco-Muslim" world, and that Constantinople became Istanbul. If democracy is an inheritance from the Greeks, then it, like the philosophic city of speech, is our Al Andalus, holding Jews, Christians, and Muslims. If globalatinization proceeds through invasion and conversion, from the pagan to the Christian (and back again), in the western empire, it is no less present in the invasions and conversions that led Rome's eastern empire from the pagan to the Christian to the Muslim. If globalatinization leads to the democracy to come, then its past and future heartland encircles the Bosphorus.

Derrida's second teaching is that democracy is suicidal, that the death of democracy is a structural inevitability, a process without agents or the possibility of escape. Yet his evidence, his arguments, our learning, our own experiences, and above all the case he cites, speak against this teaching. The defeat of democracy—the defeat of democracy in Algeria, in France, in all the places where it is defeated—is not a logic; it is the political work of specific political actors, those animated by what philosopher Jacques Rancière aptly calls "the hatred of democracy."[7]

Derrida's third lesson is closely allied to the second: that democracy has no place in the present. It belongs to the future and to the past. It is constantly deferred, sent off, delayed, deflected.[8] It belongs either to a future, a time to come that may never come; or to a lost Greek past, one that may never have been. Its presence among us is spectral, ghostly. Yet Derrida's evocation of the *revenant*, the returning specter, reminds us that we can see in Derrida's undead a democracy that is not dead. If democracy haunts the past, it can be, has been, called up in the present. If democracy is to come, it remains a possibility that has not been and cannot be foreclosed.

This is a twice-haunted text. Derrida is haunted by the democracy he fears, and by the Muslim whose fraternity he has refused.

Islam appears in *Rogues* as Ishmael to Isaac, as the brother excluded from the covenant with the divine. Muslims are, like Ishmael, cast out of the Abrahamic inheritance that runs in Derrida's writing, as in Jewish and Christian scripture, from Abraham to Isaac. They are cast out from the inheritance of democracy. Muslims are alien to democracy, which belongs to a "Greco-Christian and globalatinizing tradition."[9] One can read a similar argument in "Faith and Knowledge." Derrida writes that the concepts of democracy and secularization, "even of the right to literature," are not "merely European, but Graeco-Christian, Graeco-Roman."[10] Derrida works, in *Rogues* as he did in *The Politics of Friendship*, to mark the Muslim as the altogether alien, the enemy, the one who must be cast out of the Abrahamic lineage and from the philosophic lineage that stretches from Jerusalem to Athens.

Derrida was haunted by his exclusion of Islam. He saw that in the West, in France, he was Isaac, the chosen one, the one who could be taken within the covenant, while the Arab Ishmael was sent to wander in the desert. He saw Algerian Muslims refused as he, the once-Algerian, was embraced. As he worked at the Sorbonne and the École normale supérieure, other once-Algerians (or those whose parents or grandparents were once Algerian, or Moroccan, or Tunisian) looked for work in the Parisian suburbs, the places political scientist Gilles Kepel called the *banlieues d'Islam*. As he became an ever more cosmopolitan intellectual, they were confined to the jobless suburbs of Paris.

Muslims are citizens of the République. They can be found in every sector of French life. Despite this very ordinary integration, the familiar presence of Arabs and Arabic, Muslims and Islam, in France, it is still possible to mark Islam as alien to the Republic and to republican values, and so to place Muslims outside the boundaries of an ideal France. This was the position Derrida endorsed in *Rogues*

This is also the position Derrida's work speaks against. A longtime reader of Derrida who knows something of Islam might reasonably have expected different things from him. Derrida testified to the ethical demands of bearing witness. One can hear in that demand the echo of the *shahada*. Derrida would have heard the *shahada* often in the nineteen years he spent in Algeria. The *shahada*, which means "testimony" or "witness," is part of the *adhan* that calls Muslims to prayer five times a day. Derrida spoke from and as and for the Jew, acknowledging the echo of the *Shema*, remaining silent about the *shahada*. He heard bearing witness as a calling, as it was in the Algiers of his childhood. Derrida spoke against the author and authority. He argued for an understanding of authority that saw it flowing outward, constantly disseminated, constantly seeding new meanings. He recognized that difference summons the new. Derrida's contributions to philosophy bear the mark not only of Jerusalem and Athens, but of the streets of Algiers. The sound of the call to bear witness carries not only the *Shema* but the text of the Koran within it.

At each point where he marks Islam as the other of democracy, Muslims as alien, and Ishmael as the enemy, Derrida gestures to another possibility: for Islam and for democrats. The road he does not follow takes Ishmael as a friend and a brother rather than an enemy, marks out a meeting place in Greek philosophy, and gives us democracy not as a dangerous course to be endlessly deferred but as a timeless place we can reach together.

Derrida says *adieu* to Ishmael and to democracy. He hears salvation in the "latinity" of *salut*. Perhaps we should learn enough Arabic for simple greetings, enough to say *Ahlan wa sahlan* and *Marhaba*. *Marhaba*, which is used as English-speakers use "Hello," carries within it the idea that the one greeted is welcome, that there is plenty of room. Arabic words, like words in Hebrew, are formed from roots. Each root leads to a tree of words. The root of the word *r-h-b* gives us *rahb*, which means spacious or roomy but also "unconfined" and "open-minded, broad-minded, frank, liberal." It is also the root of *rahaba*, the word for the public square. *Marhaba* is a good greeting for liberals, who at their open-minded, broad-minded best, can find that there is plenty of room in the public square.

The Egyptian poet and scholar Farouk Mustafa translated *Ahlan wa sahlan* as "you are among your people and your keep is easy." Like *Marhaba*, the greeting marks a welcome, and a curious one. *Ahlan wa sahlan* is not said simply to one's own, to family and friends and fellow citizens. It is said to foreigners, to travelers, to people who are not, in the ordinary sense, one's own. Like the American "Come in, make yourself at home," it is said to people who are not at home, who might be turned away. The greeting recognizes a difference only to set it aside. *Ahlan wa sahlan* recognizes that there are different peoples, that people belong to different nations, and that they might find themselves in a foreign country, among an alien people. This greeting marks the possibility that the other, the alien, the wanderer, and the refugee might be met with a welcome rather than with fear.

We can find these resources in European languages as well. One need not say adieu to democracy: one can say welcome. Welcome, *wilkommen*, *bienvenue*, *benvenidos* all speak to the possibility that the other could be met with pleasure and celebration. It is possible to hear, in all these languages, "It is good that you have come, you have done well to come here." The words mark the pleasure of meeting a different sort of person, with strange and exotic clothing and customs, with news and new stories. They mark, too, the luck of the stranger who finds food, shelter, and companionship. These words mark the moment of meeting, the relation of host and guest as one of shared pleasure and good fortune.

Throughout his work, Derrida protested against the possibility of friendship and welcome. He wrote a moment of hostility into hospitality, renaming it "hostipitality." *The Politics of Friendship* is full of longing for friendship, for the lost friend or the lost possibility of friendship. Friendship is grief for Derrida. The friend is always already lost, a ghost or a memory. The enemy is always hiding in the friend. "O my friends," Derrida cried (for Aristotle surely did not), "there is no friend!"

We can, with a little Arabic, find friendship where Derrida could not. *Ahlan wa sahlan* is a curiously earthy greeting. It speaks directly to the simple concerns of life:

food and shelter. The shared need for these things, and for companionship, runs beneath and beyond the differences of place and people. In much of contemporary Western philosophy, bare life is associated with pain and fear, with the abandoned refugee or the most abject in the camps of the Holocaust. Those people, those places, must be remembered. But the experience of bare life and the hazards of bare life—the need for shelter in a harsh frontier, the need for food in the desert, the need to find protection—also calls forth the commons. Need drives us to politics and a common life. The fragility of life in hard times and hard places turns people to one another. This was the fundamental recognition of the fourteenth-century Muslim historiographer Ibn Khaldun.

People in hard places, Ibn Khaldun argued, must have two virtues if they are to survive. They must have fortitude, and they must depend upon each other. Those who learn these things and survive, prosper. Power comes to them because they can act in common.[11] Need has made them political and taught them power.

Ibn Khaldun offers an alternative to Derrida, Giorgio Agamben, and all those who follow Carl Schmitt in saying that politics is founded in enmity. Derrida locates himself in a Greco-Christian tradition that he presents as alien to Islam. He knew well that this was not correct. Greek philosophy has been a cosmopolitan, mongrel meeting place rather than an exclusive club. Greek philosophy belongs as much to the Muslim as to the Christian tradition—and they have drawn from it, continued it, kept it alive in hard times. Like Aristotle and Plato, Ibn Khaldun founds politics in friendship.

In Ibn Khaldun's account, the friendship that founds politics comes into being when people find that they can depend on one another. This account confounds much of what we in the West have been taught to take for granted. For Ibn Khaldun, individualism and the commons are not opposed. Those who live on the frontier are more self-reliant (because they must be) and more committed to the common good (because they must be). Individuals are more individual: more self-reliant, more independent, more able to provide for themselves. They are likely to be stronger and braver. The harsh circumstances in which they live have obliged them to learn courage, steadfastness, and fortitude. But their individual strength does not keep them apart. It draws them together. The same harsh circumstances that teach them strength and courage also teach them trust. The idea that a common experience of danger or hardship draws people together is a common one. Soldiers who serve together come to see themselves as a band of brothers. Settlers on a windswept, barren plain learn to work together to protect their farms.

Derrida saw friendship as a luxury good. Ibn Khaldun recognized it as a necessity. Derrida's late account of democracy figured it as the place where enemies meet: the turn of a wheel that raises some and throws others down, perhaps beneath it. Wendy Brown has observed how foreign this is to democracy. This is precisely what democracy would not be: not outside, not unilateral, not over, not a matter of "winning out over." Democracy is, on the contrary, ruling together, ruling and being ruled in turn. Democracies are manifold, many-sided. There are many sides to any question and many sides contesting. Democracy has many dimensions, and on each dimension one may win or lose, and one will be ruled and rule in turn. Opposition is not enmity. Or perhaps it is.

Perhaps democracies have made enmity their own. Perhaps democracies have the power to tame enmity. Tyrants, as philosophers from Xenophon to Arendt have recognized, live in constant fear of opposition. They see enemies everywhere. They live in fear. They live by fear. Their safety depends on making their enemies fear them, and everyone is their enemy. Fear spreads, and such regimes end, as Arendt observed, by eating their own.

In democracies, enmity is made ordinary. Democrats live with the enemy. We argue with our enemies in our homes and at work; we hear them on the radio and watch them on television. We see their blogs. We campaign against them, write against them, vote against them. We hate them and we know that they may win: in this debate, this election, this bill, this law. We set our hearts and lives against them. When they win, we submit.

Whether we win or lose, we do not fear them. Or, more precisely, we have learned to govern our fear. Enmity is not easily domesticated. When domesticated, it may still show its claws. We can hear the gunfire in the parking lot of an Arizona grocery. We can see the aborted fetus. We can see the bullets hit the doctor who performs abortions. We live—all of us—with our enemies as well as with our friends. We live with danger.

Democracy is a hard discipline. Democrats are required to live surrounded by enemies and opponents. They are required to walk among their enemies without fear. Democracy is rooted in courage: in wild reckless courage and in steadfast endurance. The marchers who faced fire hoses and dogs on the bridge at Selma, who stood steadfast on bridges over the Nile as water cannons mowed them down, called us to witness their title to democracy. They had the courage to act when there was no hope. When Egyptians took to the streets in late January of 2011, they acted against the prevailing wisdom and their own wholly rational fears. Marchers filled the streets, moving like a river through the city, calling forth democracy, calling forth a free people, "*shaab hurri.*"

The Arab Spring did more than prove Derrida wrong. The people of these revolutions reminded us of the virtues of democracy. Democracy depends on daring, on that wild, reckless courage that defies insurmountable odds (the odds are always against democracy) and prompts people to sail forth into an unknown, unknowable future. Democracy depends on fortitude, on steadfastness, on the ability to endure hardship. Democracy relies not only on the courage one sees in a daring act, but on the courage that enables people to endure what cannot be endured, to face what cannot be faced, to stand up and begin again.

Derrida places democracy in the past and the future. Democracy belongs to a fabled and particular past, to the Greco-Christian and globalatinizing forces that made Europe. It is "ambiguously secular": at once secular and also Judeo-Christian. Democracy can belong, in this understanding, only to people who are one people, who share the same customs and habits, for only those people, we are told, can care about one another. It comes under the signs of unity and sameness; it is, as Whitman wrote, "ensemble." Democracy is Western, Christian and Jewish, but it is not for us, it is only *a venir*, to come.

Derrida's writings on Muslims indicate not only his anxieties about this all-too-alien other, but about democracy itself. He writes, in *Rogues*, that the name "rogues" belongs to the rioting youth, the *shebab*—and he recognizes the anger of democracy in them. The rogue belongs, he writes, "to what is most common and thus most popular in the people. The *demos* is thus never far away when one speaks of the *voyou*."[12] The rioting *shebab* of the *banlieues* are close to the *demos*, close to democracy. So too were other rogues, the Algerians who threatened to vote the Front Islamique du Salut into power. They were close to democracy, only to have it snatched away. Derrida accepted—indeed, propounded—the view that this democracy, the democracy of Islamists, would have put an end to democracy. Yet he shows us a democracy ended not by Islam, but by the partisans of "laïc subjectivity" and the "Enlightenment." Perhaps we can see democracy otherwise.

If politics is founded not in enmity but in friendship, perhaps we can envision "*an alterity without hierarchical difference at the root of democracy*," as Derrida says, or, as one might say more plainly, perhaps we can have a democracy of equals, individuals working, arguing, thinking, and making a politics together.[13]

If we read the Greeks as a common heritage (one that extends beyond their national or cultural offspring to all who might find themselves in a city of speech, or on the rough frontier), we need not bind ourselves within the confines of the merely European.

If we can make common cause with the rebellious *shebab*, the car-burning rogues of the French suburbs, we will find ourselves closer to democracy. We will find ourselves not just as Westerners, but as democrats.

If we take the philosophers of the Muslim world as our own, part of a more capacious canon, we will find guidance on our way. The most beautiful and most honest description of democracy I know is a passage that another

Derrida might have called "Greco-Muslim." I quote it often, because it seems to me to capture the promise and the dangers, the joy and the terror of democracy. The passage comes from al Farabi. It is almost, but not quite, a quotation from Plato's *Republic*. Al Farabi writes of the democratic city:

> On the surface, it looks like an embroidered garment, full of colored figures and dyes. Everybody loves it and loves to reside in it, because there is no human wish or desire that this city does not satisfy. The nations emigrate to it, and reside there, and it grows beyond measure. People of every race multiply in it, and this by all kinds of copulation and marriages. . . . Strangers cannot be distinguished from the residents. All kinds of wishes and ways of life are to be found in it. . . . The bigger, the more civilized, the more populated, the more productive, and the more perfect it is, the more prevalent and the greater are the good and the evil it possesses.[14]

Plato's original description gave us a condemnation of democracy.[15] Though he could describe its seductions, he could not see its virtues. Al Farabi does not strip away Plato's account of democracy's dangers. He leaves that standing but alters Plato's wording to acknowledge democracy's promise and possibilities. Al Farabi's description of democracy departed from Plato's—and in a democratic direction.

As al Farabi observed, democracies have the potential for both good and evil. They can be as they choose, but whatever course they follow, they are likely to pursue it with intensity. Nor are the differences between them exhausted by variations in their merit. There will be as many democracies as there are peoples—and more, for, as we have seen, democracies draw different peoples together. There may be, therefore, an infinity of democracies, each unlike the others. Among the array of democracies there might be those that would choose to remain as they are, to keep out all foreigners, to cultivate the homely richness of a single culture. That would be their right, and perhaps their worth and their beauty. There would be others, like my own, that would glory in the presence of the many. We are not there yet, but that is what we still strive toward.

For us, democracy is still not yet, still to come. Perhaps it is, in Sheldon Wolin's apt term, fugitive, hidden where fugitives have always hidden. Ibn Khaldun and al Farabi suggest that we look in familiar places, in the city and on the frontier. Derrida suggests we look in the suburbs. They are all saying very nearly the same thing. We should look to the ungoverned and the ungovernable, to edges and boundaries, to the mixed cosmopolitan spaces of cities and frontiers. Derrida writes that where the rogue is, democracy is never far away.[16] He knew the demos of his time. He knew it should encompass the jobless rioters of the Parisian suburbs, the *banlieues d'Islam*.

Derrida called the democracy he feared *voyouterie* ("roguery," or perhaps "outlawry"). There is always an element of the rebel and the outlaw in the democrat, for democracy is before and beyond the law. The rebel, the bandit, and the outlaw remind us that democracy is not as liberalism would have it, a creature of procedures, law, and regulation. Democracy is linked to revolution, always and everywhere.

There is another term that Derrida might have used speak of the democratic scum (*canaille*, as Sarkozy called them). One could call them *shaab*. The word has seen hard use in Arabic. It refers to the people, but to the people in their ordinary rather than their sovereign state, to what Westerners once called "the great unwashed." *Shaabi* refers to the poor as well as to the people. These words refer to the people as those who fear democracy see them: the poor, the uneducated, the uncultured, the hungry, the angry, the dangerous. These connotations live in many European languages as well. When the French speak of the popular, they do not, as Americans might assume, speak of things everyone likes, but rather of things that belong to the common people.

Al Farabi's description challenges many contemporary anxieties about democracy. First, he suggests that democracies are inevitably and magnificently diverse: "The nations emigrate to it and reside there," and they populate the ever-growing democratic city with the children of their mixed unions. Democrats do not fear the exotic, the stranger, the other, the new immigrant: they desire them. They want more: more people from more places, more exotic, more varied in their looks and habits. "People of every race multiply in it." They are not afraid of difference: they embrace it; they make love to it; they make it bring forth new people. The idea that democracies belong only to small homogenous communities pales before this vivid picture of democracy.

Al Farabi (and, for that matter, Plato) saw democracy as wildly, passionately cosmopolitan: "strangers cannot be distinguished from the residents." The democratic city al Farabi sees—that he believes results from the driving character of democracy—is not small and homogenous, with a single culture and a simple life. It is large, and growing: "the nations emigrate to it." "Everybody loves it and loves to reside in it." It attracts immigrants, and the immigrants are welcome. They disappear in the wild variety of the democratic city.

These varied and impassioned people are all in hot pursuit of happiness. They build their city to please themselves: "all kinds of wishes and ways of life are to be found in it." They choose to live in the company of people whose ways are different. They may have come to the city from far away, or perhaps simply from some smaller, less democratic place nearby. They have chosen to make different lives for themselves. Their city becomes ever larger and more civilized. For al Farabi, civilization does not belong to cultural unity alone, but to the willful mixing of cultures one finds in large cities.

Al Farabi himself came from the back of beyond, past Bukhara, in Turkestan. He traveled through the great cities of his day: Baghdad, Cairo, Aleppo, Constantinople. He studied in them, worked in them. He lived a life like our lives: in which the boundaries of East and West are constantly crossed, and one's education comes from Muslims, Christians, Jews, and the pagan philosophy of Plato and Aristotle. The rootless cosmopolite al Farabi is one of our kind, and whether or not he was a democrat, he seems to have been happy with them.

The frontier vision of Ibn Khaldun and the cosmopolitan democracy of al Farabi are as familiar to American democrats as cowboys and New Yorkers. The Western (but perhaps more than Western) people of Berlin and Paris, London and Madrid could see themselves, their lives, in al Farabi's democratic city. The Western (but not merely Western) people of the Scottish Highlands and the Norwegian fjords, the Pyrenees, the Camargue, and the deserts of the American Southwest have known the hardships and still share the values of Ibn Khaldun's frontiersmen. Political philosophy in the Muslim (but not simply Muslim) tradition offers visions of democracy, cosmopolitanism, immigration, and integration that are profoundly familiar. Facing this foreign familiar, we can find ourselves saying welcome, *ahlan wa sahlan*, you are among your people here.

Part II

In the Western Street

CHAPTER 7

Where Is Europe?

Pope Benedict XVI, the head, if not of Christendom, at least of one of its larger sects, has affirmed in Germany and Bulgaria, in speeches and in writing, that Europe has Christian roots. That is true, but not the whole truth. Europe has never been quite synonymous with Christendom. Europe has also been the home of the greatest threat to Christianity: atheism, the faith Žižek called "Europe's greatest legacy." Modern Europe orients much of its politics around shame. Europe remembers the Jews who shaped it, were persecuted and killed in it, exiled from it. The practice of democratic assemblies and a transparent law appeared not in a Christian, but in a pagan, European past. Europe has been shaped by Islam. Muslim empires shaped Europe in the past. Muslim citizens shape Europe now. The pagan, the Jewish, the Muslim, the atheist, and the Christian Europe live cheek by jowl, layered in the stones and souls of that place.

There is a pagan Europe, still alive in North and South. There is a secular Europe, an atheist Europe. There is a Jewish Europe and a Muslim Europe. These are not separate, but strands woven together, a tapestry bearing the colors of one vividly in one quarter, while another shines in the next. The European academy, European letters, European design, and the European street are shaped by the work and writing of Jews and Muslims. Those who stoke the fears of "Eurabia" inhabit a Europe shaped by those they reject.

Secularism, liberalism, capitalism, and all the ornaments of European culture, all those things in which Europe takes pride—and many that they continue to debate—are shaped by Jews as well as Christians. The very efforts to isolate and exclude Jews made them central to the shaping of European institutions. They were confined to economic activities Christian authorities marked as demeaning or illicit, and they made themselves central to European economic practices and institutions. They were condemned for (and condemned to) charging interest, and made interest the engine of European economic development. They were exiled to the margins of European commerce, and they impelled the movement of money beyond Europe and called it back again. They were the marked people of Europe, told what they must do and wear, where they might or might not live, never quite full subjects or citizens. Their inclusion and emancipation became, as Marx observed, the lynchpin of liberal institutions. Secularism was critical to the inclusion of the Jews, and Jewish thought to the shaping of secularism. The thought of the Enlightenment moved through Spinoza to Horkheimer and Arendt. European science was made by Einstein and Freud, European arts by Kafka and Mahler, European politics by Disraeli and Marx.

Modern Europe also has Jews at its heart. The Nazi past weighs heavily on Europe. That past shapes law and philosophy, politics and popular memory, the streets and the arts. Few decisions are made without considering their relation to the Nazi past. It is not only that laws forbid National Socialist parties or Holocaust denial; it is that one reads outside a train station, "From this station, trains departed to Dachau and Theresienstadt," or sees embedded in the street the *Stolpersteine* (stumbling stones) that record the names of Jews taken from the houses behind them. It is not only that philosophy, literature, and the arts still orient themselves around the Holocaust. It is that questions of bearing witness, of collaboration and betrayal, of the other, of hospitality and the possibility of inclusion are still tied to the experience of European Jews two or three generations past. Judaism haunts Europe. The contributions of today's Jews enliven it.

Europe is not, and has never been, as Christian as some Christians would have it. Crafting a Christian Europe has been—and remains—a work of conversion, conquest, and craft. Christian missionaries saw Europe not as the center of the Christian world but as the world's desolate heathen periphery. The missionaries who took the good word to northern Europe did their work hand in hand with the power of kings, displacing more democratic institutions. Their persuasive powers relied not solely on pacific evangelism, but on force. Christianity, though Christians like to forget it, spread through Europe by the sword. Christianity has taken root there, but like the tulip and the rose it was an alien planting and it was watered with blood.

The terms of the arrival of Christianity in Europe, allied with foreign powers and profiting from the ambitions of kings, shaped Christian institutions. Derrida's claim that democracy or democracy to come was the work of Greco-Christian and globalatinizing forces is not quite correct. Greece was lost to democracy before it became Christian, and Christianity did not restore it. The Rome that spread Latin through Christianity had long abandoned the Republic for the Empire. Throughout Europe, Christianity overcame democratic practices and institutions, and established aristocratic hierarchies in their place. Derrida's Greco-Christian and globalatinizing forces were hardly the fertile matrix from which European democracy was to grow. These forces had left behind both the equality of primitive Christianity and the democracy of the ancient Greeks.

If Western civilization was (or was to be) Christian, Christianity was not Western. The oldest saints of the church came from the East, from what is now the Muslim world: from Turkey, North Africa, and Arabia. Old Saint Nick comes from that uncertain zone, now Turkey, where East and West, Christian and Muslim, Europe and Asia, meet. Europe's Christian roots go deep into the soil of Bethlehem and Antioch, Jerusalem and Constantinople. Islam is rooted there as well. In these places, as in the European past, the roots of three religions are entangled.

There were moments when Europeans recognized the importance of the Christians outside the bounds of Europe. The Crusades had reminded the inhabitants of Christian Europe of Christians in the Holy Land and, by drawing Crusaders to the battle, brought Western Christians East. Colonization (justified in no small part by the imperatives of evangelism) depended on the idea of Christians and Christianity beyond Europe. Crusade and colonization coincided in the pleas of Columbus to Ferdinand and Isabella. The East would be reconquered by moving West; the origin site of Christianity would be liberated by conquests in the newly discovered lands. The conquest of the New World offered ample ammunition for the imperatives of the Crusade. Conquest in the New World would finance the reconquest of Christianity's ancient homeland. The recognition that the new Indies of the West did not lead readily to the India of old did not sever the tie between crusading and colonization.

Crusading began an inexorable move westward. The capitals of Christianity had already moved to Rome and the cathedrals of western Europe. The crusading imperative changed direction as well. As Columbus had sought to find the Indies by sailing West, so the crusading imperative pursued its mission of universal conquest through a change of direction. That which was once a way station became a destination; that which was once the means became the end. The shift enabled Spain to reconstitute itself as the center of the Christian world, between Christianity's past and its future. Capitalism mediated crusading and colonization.

The gold and silver that washed back from the New World stopped in its move eastward and pooled in Spain. In every Spanish city the saints wear the gold of the Americas. Gold crusted the cathedrals. If Christianity rotted beneath it, a little more gilding would hide the decay. Colonization, carrying the warrant of the crusade, made Spain ever more and less Catholic, ever more and less Christian. The universalism of a catholic and apostolic church gave way to caste, conversion to carnage. Salamanca debated whether the people of the Americas had souls.

Capital increased and agriculture declined. The wealthy, able to profit from the increase in foreign trade and, later, able to trade in (as well as to consume) the luxuries that importation afforded, became wealthier. The poor became poorer. Spain, which once exported food, began to import food as its own agriculture withered and failed.[1]

In its cosmopolitan conquest and appetites, Christianity remained a catholic faith, affirming its universality imperfectly, erratically, and in the interest of capitalism.

The confluence of capitalism and Christianity governed in Protestant Europe as well. The Dutch and the British sent missionaries with their traders (and traders with their missionaries). Neither capitalism nor Christianity saw a reliable ally in the other. Neither saw itself in the other's service. Yet they possessed a symmetry of form (and short-term ambitions) that made each the other's firmest support. Capitalism and Christianity were formed by a shared universalism, by the combination in each of a principled cosmopolitanism and an imperative to individual salvation (variously construed). Capitalism and Christianity (especially in its Catholic form) were animated by notions of abstract and alienable value, and developed technologies for the representation and enhancement of value and the circulatory translation of the material to the ideal. The movement of goods, people, and ideas in the twin currents of capitalism and Christianity kept the world spinning on a European axis.

Capitalism, once merely the supplementary means to a project of universal evangelism, became a supplement in the Derridean sense: adding only to replace. The means to the crusade became its end. The acquisition of capital replaced the conversion of heathen and infidel as the primary object of the Catholic and Christian kings—and their liberal successors. The liberal philosophers James and John Stuart Mill worked day jobs for the British Empire, governing India from London. They advocated imperialism in their philosophic as well as their official positions.[2] Secularized Christianity was no less assiduous in spreading the gospel of conquest.

The confluence of capital and Catholicism in the Reconquista had forced Jews and Muslims out of Spain. They flowed, masses of refugees, learned and ignorant, wealthy and poor, across the Mediterranean—and northward. Amsterdam became their all-too-capacious convivial home. Marvell wrote that Amsterdam embraced "Turk-Christian-pagan-Jew" and "staple of sects and mint of schism grew." The Netherlands flourished with this great migration. The refugees who came from a newly Catholic Spain brought commercial acumen and resources with them. They also brought learning, scholarship, the arts, and a breath of the South. These Mediterranean migrants to the North were no more welcome in some circles than modern migrants. For the less tolerant of the Enlightenment, this transplanted Mediterranean of commerce and conviviality threatened all stable power. Yet these not-always-welcome immigrants helped make the Netherlands a wild, brilliant place. Simon Schama called it "an embarrassment of riches." Everything circulated there: people, wealth, religions, cultures, and ideas. Refugees came in and writing flowed out: writing of all kinds, but, above all, the uncensored writing of political dissent. The Netherlands treated the presses much as Qatar treats al Jazeera today, permitting much freedom of speech and tolerating much dissent, as long as most of it flowed outward.

In the turmoil of the twentieth century's European wars, European intellectuals shaped myths of the origin of Europe. Paul Valéry's vision of Europe sought to overcome the exclusion of the Jew that had defined not only the idea of Europe but the European politics of his own time. A Europe that saw Athens, Rome, and Jerusalem as its heritage could refuse the antisemitism that had played so profound a part in European politics. The contributions of Freud, Marx, and a host of European Jews who had crafted European culture from a position of legal, political, and social subjection could be counted as part of the European patrimony. "France," the Yiddish proverb holds, "is a country that eats Jews." Valéry did exactly that: incorporating Jews in Europe and colonizing a Jewish past for a Christian present.

Valéry's success is evident in the works that followed. In his influential *The Idea of Europe*, Denis de Rougemont quotes Pius II's account of a Christendom refusing Eastern Christians and writes, "Let us note the significant triad: Greece, Italy, and Christendom, used here to designate all Europe; the first attempt to define our culture in terms of its three principal sources, Athens, Rome and Jerusalem, a definition Valéry was to popularize in the twentieth century."[3] Valéry was successful indeed, for Pius didn't mention Jerusalem. Rougement reads the European past in the shadow of an imagined future, and Pius through the lens of Valéry.

Many accounts of the emergence of European identity emphasize the Muslim, Arab and Turk, as the enemy against whom a nascent Europe defined itself. In these accounts, Europe becomes conscious of itself before the gates of Vienna, hearing Roland's horn in the Pyrenees. The Crusades fill children's stories with myths of courage and chivalry. The English have Richard the Lionheart, the Spanish have El Cid. If the modern inheritors of Bernard's crusade—Le Pen and Wilders, Sarrazin, Schlussel, and Breivik—are less respectable, what of it? They have a glorious past. If some of these crusading heroes—El Cid and Sarrazin—bear Arab names, well, that is easily forgotten.

The Empire of Osman called more than Europe into being. Rougement links the emergence of Europe with the idea of cosmopolitanism. He argues that Guillaume Postel, in his 1560 work *De la République des Turcs*, was the first to call himself a "cosmopolite." First or not, Postel's use points to this Ottoman effect. Europeans recognized the presence of Christians and Jews in the empire. They knew that the Sublime Porte of the Ottoman Empire ruled territories not unlike their own. They knew that Christian kings had allied with the Sublime Porte, that military commanders from Venice and elsewhere had served it. For some the recognition of these things made visible the possibility of what we now call globalization. One could move between civilizations. One could belong not to a nation or a people or a religion, but to the world. This was not the most common or the most valued path, but it would become central to one form of late modern European identity.

Other enmities changed the boundaries of Europe and the West. Tocqueville argued that the future would belong to Russia and America. Neither Russia nor America was seen as European. Voltaire had feared the rise of Russia and recommended balancing it by an alliance with the Turks. Hegel left Russia to Asia and named America the *Abendland*, the place of an unknown (perhaps unknowable) future. Two world wars and a Cold War were required to fix America firmly in the West. In that time, the West itself had moved westward. America, once an alien place of emigrants and savages (or perhaps merely savages of two sorts), had become civilized. The same period saw the heart of Europe lose its grip on civilization.

Russia moved from the periphery of the West to well outside it. The Cold War view of Russia as the other of the West was not new, either to Europeans or to Russians. The Marquis de Custine wrote in his *Russia in 1839*, "Russia sees in Europe a prey, which our dissensions sooner or later yield to it." Marx contrasted Russia and the West in the *New York Herald Tribune*: "The people of the West will rise again to power and unity of purpose, while the Russian Colossus itself will be shattered by the progress of the masses and the explosive force of ideas." Alexei Chadaev and other Slavophiles were insistent in their belief that Russia did not belong to Europe. "Russia," Dostoevsky wrote, "is something independent and peculiar, not resembling Europe at all."[4]

The Russian Revolution recast the question. Carl Schmitt wrote of "the Russian masses estranged from Europe" in *Roman Catholicism and Political Form*. With "the class-conscious proletariat of the big cities" they constitute "two great masses opposed to Western European tradition." The Soviet Union held both the archaic Russian masses and the proletariat. Schmitt declared, "From the standpoint of traditional Western European culture both are barbarians. Where they have a sense of their own power, they proudly call themselves barbarians."[5] Rougemont, too, saw the opposition as the definitive clash of civilizations. "Cannot the debate between Russia and Europe be reduced to the fundamental debate between the East and the West concerning the role and nature of civilization?"[6]

After the Second World War, the old question "Does Russia belong to Europe?" gave way to Atlanticism. The clear opposition of the Soviet Union to the liberal democratic nations of postwar Europe made Western Europe appear as the eastern boundary of a West centered in the United States. Europe was enfolded in what was called the Free World. The name concealed the continuing presence of fascism in Spain and Portugal, the junta in Greece, white supremacy in the United States, and other defects in the not quite, not yet Free World. The opposition of this new East and West, the First and Second worlds that would battle over the Third, cast the old theological divisions into shadow. Before "godless communism" all monotheisms seemed safe and sacred.

The Europe that emerged over these long centuries was never clear in its boundaries, never uncontested.

Spain, Scandinavia, Russia, and Britain all saw themselves at some times, through some eyes, as something other than European. Miguel de Unamuno wrote, "Two words sum up what the rest of the world expects of Spain. These two words are 'European' and 'modern.'" Unamuno refused both the European and the modern—and in the name of Christianity. "Here is an expression 'ancient African' to be set against 'modern European' and every bit as good if not better. St. Augustine is African and ancient, so is Tertullian. And why should we not say, 'We must Africanize ourselves in the ancient way', or 'we must ancientize ourselves in the African way'?"[7]

Unamuno's understanding remakes the world. The West disappears in it. Augustine and Tertullian are not Roman, but African. Their movement to Africa is not part of that globalatinizing project in which the West extends its power and authority and all that comes within it takes its form. Unamuno's iconic Romans are no more Roman than African. On the contrary, in Augustine and Tertullian the Roman becomes African. Christianity belongs to the African as well as the European. Unamuno reminds us that the extension of Roman power did not erase the cultures of the conquered, or proceed without affecting the Romans themselves. The globe was Latinized—to some extent—and as it was, the Roman world was altered. Rome was Africanized. As Roman culture spread to territories under Roman influence and Roman rule, so Roman culture became more African, more Asian, more European, more cosmopolitan.

In Unamuno's vision of the world Spain might, in becoming more African, become more Roman and more Christian. Unamuno's Spain at once accepts and confounds Derrida's vision of a democracy that is the work of Greco-Christian and globalatinizing forces. Unamuno's Spain is Christian, Roman, and African, at once cosmopolitan and proudly provincial.

At the turn of the millennium Unamuno's embrace of African Christianity acquired a new resonance, as Africa advanced its claim for centrality in global Christianity. Thousands of miles to the north and west, Anglicans and Episcopalians in Europe and America turned to conservative African bishops for solidarity and support. Once again, conservatives argued that Europe had failed them. Once again, they turned to Africa for the salvation of their faith.

Modern Europe has seen the passion for a lost, antique Christianity, but it has also seen wild forms of syncretism and the desire to escape Christianity altogether. Yirmiyahu Yovel has written of the waves of conversion that swept Spain in the time of Spinoza. There could be Christians, Muslims, and Jews in a single family—or a single life. One person might convert, not just once but twice or more, moving between faiths that seemed to lead to one another. Mixes of these faiths appeared throughout Spain, their followers unconscious of heresy or innovation.[8]

In Italy, the direction of conversion usually pointed toward Mecca, with converts motivated by a dangerous desire for greater equality. The *rinnegati*, renegades, converted to Islam and went into the service of the Sublime Porte. Many of these were talented and ambitious men who found that they could rise only so far, even in the most republican city-states of Europe, since they were not of the nobility. The Ottoman Empire offered them a field in which only one post was denied them, that of sultan. Conversion, or service across confessional lines, was not limited to the privileged, the talented, or the ambitious. There were also conversions among ordinary people, peasants, farmers, and small shopkeepers. Scholars have often noted that Islam's egalitarianism made conversion attractive to Hindus who wished to escape the caste system. Europe, in the early modern period, had its own caste system, and people who wished to escape it. The conversions, estimated in the hundreds of thousands, were referred to as "a hemorrhage of men."

In Scandinavia, democracy begins not with Greeks, Christians, or Romans, but with themselves. The *things* and *althings* of Scandinavia, assemblies in which not only all freemen but all free women had the vote, owed nothing to the Greeks or Romans. Christianity served only to diminish the democratic practices of the North. One might, considering Scandinavia and Greece, mindful of the modes of government among the first nations of the New World, argue that democracy has its origins and finds its most favorable climate among pagans. One might, looking at the map, argue that where the Scandinavians went, democracy followed. The years of Norse dominion in England, Scotland, and Ireland established democratic institutions—and, perhaps more importantly, a taste for more egalitarian practices. When Scandinavians went Viking, they redistributed capital. When they settled the territories they raided, they sowed democracy.

The British too sought to mark themselves off from Europe. Their manner of doing so casts further doubts on the easy association of Europe and democracy. For many Britons, the Continent was a territory given over to authoritarian rule, where early experiments in democracy dissolved into chaos and later ones into terror. Constitutionalism, republicanism, and self-rule were practices, the British taught, that reached their apex not among the Greeks or the Romans (much less their Continental offspring) but in Britain and the British Commonwealth. Montesquieu and other philosophers brought this view to France. Canada, the United States, India, and South Africa saw this history as their lineage.

If Spain, Italy, the Netherlands, Scandinavia, Russia, and the United Kingdom have been less European than Europeans imagine, Turkey has been more European than they have been willing to admit. Constantinople was the capital of the eastern Roman Empire. The Ottoman Empire, in its later days, was called "the sick man of Europe," a phrase that testifies to the assumption that the empire was European. The inclusion of Turkey in the European Union is, however, fraught both institutionally and discursively. When, why, how did Turkey cease to be European?

If Turkey has one foot in Europe and another in Asia, Israel would seem to belong wholly to the Middle East and Asia. Yet Israel is often seen as European: by friends and enemies, by itself and others. Critics and supporters alike point to European Zionism and the consequent arrival of European settlers in the late nineteenth and early twentieth centuries. The pogroms that drove Jews from Russia, and the revolutions that followed, were European events, unsettling European states and driving European Jews from Europe. Herzl and Weizmann were European founders of a European political movement, active in European intellectual, cultural, and political affairs. They spoke European languages. They worked within European institutions. Their vision of the state of Israel was shaped by European intellectual debates; their work for it took place within the confines of European politics. When young American Jews take heritage tours to Israel, they commonly begin in Europe. The camps of the Holocaust precede the arrival in Israel and serve as the Egypt of a modern Exodus. In these accounts, Israeli history grows out of Europe and remains tied to it.

Where is this Europe then? Does Europe extend where languages and cultures flowed with capital and colonization? Is Europe in America and Canada, Australia and Israel? Are the *porteños* of Buenos Aires European? Are the French-speaking architects and economists of Beirut and Tunis European? Is Europe a place or an idea? And what is Europe when it's at home?

The European Street

The Christian-secular majority culture knows that the road to European values was long, that there have been many setbacks along the way, how hard it has been for Europeans to learn tolerance. The distrust in the new arrivals is rooted in Europe's distrust of itself, says Jürgen Habermas. This distrust is well-founded. It descends from the experience Europe has had with itself.

Commenting on a conference featuring Habermas and Tariq Ramadan, a German reporter wrote, "The Irish are first and foremost Irish, the Danish Danish, the Germans German, the Belgians either Flemish or Walloons; the immigrants who are not given the chance of becoming Irish, Danish or German, but who we expect to be more European than the Europeans have ever been themselves, have little choice but to become Europeans. They will be the first real Europeans."[9] In this journalist's reading, Europe is twice indebted to the Muslim. It is against the Eastern Muslim that European identity was conceived—and it is in the Western Muslim that European identity is realized.

North and South, East and West, Europe is doing what it has done before: enfolding immigrants, changing them, and being changed by them.

In the streets of Spain, there is a Europe shaped by more than Christianity. Madrileños know their city was founded as a Muslim fortress by Muhammad I. A taxi driver, pointing out the sights, gestures first to the iconic bullring, Las Ventas, and then to a vast new mosque. Both are, in the taxi driver's view, Spanish landmarks, and both are beautiful and to be praised. This is a living history. Islam is written into the stones of Granada, Cordoba, and Seville. That writing might inscribe it in the past, but it is also present on the street. Tourists from all over the Muslim world come to Cordoba. They file in with Spanish schoolchildren into the Tower of La Calahorra to hear animated figures of Maimonides, Ibn Rushd, Ibn Arabi, and Alfonso X address the audience. Each speaks of acceptance, of his affection and regard for aspects of the others' faiths. The exhibit is a little preachy and the text may be a little too sophisticated for the smaller schoolchildren, but it testifies to the pride of Spain in its Andalusian past, the pride of Cordoba in its miscegenate culture.

All three faiths still live in Andalusia. They still mix. They still exchange people and ideas. Catholic schoolchildren on field trips pose at the feet of the statue of Maimonides. Modern Spaniards, like the Spaniards of the past, still move between the Abrahamic faiths. Spain has seen a wave of conversions to Islam since the late sixties. In the words of a *New York Times* writer, "While immigration is gradually spreading Islam across Europe, a homegrown movement is giving it added momentum in Spain. Here a generation of post-Franco intellectuals is reassessing the country's Moorish past and recasting Spanish identity to include Islamic influences." Spain's identity, the *New York Times* should have recognized, does not require recasting to include Islamic influences. It is grounded not in nostalgia for the past, but in the practices of the present. The Granadan leader of the city's Muslim community told the *Times* reporter, "We reject the romantic idea of a return to the Islam of the past. We've created a new community of this place and this time." Teenagers practice their flamenco steps in the courtyard of the Mezquita. Spanish Muslims dress, like the Granadan Hajj Abdulhasib Castiñeira, in "a glen plaid jacket and suede brogues."[10]

Al Andalus is often presented as a singular paradise, incomparable and lost. But Andalusia is not alone. There other sites that present a Europe that enfolds Muslims within it. They offer alternative pasts and open to alternative futures. They invite the West to recall other pasts, to explore the possibilities of other genealogies. They revive sleeping cultural memories.

They are not uncontested. They are sometimes found in hostile terrain. One day in the fall of 2007, I set out to visit Dutch mosques. A prosperous, well-educated Dutch woman, a neighbor of the late Theo van Gogh, told me, with evident distaste, that her neighborhood was full of them, and marked two on a map. Her colleagues, young, artistic, and much less dismayed by the presence of Muslims, told me of another, which they characterized as "liberal." "Hussein goes there," they told me. This prompted a dismissive shrug from the woman, who appeared to doubt the liberality of both Hussein and the mosque. All three knew and worked with people who attended the mosque, though they had very different views of its politics. All three mosques were an easy walk away. I never found two of them.

   I found the Muslim neighborhood easily enough. I had seen women with headscarves on the buses and in the streets. I began to see more, along with the telltale signs of an immigrant population: stores advertising phone cards and cheap airfares. There were halal restaurants, and, in an open-air market, stalls selling *rai* CDs along with Dutch herring and Belgian *frites*. The directions were clear, my map was marked, but I couldn't find the mosques. I began to walk block by block, repeating my steps. The time for the call to prayer came and went without a sound. I saw groups of men, bearded and wearing the headwear of the very observant. I had to be close. Still no mosque. I stopped at the Euphrates Grocery and asked, in my simple Arabic, "Where is the mosque?" The proprietor seemed a bit surprised but gave me directions first in Dutch, and then in Arabic. Still no mosque. I approached a group of women, older women veiled in the traditional fashion (with open faces and long black wraps) and younger ones, hair uncovered, and dressed in jeans. The older women spoke Turkish, the younger Dutch and, luckily for me, a little English. The older women, smiling and gesturing, sent a daughter to show me the way to the mosque.

I had passed it many times. We entered through a small grocery store. The door to the mosque was in the back of the grocery. I covered my head (my choice—I was brought up to be polite), left my shoes by the door, and followed the grocer down the hall. In a room off to one side some young men were having a class in Dutch. We came to the prayer hall, followed by the mosque cat, and the grocer gestured for me to look around. There were two spacious prayer halls, one for women and one for men, a playground outside, and inside classrooms and meeting rooms. My guide took me to the men's prayer hall. In this way, he avoided entering the women's space, instead welcoming a woman into the men's space. The mosque complex was large, and it was almost invisible. There were no minarets, no arches, no signs, no green paint, nothing that might catch the eye.

It was easy, when I was in Amsterdam, to find marijuana and gay bars (even—occasionally—for lesbians), prostitutes, bondage equipment, and vibrators. They were all in the shop window, and there were lots of shops. Anything that could be sold, or that gratified an appetite, seemed easy to find: bikes and burkas as well as sex equipment. Never has the phrase "an embarrassment of riches" seemed so apt. The streets of Amsterdam do not speak, as they once did, for freedom of religion or freedom of speech. They speak for the freedom to consume.

The Netherlands of Geert Wilders, Pim Fortuyn, and *Naar Nederland* (the official website that explains what it means to be Dutch to prospective immigrants) may be the New Jerusalem of sexual liberation, but it is also the site of the crusading efforts of our time. The Dutch look anxiously at their Muslim compatriots on buses and in the streets. The proud home of freedom of speech demands that new citizens speak a script written for them. Where Rembrandt once painted Jews in the clothing of their faith, women are forbidden to wear the burka. Old sumptuary laws are revived in an altered form.

The Netherlands is not, however, entirely given over to the fears of Wilders and Hirsi Ali. The Muslim women's organization al Nisa celebrated its nearly thirty years of existence in the Netherlands with a poster campaign called "Real Dutch." The posters presented Dutch Muslim women doing iconically Dutch things—but with a sharp edge of political satire. One showed a smiling woman in a hijab about to swallow that Dutch favorite, raw herring with onions. The caption, "I like it raw," referred not only to the herring but to Geert Wilders's tasteless comment on women who wear the veil. "Cup of tea in the mosque?" another poster asked, referring to the teatime chats held by Amsterdam's Jewish mayor Job Cohen, much criticized by Wilders and his allies. Cohen had provoked a controversy by suggesting that the problem of the presence of believing Muslims could be settled as the postwar Dutch had settled the differences between secular socialists and believing Christians: by recognizing different communities as pillars supporting the nation as a whole.

A few miles south and west of Amsterdam, Dutch-speaking Flemish boys walk hand in hand with veiled Muslim girls; a waffle stand has a Turkish name. The people of Brussels are less vexed by their Muslim compatriots than they are by Flemish nationalists. There are many veils on the streets of Brussels. There are the scarves of conservative grannies and the tightly tucked hijabs of radical schoolgirls. Hijabs are worn with clothes from Zara and Mango, with jeans from Levis and 7 for All Mankind. Near the palace, there is a statue to the first king of Jerusalem, but in Martyrs Square (a monument to one of many failed revolutions) a Muslim family picnics from a parked car and another revolution takes place quietly, domestically.

One can find the same divisions in Scandinavia. Aarhus University professor Frederik Stjernfelt has been one of the most vocal opponents of multiculturalism, convinced of the hazards Islam poses to a liberal and democratic Denmark. Journalist friends of mine in Copenhagen insisted that I talk to him. He gave me tea in a lovely apartment lined with books, facing the water: the kind of home that any academic will find familiar. We are both academics, not far apart in age, with some common intellectual interests, yet we do not live in the same world, or see with the same eyes. Stjernfelt sees Islam as a threat to the West, especially Western women. I am a Western woman, yet I see a greater threat in the views he advances. In the neighborhood around us, Stjernfelt saw encroaching dangers. I saw a peaceful changing neighborhood full of promise.

Often when I talked to Danes about Muslim immigration, they would say to me, "We do things very well. They must learn to do things the way we do." I heard this from city councillors, journalists, and professors, from officials and ordinary citizens. When I suggested that there might be more than one way to do certain things well, they shook their heads firmly. "They must learn to do things the way we do." This covered more than issues of religion in the public sphere, or how women should dress. I was told that women in an immigrant center had to learn that only they could reproach their children. If a child did something wrong, the mother had to intervene and admonish the child. No one else could. The Danes thought of these strictures as not only Danish but Western. I was all too aware that I did not always do things the way they did. I felt the weight of their disapproval and the narrowing limits of the world they wanted to maintain. I was puzzled by their certainty that they could not learn or change or become better than they were. Their world is beautiful but it is smaller than some Westerners would like. When I came home, I looked at my classroom of once-Asians, once-Africans, once-Europeans, all doing things in wildly different ways, and I smiled. We do things differently here.

This is not, however, a division between Europe and America. Within each European country, there are those who argue for closing borders and those who accept Muslims as their own. Sarrazin rails against Muslims and the loss of German identity, but around him German identity changes peacefully and for the better. In the media, Merkel's strictures against multiculturalism war with articles that chronicle the integration of German Muslims. Outside the media's gaze, Germany integrates quietly. Berlin parks enfold the veiled and the unveiled and bottles of Turkish *ayran* appear in the dairy section. Everyone eats döner kebab. Germany's Turkish immigrants become more German. Germany becomes more Turkish. In becoming more Turkish and more Muslim, Germany repudiates in action (rather than simply in words and monuments) the darkness of an earlier era. However great the architect, however moving the memorial, stone or bronze cannot testify to an overcoming. It is in the peaceful mixing on the street that Germany finds redemption.

Islam is already woven into Europe—in every sense. The dome and the minaret are already imprinted on the horizon of Europe. These forms, tiles, and mosaic patterns are woven into the stone fabric of European architecture. The sound of the lute moves from Asia to Europe to the Americas and back again. The oud migrates, circulates, changing shape and sound, played once by a European, then by an Arab, then by an Arab European. The oud evolves, giving birth to the lute and the guitar. The shape of the sounds shifts as well. Greek *rebetica* and North African *rai* carry the music of the Arab East westward. The *fados* of Portugal carry Arab sounds, traveling sounds. The music of war fills the air and the ears of Europe under the walls of Vienna, and Europe adopts the military bands of the Ottoman Empire. The music becomes so laden with nationalism that it cannot be heard as alien.

All the languages of Europe bear Arab words within them. Though the French police the boundaries of their language like an Arizona sheriff, one still can go to the *talib* (doctor) if one feels *mesquin* (miserable). Arabic numerals mark an intellectual integration so profound it goes unnoticed.

One can buy harissa in the grocery store and eat tabouleh (*un petit taboule*) at a restaurant in Paris or Lyon. There is a great selection of loukoum in the Grand Marché au Bruxelles. The chocolatiers of Brussels offer alcohol-free boxes. Coffee and olives, almonds and dates made themselves at home in Europe so thoroughly and so long ago that no one knows them as other than European. All the senses testify to the presence of the Arab, the Turk, the Muslim: the sound of the lute, the sight of an arch, the feel of the carpet under one's feet, the smell of coffee, the taste of olives.

CHAPTER 8

"Islamofascism" and the Burden of the Holocaust

The Holocaust left the West with a grief too great to bear, and a shame too bitter to acknowledge. The affirmation that this must never happen again put in place laws against National Socialist parties and Holocaust denial. A collective commitment to remember and bear witness marked the West with memorials, great and small, visible and invisible, speaking to the eye and to the mind.

As the generations passed, grief remained and shame declined. We of the West become not the civilization that gave the world Nazism, but the people who defeated it. All Europe becomes Allied. The laws against National Socialist parties testify to the purity of our politics. The memorials testify to the purity of our sentiments. Because we remember, we have a license to forget. Because we remember what happened in the past, we can forget that some of the structures that made it possible persist in the present. The defenders of Western civilization need not consider the origins, connections, and survivals of the enemy they have so thoroughly disavowed.

So too with the years of blood and death, barren tyranny and constant surveillance in Eastern Europe. The fall of the Evil Empire is recorded as a victory for the United States and Europe, a victory for the West. In these accounts, the West is the constant defender of the free, opposing itself, often with little hope of success, against the totalitarianism of Hitler's National Socialism and Stalin's Soviet Union. This forgetfulness might be excused as part of an effort to make the sins of the past unthinkable in the present. What is not excusable is the effort to place the burden of our past on others. This is the work done in the word "Islamofascism."

In the opening pages of his *Terror and Liberalism*, Paul Berman tells how he came to recognize "Islamofascism." In the days of the first Gulf War, he found himself at odds with those, formerly his allies, who opposed the war. He was not, he insists, concerned about American interests. "I didn't give a damn about the politics of oil, per se, nor about 'vital interests.'" He does not mention the violation of Kuwaiti sovereignty that served as the official justification for the war. Rather, he was reminded of another war, in another place and time. "I thought that in Saddam and his government, we were facing a totalitarian menace—something akin to fascism." "The entire situation," he writes a page later, "had the look of Europe in 1939."[1]

That is to say, it looked that way to him. "The entire situation" encompassed conflicts from Palestine to Pakistan and enemies as diverse as the secular dictator Saddam Hussein and the religious militants of the Taliban. Iraqi or Afghani, religious or secular, they all reminded Berman of Europe in 1939.

For Berman, all enemies are the same enemy: the enemy of liberalism. All enemies of liberalism are akin. The communist in Bologna opposing the neoliberalism of the monopolist Berlusconi; the partisan of direct democracy in Athens opposing the austerity measures sought by the liberal (but undemocratic) European Union; the radical lesbian suspicious of liberal feminism; the Afrocentrist; the Islamist—all appear as a single monstrous enemy.

Fascism and communism were, seen properly, "tentacles of a single, larger, monster from the deep—some new and horrible creature of modern civilization, which had never been seen and never been named but was, even so, capable of sending up further ghastly tentacles from sinister depths."[2] There are, as he suggests, continuities with older demons, older monsters. The xenophobia that imprisoned Dreyfus, the pogroms, the demonization that issued in genocide, are old and they have older roots. They live on in dark places. Berman thinks they prosper in Islam.

Berman sees "Islamofascism" as the successor to Nazism and the Soviet Union, as a form of totalitarianism fundamentally opposed to the freedoms of Western civilization. The bridge that proves the crossing of Nazism from Europe to the Middle East, that proves the presence—indeed, the authority—of fascism in the Muslim world, is the Mufti of Jerusalem, Hajj Amin al Husseini, a notorious Nazi sympathizer. The Mufti has been born posthumously, attaining more power in death than he ever held in life.

In the accounts of Berman and his allies, the West stands for the freedom of the individual against those who would silence all dissent. The struggle against National Socialism was followed by the struggle against

Soviet totalitarianism. Now Islam presents the threat of a totalitarian order. The clash of civilizations continues with a constant West constantly confronted by the enemies of freedom.

There is a profound dishonesty in this. Fascism belongs to the West, and the defenders of Western civilization are obliged to answer for it. National Socialism was located in the West, emerged from Western history and Western civilization. Rome fell to fascism. Germany, and the old realm of the Holy Roman Empire, fell too. Spain fell to fascism. France fell under its rule and perhaps under its spell. England (even England) had Oswald Mosley and the blackshirts. The French had (the French were) Vichy. Admirers of the Nazis are easy enough to find, even among the Allies: Ezra Pound and Charles Lindbergh, the Duke of Windsor and Unity Mitford. Germany and Austria had the Nazis themselves. If Islam is indicted by the Mufti, what are we to say of the West?

America, Canada, and Australia—the old colonial periphery—remained largely immune to the appeal of fascism. The center of Europe, of European culture, of Christendom, was its homeland. Fascism rose there, presenting itself as the culmination of Western civilization. Fascism persisted long after the Second World War, surviving in Christendom: ruling in Spain and Portugal and still fielding parties and winning elections in the heart of Europe. The West fought fascism, but the West had also bred it, and the West maintained it long after Hitler's defeat. In fascism, the West still has something to answer for.

Western civilization still holds traces (and more than traces) of that moment. Germany may forbid the iconography of National Socialism, but it has neo-Nazis. Americans pride themselves on a space program advanced by the contributions of the former Nazi Werner von Braun. We drive Volkswagens. Academics trouble themselves over Heidegger and Schmitt, and look doubtfully at a shamed and repentant Paul de Man, but we read their work, as we should, and continue to count it part of Western civilization.

Most importantly, fascism continues as a political force in Europe. Fascism was not defeated with the defeat of Germany and Italy in the Second World War. It continued in Franco's Spain and Salazar's Portugal. It has heirs in Italy. Mosley returned from exile to lead the first round of the anti-immigrant politics in postwar Britain. Western civilization is not simply haunted by the memories of fascism; it continues to grapple with it electorally.

There is, however, no "Islamofascism." Lebanon has a fascist party, the Phalange, but the Phalange is a Christian party in Lebanon's all-too-sectarian politics, and one that has cooperated with Israel, most notably in the infamous massacres at Sabra and Shatila. Berman does not mention these massacres, though Israel's Kahan Commission censured Ariel Sharon for his part in them. When Berman writes of terrorism in Lebanon, he limits his attention to Hezbollah. When he writes of fascism there, he neglects to mention the actual, rather than merely the metaphoric, fascists. It is a lapse of memory that papers over a number of uncomfortable connections in the past and present: between fascism and the militant Zionists Meir Jabotinsky and Ze'ev Har-Zion; between the Phalange and Sharon; between Christianity and fascism in Europe and the Middle East.

The greater shame comes in denying Arab and Muslim opposition to fascism. Israel Gershoni and James Jankowski have provided a stunning and superbly documented refutation of Berman's imagined history. Egyptian newspapers and magazines published caricatures of Hitler and Mussolini in league with the Angel of Death, threatening innocents, crushing nations. The fascists were portrayed as monstrous, not once or twice but over and over again. Egyptians saw fascism as something to be feared and ridiculed. Egyptian newspapers recognized that Nazi imperialism and theories of racial hierarchy boded ill for them. *Al Ahram* and *Al Misri*, the newspapers with the largest circulation, consistently opposed fascism. Writers in both inveighed against the racial theories of the Nazis. They were not slow to recognize the Nazi persecution of the Jews. *Al Ahram* condemned Kristallnacht and the persecution of "innocent Jewish German citizens."[3] *Al Ahram* systematically condemned the Nazis for an expansionist and aggressive imperialism, dictatorship, and racism.

Berman imagines the Arab and Muslim Middle East as a world far from the intellectual life of Europe and the West, with few intellectual resources of its own. He pictures it as a world without a public sphere, without the rich intellectual culture of European café society and approaches it in a posture of reluctant understanding. Fascism attracted Arabs, Berman argues, as a means of opposing British and French colonial power. The alliance is therefore not surprising, though it remains repellent. Berman's seeming forbearance is not generosity but its opposite. There was a rich intellectual culture in Middle Eastern cities in the era between the wars, as there had been for centuries. Modernity had altered that culture, but expanded rather than displacing it. Arab and Muslim (and Christian and Jewish) intellectuals knew (and wrote) on a variety of theorists. They were not reflexively attracted to fascism. Nor was fascism a magnet for the masses. Fascism had more followers in Mosley's England.

Gershoni and Jankowski also debunk the claims that the Muslim Brotherhood were tools or fellow travelers of Hitler and Mussolini. When Berman indicts the Muslim Brotherhood as fascists, his evidence is taken from a secondary source, and one that he treats less carefully than he should. Gershoni and Jankowski rely on the writings of the Muslim Brotherhood in their original Arabic, a language Berman does not read. This may account for Berman's translation of the Arabic *kata'ib* as "phalanges," which he uses as evidence of fascism. It's not. *Kata'ib* is the plural of *katiba* and means, according to Hans Wehr (the Arabic dictionary of reference), "squadron" or regiment," or even "cavalry detachment." It is a word in common use and carries no particularly fascist connotations. If the use of "phalange" bears the stigma of fascism, Berman should look more carefully at the French.

Berman is right only about fascism's site of origin. Berman describes fascism's European roots in some detail. It is curious, then, that when fascist parties continue to be active in Europe, he has no interest in pursuing them where they are rooted. If fascism presents so great a threat to the West, should we not pursue it first at home? If it is from the West that fascism has spread, should we not fight it at the root? Shouldn't we fear the fascists most where they hold office? Shouldn't we cast a critical eye on the policies fascist parties hold regarding immigrants? Shouldn't we ask whether the West has truly overcome the antisemitism of the past?

In its contemporary form, this shifting antisemitism has shown itself in a pattern of symbolic loves and hates. The refusal of Muslims is marked by a symbolic (but only symbolic) embrace of the Jews. The refusal of Jews is marked by an (again only symbolic) embrace of Muslims. The refusal of one antisemitism is used to make the adoption of another appear benign. Worse, the refusal of one enmity mandates the embrace of another. If I embrace the Jews, I must refuse the Muslim. If I embrace Muslims, I must refuse the Jew. In this way, hatred becomes the required sign of love. The rejection of one hatred requires the adoption of another. A seeming moment of acceptance reveals itself as a simple shift of hate.[4]

That shift of hatred seizes on improbable objects. Both Berman and Caroline Fourest have seized on Tariq Ramadan, a Western Muslim, a Swiss citizen with a doctorate from the University of Geneva, who has advocated the willing integration of Western Muslims into the cultures and electoral practices of the West. All of Berman's discussions of Ramadan center not on Ramadan's books, speeches, or writings, but on his ancestry. Ramadan is the grandson of Hassan al Banna, the founder of the Muslim Brotherhood. Indeed, Berman writes, "Tariq Ramadan is nothing if not a son, a brother, a grandson." Writing of the political views of the grandfather of John Rawls or the grandmother of Alexis de Tocqueville would be thought highly eccentric. When one writes of Henry Adams, John Adams is not regarded as the determinative shaper of his thought. When we study political thinkers, philosophers, or politicians, we assume that their views are their own. They may be influenced by their families, to be sure, but those influences are as likely to produce rebellion as agreement. The grandfather, if the child knew him well, is rather more likely to appear to the child as a source of sweets (or, possibly, a vaguely terrifying figure) than as a source of doctrines.

Ancestry shapes the body rather than the mind. We ordinarily assume that people's ideas, their work, their philosophies, and their political positions are produced not by their genetics, but by their own thought. The relevant ancestors in this case are those they read, those who shape their minds—and here too the influence is as likely to produce rebellion as agreement. We cannot choose our ancestors, or shape our own genetic material. We do choose our intellectual ancestors. We all shape our own minds.

All, it appears, but Tariq Ramadan. Berman insists that Ramadan must be what his grandfather was, must carry his thought as he carries his DNA—indeed more so, for Berman assumes that the thought of Hassan al Banna passes through the blood unaltered by contact with any other. Ramadan is not a man as Berman is, able to make his own choices, shape his own ideas. He is a man shaped by blood alone, without freedom of thought or an independent will. Ramadan, as Berman sees him, is not like us. He belongs not to the rational, but to the irrational. Berman is shaped by thought and choice, Ramadan by blood and destiny. We are individuals; he is one instance of a collective. He is a Muslim. He is a Muslim Brother. He cannot be anything else.

The idea that some people should be excluded from politics by virtue of their ancestry belongs to feudal antiquity or modern racism. Berman, proud of his leftism, rejects both. Yet the same conviction that some are what their ancestry makes them animates his condemnations of Tariq Ramadan. A peasant in a feudal order is a peasant, no matter what he reads or writes, or what he does. To an antisemite an atheist may be a Jew, and a professed Christian a Jew still, whatever his beliefs. Professed beliefs are read as concealment. They cannot be anything else.

Caroline Fourest's *Brother Tariq* reads Ramadan according to the same logic. He can be only what his ancestry makes him. The first chapter of Fourest's book is entitled "'Islam's Future' or the Future of the Muslim Brotherhood?" and begins by stating that Ramadan's father was "in charge of propagating the Muslim Brotherhood's brand of Islam throughout Europe"; his mother was "none other than the favorite daughter of the founder of the Muslim Brotherhood."[5] The second chapter names Ramadan "The Heir."

Fourest quotes Ramadan's account of his realization of his European identity: "Up to the age of 23 or 24 I felt more Egyptian than Swiss. I thought again of leaving. Then I decided I was European and Swiss and should accept the fact." Reading against the plain sense of the words, Fourest writes that Ramadan remained "marked for life by the very backbone of his identity: not Egypt . . . but the Islam of the Muslim Brothers."[6]

Fourest's conception of the character and aims of the Muslim Brotherhood serves her as a sieve to sort through Ramadan's writings and speeches. Those that accord with her view of the Muslim Brotherhood are his true sentiments. Statements or speeches where Ramadan argues for women's equality with men, endorses freedom of speech or democracy, or accords with liberal principles are lies or concealments: the "doublespeak" of Tariq Ramadan. In order to know what Ramadan truly means, one must consult Caroline Fourest. Fourest thus goes one step beyond the demand that Muslims speak a script written for them by others. They may speak it, but they will not be believed. Fourest's book reveals the emptiness of the demand to "denounce terrorism" or "endorse liberal values." Satisfying that demand is futile.

This is true not only for Ramadan, but—perhaps more importantly—for all who read or listen to him. The term "collaborator" is a loaded one in France. It recalls the France of Vichy, the French who collaborated with the Nazi regime. If you don't share Fourest's opinions, or Berman's, they tell you, you are a collaborator. This is a remarkable position for people scornful of political correctness, who praise the Enlightenment and count themselves as defenders of liberal values.

Philosophers who elsewhere protest against the constitutive injustices of our time become complicit in the construction of the Muslim as the providential enemy. Žižek marks the Muslim as both the exception and the proper object of enmity for a secular, enlightened politics. In Žižek's view, the history of the modern West—that is to say of the West, of modernity—is the overcoming of religion by atheism, of theology by Enlightenment. The local means for advancing that project come from a Europe in which atheism is (historically) aligned with Christianity. Thus he writes in "A Glance into the Archives of Islam," "We usually speak of the Jewish-Christian civilization—perhaps, the time has come, especially with regard to the Middle East conflict, to talk about the *Jewish-Muslim civilization* as an axis opposed to Christianity."[7] Žižek's endorsement of atheism drives him, by his own account, to an endorsement of a Europe—one might more accurately say an atheist Christendom—against Islam and Judaism. Žižek's writing reminds us that neither Marx nor socialism has been proof against the antipathy to Muslim and Jew embedded in an Enlightenment held within the limits of Christendom.

There is more to Christianity, more to the Enlightenment, more to the West than this. There are forces within each of these that drive us away from enmity. There are ethical imperatives that drive us not only to remember past antisemitism but to overcome it in the present.

While the memory of the Holocaust remains, the term *Muselmänner* may be too familiar to require translation. We know the images of the *Muselmänner*, the most abject prisoners of the camps. We know the descriptions of their states, the place they hold in reflections on the Holocaust. Yet if the term is familiar, the meaning is still hidden. We forget that *Muselmann* means Muslim.

Muselmänner names Muslims: it names those who inhabit the camps at Guantánamo and Abu Ghraib, and certain other sites that only some can name. It names those Muslims who inhabit camps awaiting deportation. In each of these moments, the name of Muslim is given to the most reduced, to bare life.

If Western civilization is to enfold, embrace, and comprehend the Jews and in so doing claim its own Judaism, that should be done without giving license to another series of pogroms. If the West is to bear true witness to the evil of the Holocaust, then it must meet ethical demands that go beyond the construction of memorials and an ethic of remembrance. The West must close the camps and take the *Muselmänner* as its own.

The recollection of the Holocaust is not a matter of memory and memorial but an ethical imperative at work in the present.

CHAPTER 9

In the American Desert

Americans believe that all men are created equal, that they are endowed by their creator with certain inalienable rights. Those convictions have been challenged. The realization of those principles has been, and remains, a struggle. Yet the belief is real, the demands it places are great, and it drives not only sentiment but policy.

There is room here. There is room to flee your past and become something new. There is room enough to keep the old ways safe. There are Arab Americans and Pakistani Americans, Muslims from every corner of the globe. There are new converts and the children of old ones. There are large Muslim communities in Brooklyn and Dearborn, and Muslim families living among Christians and Jews. One can make a new life or a separate world under the American sky.

American faith, American myth, and the demands of American life all protested against the demonization of Muslims. There were those—there are still those—who call for that demonization. Debbie Schlussel called for genocide, saying of the death of bin Laden, "One down, 1.8 billion to go." Anders Behring Breivik, the Norwegian mass murderer who attacked a Norwegian youth camp, quoted extensively from Robert Spencer, Pamela Geller, and other profiteers of terror. Before Breivik acted, Pamela Geller hosted and protected a Norwegian correspondent threatening violence, who posted, "We are stockpiling and caching weapons" against Muslims.[1] The more established purveyors of hate, Limbaugh, Savage, and Coulter, have also traded in these unwholesome wares. They have been joined by intellectuals, pundits, and public figures: Daniel Pipes, Richard Pearl, David Frum, and congressional representatives Peter King (R-NY), Michele Bachmann, (R-MI), and Paul Broun (R-GA). But their calls for internment camps, purges, and persecution have remained ineffective. If they speak to some, they are mocked by many more. The hard-fought struggles of the civil rights movement and the shameful memory of Japanese internment have kept the country clean of such measures.

In Europe, the Muslim question turns, in no small part, on the possibility of holding fast against change. Danes demand that Muslim immigrants not only become Danes, but act like Danes. In France and the Netherlands, Muslim women must dress like French and Dutch women, unveiled. Americans do not make such demands. We know we are still at work on ourselves, still striving, still struggling to become better than we are.

In the uncertain place where the American republic meets the American empire, the presence of many peoples—drawn from many cultures, born speaking many languages, practicing different faiths—is an occasion for pride. It testifies that America is not for itself alone, but for all the world. We are still an "experiment," still a place whose uncertain, questionable fate is "in many respects the most interesting in the world."[2] The success of that experiment must be, as the Declaration of Independence affirmed, "submitted to the judgment of a candid world." In the republic, the presence of many peoples committed to a common set of democratic and republican principles testifies to the primacy of those principles. In the empire, the American capacity to "contain multitudes," in the words of the poet Walt Whitman, can be taken as proof of imperial capacity, of imperial grandeur, and a sign (for the credulous) that imperialism can accord with the values of the republic.

In an America born to liberalism and from the Enlightenment, American Christians and American secularists were both able to see Jews as American, and to make America more Jewish. Jews were, like other immigrant groups, able to retain elements of difference and pride in those differences. American gentiles adopted foods and phrases previously seen as Jewish. Elements of Jewish identity were incorporated into a broader sense of what it means to be an American. One sees this in American literary and political culture, from Israel Zangwill's *The Melting Pot* to Tony Kushner's *Angels in America*; from Hannah Arendt and Leo Strauss to Michael Lerner and Michael Walzer; in national efforts to preserve the memory of the Holocaust and national commitment to the survival of Israel. This did not free the United States from antisemitism, but it provided a limit and omnipresent counter to it, and placed the idea of the Jews at the heart of America.

The Wars in the Desert

The conviction that America offers a home to people of every place and faith spoke against discrimination after the attacks of September 11. The remembered shame of Japanese internment forestalled proposals for internment camps. There were attacks on Muslims, there was harassment, but these were never given the endorsement of the state and did not achieve popular acceptance. Instead, America seemed to project outward the enmities it refused at home.

The wars in Iraq and Afghanistan have been desert wars though they are fought in cities, mountains, and marshes. They take place in the deserts of an imaginary Arabia, inhabited by the demons we would not loose at home. They are barren wars. The War on Terror saw us desert our principles for torture, secret prisons, and extraordinary rendition. Abu Ghraib and Guantánamo are places in the trackless desert where we have lost our way. Here, far from home, we confront troubling domestic issues: the number and cruelties of our prisons; the pathologies of pornography and celebrity; the fiction of gender equality; the burden of racial inequality; the ethical demands of our many creeds; and our imperfect stewardship over the living. If we of the West are Isaac to the Arab Ishmael, it is in these deserts that we wrestle with the angel.

Those who favored the war in Iraq hoped to come to Iraq as liberators. They were, they argued, opening the way for democracy. Instead they found themselves viewed as an occupying power whose authority, like that of Saddam Hussein, depended not on the consent of the governed but on military force. Nowhere was that tragic fall more marked than at Abu Ghraib.

Abu Ghraib

In taking over the prison at Abu Ghraib, the United States took the place of Saddam Hussein. The prison, already a notorious place of abuse, came under new management, but the abuse continued. The tearing down of the Bastille was, as many historians have observed, a largely symbolic act: there were few prisoners held within its walls. The decision to keep Abu Ghraib intact and use it as Saddam Hussein had used it was both a practical and a symbolic act. Taking the prison was an act of conquest. It might have been used to mark the difference between Saddam Hussein's regime and the liberating invaders. The occupation forces chose to leave the prison standing, however, and in doing so, they seemed to step into Saddam's place. They kept the structures of Iraqi imprisonment intact. The abuses at Abu Ghraib argued that the forces of the American occupation had not only taken the place but assumed the practices of the former tyrannical regime.

In the deserts of Iraq and Afghanistan, Israel and Palestine, the harshest questions the West confronts are not about Islam, but about ourselves.

We acknowledged that a few Americans had done evil abroad. We failed to acknowledge—even to see—that America as a whole does similar evils at home. We were, as a people, willing to acknowledge the evil of sexual license, of pornography, of a culture of celebrity, narcissism, and exploitation. Acknowledging these defects served to draw the eye away from other failings we are less willing to examine.

The United States has become a carceral society, imprisoning a large portion of its own population. The design, building, maintenance, supply, and staffing of the American prison system is a major industry.[3] The role of former prison guards in the abuses at Abu Ghraib should raise questions about the practices of prison guards at home. The abuses at Abu Ghraib tended instead to fix the debate over torture and the conditions of confinement at a foreign site. These were matters of foreign rather than domestic policy; the abuses were inflicted on aliens rather than our own. The torture at Abu Ghraib was presented as errant and exceptional, predicated on conditions of war and the absence of legal constraints. The role of reservists and mercenaries with experience in the prison system was concealed or diminished.

The violence at Abu Ghraib was staged for the camera. The forms, roles, and poses derived from other forms of theatricality: tourism, pornography, celebrity. The drive to see and be seen informed the staging of violence and the photographic records of the violence, and it impelled the vortex of circulation into which the photographs were cast.

In performing these acts of violence, soldiers performed roles—assigned and assumed, official and informal, obedient and rebellious—and in doing so enacted a series of claims. These acts of violence called up a Muslim identity, gave it content, staged it, and forced it on prisoners. The content of these acts of violence provides a map of American anxieties: about Islam and about ourselves. These acts of violence staged fantasies of the Muslim. They were informed by the history of the United States. Consider the photograph of a hooded prisoner standing on a box, his outstretched arms attached to electric wires.

This photograph became an icon within days of its appearance. The image, like all icons, is full of meaning. Among these meanings is a series of references that are iconic in a sense that is at once rich and troubling. The image echoes religious images. To a European eye the pointed black hood recalls the customary garb of

Spanish penitents. In any American lexicon of images, the pointed hood belongs to the Klan. This image was seized by cartoonists like Mike Lukovich, who took the hood off the prisoner and gave it to the torturer.

Switching the hoods responded to the bigotry in the present as well as in the past. The campaign against the Arab and the Muslim tried to identify Arabs and Islam with bigotry against Jews and Christians, and made the bigotry the license for invasion, war, and war crimes. The image had a series of visual reversals that drove historical and contemporary indictments home. The hoods the Klansmen wore were white, like the race they claimed. Here the hood is black and the man is dark. The Klan wore their hoods to claim power in the name of race and culture, to assault those who challenged that power, and to hold fast to their own supremacy. Here the dark hood marks a dark man, held in the grip of power, assaulted and helpless. The fire the Klansmen used to fuel their crosses and light their lynchings was primitive and hot. Here the flaming cross is replaced by a small black box, and the fire runs through cold wires.

Susan Sontag also saw the American past in the photographs from Abu Ghraib. "If there is something comparable to what these pictures show it would be some of the photographs of black victims of lynching taken between the 1880's and 1930's, which show Americans grinning beneath the naked mutilated body of a black man or woman hanging behind them from a tree."[4] What was noteworthy, for Sontag, was the willingness of those photographed with the bodies of the tortured dead to own their acts; to stand unashamed before those to whom they sent the photographs: their families, their friends, and perhaps a larger, more abstract audience.

Sontag was wrong. The photographs of lynchings are (like those of Abu Ghraib) bound with a history of secret violence. They were recognized as illegal, even by those who performed them. The politics of lynching was a politics of separatism. It was white supremacist, Protestant, connected, in most cases, to a mythology of the defeated Confederacy, and refusing integration into the Union. Trophies of lynching circulated secretly, among those committed to the secret societies that advanced white supremacist claims. Secrecy is tied, here as elsewhere, to an antidemocratic politics of hierarchy and exclusion.

In an atmosphere of millenarianism, Christian Zionism, and evangelical justifications for empire, the posture of the photographed prisoners challenged Christian ethics. The hooded man with arms outstretched, prisoners handcuffed to the cell doors, and the prisoner who stood covered with dirt and feces before a military guard, stand in form of Christ crucified. These images directed a series of imperative challenges and questions to Christians.

Fernando Botero, in a significant departure from the characteristic references and emotional valences of his work, painted the tortured of Abu Ghraib as Christ and the saints were painted: in their suffering. *Abu Ghraib 53* recalls both the piles of prisoners and the wounds of Saint Sebastian. *Abu Ghraib 66* echoes paintings of Christ carrying the cross, bearded, lips parted in pain. Botero heard the divine in the photographs of suffering humanity. He had canonical warrant. "As you did it to one of the least of these, my brethren, you did it to me."[5] Not only Christians are reproached here. The sight of the dead, the tortured, the imprisoned, those reduced beyond humiliation, throws a shadow over the democratic faith.

The trope of veiling that casts the Muslim world as the abode of concealment and oppression should draw attention to other strategies of concealment and the governance of sight. Members of the press are subject to restrictions on what they can show, the people on what they can see. A veil is drawn over coffins returning to Dover Air Force Base, and over photographs and videos of the abuse of women prisoners at Abu Ghraib. The use of embedded journalists may make more of the soldier's life visible, but it means that the one embedded sees not simply through the eyes of a journalist, but through the eyes of a comrade. Americans see, albeit partially and belatedly, photos of Abu Ghraib. We do not see the secret prisons whose existence is known. We hover outside Guantánamo, between America and another place, using what lenses we can find to get a glimpse of what is done in our name.

Much is concealed from Americans, but we are increasingly subject to surveillance. The Patriot Act licensed previously forbidden forms of intrusive surveillance. Airport security made these commonplace and taught us to say thank you for them. The installation of security cameras by municipalities, and, much more pervasively, the use of security cameras by commercial establishments, is rarely considered a matter of surveillance. These seem to be seen instead as benign and desirable means of preserving our safety, regulating traffic, and permitting the identification of the occasional criminal. Debate over secrecy and surveillance has not encompassed, much less challenged, these practices. Americans know they are watched, and know that they do not always know who is watching, when or how they are watched. Americans know there are secret prisons, ghost prisoners, secret files. Americans know that much is hidden from them. Americans, and indeed a candid world, knew that much of the war in Iraq was concealed. Journalists were limited in where they could go, whom they could cover, and under what conditions. They have accepted these constraints.

In such an economy, that which is seen seems to testify to openness and transparency. For those who knew that they were not permitted to see coffins returning to Dover Air Force Base, photographs of the inside of an American prison in Iraq seemed to offer unexpected access. For those who knew they were shown what the occupation forces and the administration wished them to see, photographs of torture seemed to rupture the constraints enveloping coverage of American military procedures and practices. In this context, the Abu Ghraib photographs seemed to offer unmediated access to the previously hidden: sudden, unexpected stolen knowledge that had escaped governance.

The photographs of the violence at Abu Ghraib were, however, not transparent but thoroughly mediated. They were circulated as digital media, and through digital media. They were presented, edited and censored, by the state and commercial networks.[6] Not all the photographs were made public. Government officials continue to object to release and discussion of much of the evidence obtained, notably the videos and photographs showing the abuse of women—this even after some of these photographs had been released outside the United States. The photographs that were shown were cropped and censored in a variety of ways, including the editing out of the casual presence of the torturer and attempts to obscure the identity of the victim. The photographs were staged, composed, and performed in accordance with media conventions, notably those for pornography. They did not offer open and unmediated access to the heart of darkness. They put on display performances of violent degradation that were willful, artful assertions of authority.

The Abu Ghraib photographs testify to the limits placed on—and accepted by—the media. They also testify to the ways in which the practices and conventions of the mass media have undermined structures, practices, and expectations upon which democracy depends. The Enlightenment taught Westerners to look upon the press, and, later, on the mass media, as central to democratic politics. Insistence on freedom of the press followed the confident belief that the media would oversee and chasten government and economic power, to make dissenting voices heard. Market expressions of the people's passionate desire to know would spur the media to greater oversight, greater diligence, greater daring. It has not been so. Sheldon Wolin demonstrates how capitalism has made the media servants not of subscribers, but of owners and advertisers. Rather than being spurred on by the people's desire to know, the media is ever more closely constrained. Oversight diminishes; the media are fed by the political and economic powers they once challenged. Dissenting voices are silenced, not by the state, but by media who act as strict and unlicensed censors: exiling dissident views to the fringes of discourse or silencing them altogether.[7]

The mediation of the Abu Ghraib photographs goes beyond the process that presented them to the world as a witness (at once for and against) the American regime. They also carry references of visual practices that point to more ordinary pathologies of celebrity and pornography.

These photographs and videos were taken by soldiers who showed them to one another and, in some cases, sent them home to friends and relatives. They cast atrocities in the idioms of snapshots, home movies, pornography, tourism, and memorabilia. These are the visual conventions of the banality of evil.

The soldiers at Abu Ghraib were not mere consumers of pornography. They were authors, directors, producers. They knew the conventions of the genre, and they violated or accepted them as they pleased. The photographs cast them as authority figures. They wore their uniforms and signs of rank; they held weapons; they posed outside the cells, above the pyramids of bodies. They showed themselves arranging the bodies in pyramids, attacking the prisoners, stitching their wounds. They recorded their authority. Staging these scenes for one another, for family and friends, gave them a small celebrity. A larger unsought audience gave them a larger, infamous place in the media.

When the photographs, sent home from the war, were circulated among family and friends, they bore a family resemblance to the snapshots and videos of tourism. The tourist moves freely in the world. The tourist comes to a chosen destination. The photographic conventions of tourism set the freedom of the soldiers against the manifold imprisonment of the Iraqis. The Iraqis are confined in shackles, in cells, in a prison, in a country they cannot leave, whose boundaries they cannot close. The soldiers entered Iraq and move about within it. They control the space of the prison and move in a relaxed, often casual, fashion in the photographs. They are volunteers, who entered the military of their own volition. The conventions of tourism affirm this freedom and conceal its limits and fictions. We have learned that stop-loss orders can keep soldiers in the service as conscripts rather than volunteers. We have learned that volunteers are less free than we might imagine: compelled not by the draft but by economic need and a dearth of opportunities.

The records the torturers made of their acts at Abu Ghraib seem to affirm their power and their freedom. They argue for a radical difference between the prisoner and the torturer, the one a dog, the other a master. This does not hold. Nietzsche's Second Essay in *On the Genealogy of Morals* reminds us that the link of violence to power is a perverse one: the enjoyment of pain depends on the recognition of likeness with the one who suffers. If the photographs record some moment of pleasure for the war criminals who staged them, they reaffirm, silently and insistently, a common vulnerability to pain. If the acts seem to mark the prisoners as alien, animal, and other, they also recall aspects of ourselves we have alternately owned and disavowed. If the acts seem to look outwards toward the Arab, they also testify, silently and insistently, to an American history that is sometimes thought best forgotten.

Guantánamo

The violence at Abu Ghraib was theatrical and spectacular. The violence at Guantánamo was rational, ordered, regimented.

The prison at Guantánamo is located on an American naval base at the southeastern end of Cuba. The United States pays rent for the base to the government of Cuba, which does not accept the rent or acknowledge the legitimacy of the base or the lease. The base is often referred to as "a legal black hole." Guantánamo is legally and historically American and un-American. It is inside and outside American territory, within and without American governance, governed by and exempt from American law. Guantánamo is a limen, a threshold, a gateway, between what is permitted and what is forbidden to Americans.

Guantánamo may have been at its worst when it sought to be most inclusive and most deferential to religious freedom. In Guantánamo prisoners were held in cages made of chain-link fence. They look not unlike the cages used to hold lab animals. Their transparency deprives the prisoners of privacy. They are inhuman, yet they are also inscribed with a perverse text on cultural tolerance. Each cage is furnished with a Koran, and a hanging sack that keeps the Koran off the floor. Each cage is marked with an arrow that enables the prisoners to pray facing Mecca. This was the dark reversal of a cultural sensitivity that could take still more shameful forms.

The use of dogs was frequently described as a strategy meant to exploit a distinctively Arab dislike, and fear, of dogs. The abuse and accounts of the abuse transformed a common human vulnerability into a vulnerability peculiar to one culture and a site of the power of Western over Arab culture.

The use of dogs came to Abu Ghraib from Guantánamo. Dogs had been used to "fear up" prisoners there, and their use went beyond the animals themselves. The interrogation log of Mohammed al Qahtani records for December 20, 2002 (day 28 of his interrogation), "Told detainee a dog is held in higher esteem because dogs know right from wrong and know how to protect innocent people from bad people. Began teaching detainee lessons such as stay, come, and bark, to elevate his social status up to that of a dog." Later, the interrogator writes, "Dog tricks continue . . . told detainee he should bark happy for these people . . . told detainee he should growl."[8] Guantánamo is an uncanny place: a "black hole" whose legal and jurisdictional particularities are carefully parsed; a military base in a country Americans are not permitted to visit directly. The site is replete with Kafkaesque bureaucratic perversities, and, as Alex Danchev has noted, "in Kafka's world, humiliation takes canine form."[9] The determination to "Gitmoize" Abu Ghraib entailed the introduction of dogs along with increasingly strenuous procedures for "fear up" and "ego down."

Causing a human being to huddle in fear before a dog is a particularly powerful way of indicating that the human being is less than that dog, less than an animal, reduced by fear of an animal to animal fear. The act illustrates the effects of the violation of human rights it enacts. The language of rights is not, however, adequate to the act. This is not a violation of a code or status that remains otherwise intact, a defect in a system. The act strikes at humanity altogether. The dog is used to make the prisoner appear as an animal, act as an animal, confront the animal before him and in himself and find himself wanting.

This use of dogs reduces the human twice over. It is not only that the human being who cowers before the dog appears (in the absence of respect for rights, in the absence of language, outside politics) as no more than an animal, and a weak one at that. There is a double loss, for the human who holds the leash is transformed as well. The mouth of the dog becomes the hand of the master, and the master forfeits humanity in the inhuman act.

The weaponized dog belongs not to the rebellious American colonies who made a nation, but to the imperial conquistadors. The weaponized dog belongs not to the America of inalienable rights, but to the refusals and denials of those rights. The act belongs to a time before America, to the "not now" and "never" that whisper against "not yet."

Tzvetan Todorov dedicated his book *The Conquest of America* to the memory of a woman the conquistadors cast to the dogs. This book reminds us of a history that begins not with refugees from political persecution or rebellious democrats, but instead with greed and religious fanaticism. This history is the history of America as a carceral state. This is the history of American empire. It is not the only history, even of these events, but it is a history we are called to record.

This is the history of conquest. This history records the decimation and confinement of the first nations, the Trail of Tears and the emergence of the reservation system. This is the history of the crowded holds of the Middle Passage, of slave quarters, slave trading, and segregation. This is the history of the plantation and the overseer. This is the history of the prison system. This history records the Cold War, Hiroshima and My Lai, McCarthyism and a culture of surveillance. This is the history of restrictive immigration laws, of housing covenants and border fences, of gated communities and midnight raids. This is the history of the coyotes who bring immigrants over the border and abandon them in the desert, and of the employers who exploited them. This is the history of redlining and subprime mortgages, of usury, eviction, and foreclosure. In this history, greed makes use of violence. In this history, imperial power leads not to greatness but to shame and diminution. Imprisonment follows the footsteps of empire. This history testifies against an easy, natural alliance between capitalism and democracy.

Mindful of this history, we are obliged to question those histories that couple the expansion of America across the continent with the expansion of the American electorate, civil rights, and political liberty. That expansion also brought the Trail of Tears, the reservation system, and the Mormon Wars. Imperial power was accompanied by imprisonment: the building of walls, the enforcement of borders, the proliferation of prisons and detention centers. The expansion of American territory across the continent and American dominion overseas were followed by a decline in freedom at home and abroad.

There are closer and more haunting memories. Those who watched the civil rights movement unfold remember the uses of dogs against African American marchers. These acts, like those at Guantánamo and Abu Ghraib, were photographed and the images circulated. We saw photographs in the newspapers that froze the snarl of the German shepherd and enabled us to count every tooth. The photographs caught the forward lunge of the leashed dog. We saw the marchers thrust back as sharply as they had been by the fire hoses. We saw the uniformed man who held the dog and urged it forward. Television captured the sound and movement of the march and the attack. The images testified to the strength and courage of the marchers. Conventional certainties decayed. A dog could be a weapon, a policeman an enemy. Children learned to question the license a uniform grants. They learned to question the distinction between friend and enemy and its relation to the political. They learned more. There is a passage in *The Republic* where Plato takes up the question of the just man. Plato writes that the just man must be stripped "of everything save justice," and in that naked deprivation the reader will see what justice is. So it was with the photographs from Alabama. The marchers, stripped of the protections of the state, held their rights still. They became rights and right incarnate, and the rights they stood for stood or fell with them.

Seeing dogs used against the unarmed evoked powerful and disturbing memories, reminding Americans of our failings as a nation. The uses of dogs at Abu Ghraib recalled the use of dogs in Alabama. The photographs raised questions about the actions and the legitimacy of those who, like those earlier dog-handlers, wore the uniform of the state and acted in its name. They placed the prisoners in the position of the civil rights marchers. The man who is "stripped of everything," naked before the power of the state—whether at Selma or Abu Ghraib—still holds the rights that power denies him. The rights he holds in himself—civil, human, natural—stand or fall with him.

Americans once found their soul in those who affirmed, "We shall overcome, someday." The civil rights marchers kept open the possibility of an America that we have not yet achieved. The men who held the leashes in Alabama wore the uniforms of the state but not the nation. They were provincials, and because of this their act could be read, easily and precisely, as the act of a part against the whole. The role of the federal troops at Little Rock, and the discourse of states' rights, made the denial of national responsibility for racism easier. Racism, Jim Crow, and white supremacy came to belong to a place (the South), a time (the past), and an order (the Confederacy) at odds with the nation in the present, the nation as a whole, the nation's history. The long-standing segregation of American sins—in the South, in the past, in the defeated Confederacy—was not honest, but it was plausible. Though it was a lie, it had the virtue of permitting the nation to acknowledge the acts it came to disown and disavow. The acts belonged to our past, our South, and so they were our sins, but they were sins that we might claim to have fought and defeated. The sins of Abu Ghraib and Guantánamo, the massacres by drones and men, cannot be so easily disowned. These are the work of our soldiers in the present. They call for a more thorough overcoming.

CHAPTER 10

There Is No Clash of Civilizations

The "clash of civilizations" is an article of faith, accepted by Left and Right, by politicians and philosophers. Samuel Huntington gets the credit for the clash of civilizations now, but there were earlier, and more eminent, partisans.[1] That understanding animated Ernst Renan's literary debate with Jamal al Din al Afghani in nineteenth-century Paris. It has a long and distinguished history. But it is not true.

Where we meet Islamic civilization in the West, we find not a clash but work on a common life. The evidence for this may be sparse in the work of scholars or the speeches of politicians, but it is very easily found. If you turn away from philosophers, politicians, and the press, there are many instances of conviviality. Every day, in defiance of the clash of civilizations, ordinary people find ordinary ways to make a life together.

Those lives are not without conflict. This is no utopia; this is home. There are frictions in the neighborhood. There are tensions, clashes, and occasionally crises. People irritate each other. But they also ride the same subways, live in the same neighborhoods, play on the same teams. They buy from each other and sell to each other. Where it counts the most, they work together. Paul Gilroy has used the word "conviviality" to describe the most important proof that we are making a life in common.[2] He noted that in hospitals (and, one might add, in the military and in schools) one looks around and sees Muslims, Christians, and Jews, immigrants and the native born, working together, relying on each other.

This is the story of Islam in the West we live in. This is an account of a West in which Muslims are at home, and Christians, Jews, Hindus, Buddhists, Zoroastrians, and secularists are at home with Muslims. This is an account of how people make themselves and their worlds out of materials that we are told are essentially opposed and impossible to integrate. These integrations are not only possible; they are commonplace. Where we live, we of the West, the "clash of civilizations" falls before the ordinary demands, frictions, and opportunities of living in the world, a world that is always and everywhere alien and familiar.

This is the story of where we live, we of the West. These everyday projects of hybridity and synthesis surround us. I have chosen a few from the many I have seen. I might have chosen many others. I chose these because I found them engaging, revelatory, and familiar. Some come from the mainstream of my cultural milieu, others from the edges. Anyone who looks for these moments of hybridity and synthesis will find them easily (though more easily in cities than in the countryside). They speak to every sense: to sight and sound, to touch and taste. They are inscribed in diverse scripts and media. They travel. They change and are changed. They are always on the move—and they reproduce. They grow.

This world is stronger, more beautiful, more demanding, and more just than the world Huntington saw. It is more faithful: true to the ideals of the many religions enfolded here. This world holds to the ideals of the West: to the belief in liberty, equality, and fraternity. The habits, the places, the sights and sounds, the streets we walk every day bear witness to the work we have already done in common.

"Western Muslims are at home," Tariq Ramadan writes, "and should not only say so, but feel so."[3] They should regard themselves as simultaneously fully Western and fully Muslim, not as displaced members of their ancestral cultures, still less as partisans of a civilization with which their present homeland is at war. "Our purpose and aim consist in discerning and abstracting Islam from the incidentals of Arab and/or Asian culture, tradition, and dress in order to arrive at a conception of the universal principles to which Muslims in the West must hold if they are to remain faithful and then to dress them in that culture." Ramadan expects that only at "the end of this process, the means of becoming a European or American Muslim will emerge."[4] There are already many American and British Muslims. There are many people on their way to being Dutch and Danish Muslims.

For scholars, as Hegel observed, the "owl of Minerva flies at twilight." Those people who face the daily questions, demands, and duties of being Muslim in the West, of having Muslim friends and family, colleagues and neighbors, must find their way home before twilight. Of necessity, they go before scholars, making Western Islam real in the world before it has achieved a scholarly recognition.

Islam Is in the House

Michael Muhammad Knight's novel *The Taqwacores* opens the house of Islam. In it, Knight made a "map that precedes the territory" which brought that territory into being.⁵ He pointed out not one way, but many ways to be Muslim in the West. He shows us a wild variety of Western Muslims. They are fictional, but they are fictions drawn from the American ordinary and returning to it.

Knight is a Muslim convert, a musician, and a student of Islam in America. He was, and perhaps remains, one of the lost boys from whom Islam makes so many converts in the West. *The Taqwacores* is a novel about a house of college students in Buffalo, New York. The students (and other not-quite-students) are all Muslims, united—and divided—by their faith in Islam and their love of music. There is Umar, straightedge Sunni; Rabeya, the veiled feminist, her burka covered with the insignia of punk bands. There is Jehangir, charismatic and capacious in his conception and practice of Islam. There is the Amazing Ayyub, with "Karbala" tattooed across his chest, Rude Daud, the Sudanese ska man, and more. The narrator, Yusef Ali, is straight and sedate, and at home with this more transgressive company.

The Taqwacores is a utopian novel, and like most utopias—and most college houses—it ends badly.⁶ The climactic concert results in a death, brought in from outside. Yet even before the dark outside world intrudes, the utopia portrayed is imperfect. People quarrel. Nothing is tidy, nothing perfect. There are unreconciled differences. People get left out; people get dissed; people get hurt. This is what gives the novel its power. The characters—and so the readers—enter a place where more forms of Islam, and of the West, are possible.

Knight constructed a world in this small *beit al muminim*, this little house of the faithful. The imaginary world he made spoke to young Muslims in the United States and Canada. The novel circulated privately; then, published by Soft Skull in Brooklyn, it took off and became the basis for a film. More importantly, it fueled the rise of a series of Muslim bands including the Kominas, Vote Hezbollah, and Al Thawra Miskeen.[7] Knight's novel was, in Baudrillard's phrase, "the map that creates the territory." I've heard the Kominas play a Taqwacore concert at Haverford College and talked to the band members, who drove down from Brooklyn. Other bands proceeded to make themselves heard and seen. The Kominas partnered with Secret Trial Five through an unofficial (and apparently unappreciated) performance at an Islamic convention.[8] Knight brought newness into the world.[9]

The imagined house and the music it called forth were both instances of mixing, *mestizaje* and mixité. Ancestries are mixed. Languages are mixed: Arabic and English and a little Urdu. Men and women mix, but there is only one woman in the house, Rabeya, and Rabeya remains veiled. The other (possibly) Muslim woman is more Western and less clothed, and sits uneasily just beyond the boundary. Gender politics, as this suggests, is not Knight's strong suit. Sexual politics—among men—may be. The novel's most effective accommodation is of diverse forms of male sexuality. The men are queer, gay, and straight; they practice celibacy, masturbation, and a variety of forms of intercourse. Sex, at this site, takes second place to the demands of friendship.[10]

Friendship rather than sexuality founds the household, and the egalitarian imperatives of friendship govern it. Prayer is its other anchor. Knight's believers pray together and they pray a lot, usually on schedule though not always according to regulations. Prayer stabilizes the characters as Muslims and underlines the Muslim character of the novel. Irregular sexual practices, drinking, drugs, and doctrinal heterodoxy are presented as small personal failings and deviations that do not put in question the believer's fundamental adherence to Islam.

The Taqwacores is the literary and (in the real Muslims it captured and inspired) the practical instantiation of Tariq Ramadan's call for a Western Islam. Ramadan's firm insistence that Western Muslims cede nothing to national custom, that they insist on their own capacity to practice their faith, licenses a new Muslim, one who recognizes, with Knight's Rabeya, that "it remained her own Islam as she saw fit to live it."[11]

Music, as people choose to make it, is a means of crafting convivial lives in unexpected places. Walter Armbrust's collection *Mass Mediations* offers articles on the struggles over political and musical authenticity among Iranians in Los Angeles; Ted Swedenburg's *Hawgblawg* chronicles the continuing evolution of several Andalusian musics from the University of Arkansas.[12] In *Heavy Metal Islam*, Mark LeVine, a professor of Middle East history, sets out to find—and play with—heavy metal bands in the Middle East and North Africa.[13] Outside the academy, Juha, a band characterized (accurately) by my colleague and friend Bob Vitalis as "gay Hawaiian Palestinians," draws on each of the elements in this curious trinity to fashion songs that challenge not only the clash of civilizations thesis, but the politics of sexuality. The American boys in Juha sing not only, "See that soldier on the hill / thinks his are the chosen. / When the kiddies throw the stones / he blasts their heads right open," but also "sniggers when we belly dance / but he knows what size dress he fits."

Juha fields its challenge to Huntington's thesis in the way the songs are made. These combine found sound and spoken word with more conventional (I use the term loosely here) music. Don Ho's Hawaiian kitsch classic "Tiny Bubbles" is woven with the call to prayer and Arabesque passages. This is radical in a double sense. Juha's fusion of Don Ho and classical Arab sonic vocabularies recalls one of the origin points of Western popular music.

On the other side of the Pacific, in California, Dick Dale, the son of Lebanese immigrants, adapted the tremolo style of oud playing and the Hijazi scales to produce a distinctively American sound: surf music.[14] In *Al'America: Travels through America's Arab and Islamic Roots* Jonathan Curiel shows the extent to which Arab music was consciously interwoven with the development of rock in the wake of Dale's "Miserlou." Curiel follows that influence through the Rolling Stones, Jefferson Airplane, Jimi Hendrix, and the Doors. He recalls the Grateful Dead's "Blues for Allah" and the interview in which Robert Plant tells rock critic Robert Palmer about the influence of legendary Egyptian singer Umm Kulthum on his work: "You can hear it in the longer sustained notes, the drops, the quarter tones. You hear that in 'Friends' or 'In the Light' and lots of other places too."[15] It gives new meaning to Caliphornia.[16]

The most fertile musical site may be that place where rap, hip-hop, and spoken word mix and produce. The long influence of Islam on the African American community may be part of the reason for the presence of Islam in rap and hip-hop. There are Muslim artists: Mos Def, Busta Rhymes, Ghostface Killah, Ice Cube. Perhaps more interestingly, there are Muslim references in work by non-Muslim artists. Nas, who is pictured on his record company bio wearing a cross, quotes the surah al Nas in the liner notes to *I Am*. P. Diddy samples the *adhan*, the call to prayer, on *No Way Out*. Throughout the Middle East, rap and hip-hop have become central to popular culture. The identification of rap and hip-hop with the region is so strong that academic conferences on the Middle East regularly feature concerts.

Scholars of the Middle East are—unsurprisingly and appropriately—preoccupied with those fusions and exchanges that involve the influence, adoptions, alterations, and adaptations of Western cultural styles and media into Arabo-Muslim musics. What has not been sufficiently recognized is that cultural influence goes both ways. Western musicians are becoming more Arab, more Muslim.

As African Americans and African American rap have come to signify struggle for the *shebab* of the Middle East and Europe, Islam has come to signify pride to many African Americans. The conversion of Malik El-Shabazz, Muhammad Ali, and Kareem Abdul Jabbar made Islam a sign of resistance and achievement. This finds a number of musical expressions, including the rap of the Five Percenters. If little of Islamic doctrine survives in the radical heterodoxy of the Gods, what remains is the sense of Islam as a source of pride for people of color.[17] The changing political context has changed the meaning of Islam and the signs of Islam in American public life without altering its link to pride and resistance.

There are also newer, and perhaps less expected, sources of musical dissent from the "clash of civilizations" thesis. Steve Earle's controversial album *Jerusalem* fielded two notable challenges to the Huntingtonian orthodoxy. The title song attacked the thesis of primordial conflict directly: "the man on my TV told me that it had always been that way / And there was nothin' anyone could do or say." Earle then proceeded to a lyrical invocation of the Abrahamic tradition as a site of unity: "I believe there'll come a day when the lion and the lamb / Will lie down in peace together in Jerusalem." This vision was allied to a critique of the Israeli occupation—itself remarkable in the American cultural context. Earle followed this with "John Walker's Blues," written from the perspective of John Walker Lindh. Earle made the *shahada* central to the song but sang it in his own voice: carefully pronounced Arabic bearing witness in a Texas accent. Questioned about his sympathetic portrayal of Lindh, Earle responded that he had a son like that, "and it was hard to keep that dog on the porch." Earle's claiming of Lindh is further—and in my view, more powerful—evidence for conviviality. It is not only, as Ramadan wrote, that Western Muslims know themselves as Western and Muslim; it is also that non-Muslim Westerners know this Muslim West as their own.

Knight's fragile utopia is made of music and Islam. LeVine makes metal the meeting place of Islam and the West. For Earle, Muslims are part of the family. We are often asked to see the visual—the cartoons, the veil—as the terrain of conflict between Islam and the West. Here we are called to music as the moment of unity and pleasure.

Perhaps the role of music in the making of Western Islam (and a more Muslim West) owes something to sound. In speech, even in the inarticulate cry, sound wants to be heard. Sound travels; sound circulates. Perhaps it owes something to the Arab. The inventors of the oud were also bound up in multiple practices of the spoken word: oratory, recitation, critical satiric poetry. Perhaps it owes something to Islam. Islam begins with the command "Recite." The Muslim day is (or ought to be) punctuated by the call to prayer. Islam is a calling. Tariq

Ramadan has suggested that Western Muslims abandon the old construct that divided the world into the *dar al harb* and the *dar al Islam*, and instead regard their West as the *dar ash-shahada*, the place of witness, or the *dar al dawa*, the place of the calling.[18] Cities in the West have silenced the call to prayer. Musicians have given voice to this silenced Western Islam. They have made it sing, growl, and scream.

Our Homeland the Text: Novels, Graphic Novels

The clash of civilizations foregrounds the visual—commissioning cartoons of Muhammad and legislating against the veil. Outside the realm of legislation, what we see on the street and in our homes often resists the idea of a clash of civilizations. In dress, in novels, and in graphic novels, we see the shaping of a common life, lived differently.

Like other profoundly industrial objects in a post-industrial moment, graphic novels are instances of the industrial artisanal. They do not have a broad mass circulation. They have distinctive styles. Some draw on the aesthetic conventions of superhero comic books. Joe Sacco's *Palestine* and *Footnotes in Gaza* visually echo the style of R. Crumb. Marjane Satrapi's use of silhouettes in *Persepolis* recalls Kara Walker's, though without the edge or the historical resonance. G. Willow Wilson and M. K. Perker's *Cairo* and *Air* (especially the latter) have a steampunk aesthetic. Baru's *Road to America*, which follows the short and tragic career of an émigré Maghrebi boxer, is also informed by the stylistic nostalgia of the noir.

The styles employed in these graphic novels are, of course, part of the text. Baru's noir style is allied to a reactionary politics and attempts a late and hostile revision of the Algerian revolution. Baru's character, attempting to become a successful fighter and ultimately emigrate from France to the United States, is defeated by the Mafia-like activities of exiled revolutionaries who try to corrupt him. Baru's effort to construct Algerian revolutionaries as thuggish enforcers of political orthodoxy, recruiting by impressment, is particularly regressive in the context of contemporary French politics. Hostility to the immigrant and the descendants of immigrants, the foregrounding of criminality—these motifs echo the politics of Sarkozy and Le Pen.

If one turns to graphic novels in the confident expectation that conviviality leads inevitably to solidarity, one is certain to be disappointed. In Marjane Satrapi's *Persepolis*, class hierarchies are affirmed and reinforced. Old aristocratic claims are fielded. Consumption is presented as the privileged and proper site of resistance and redemption. The poor are contemptible (unless they were once rich); the rich are admirable (unless they are newly rich). Islamists are poor, uneducated, and bent on humiliating the privileged. The privileged—that is, those like Satrapi's family, who claim descent from the Qajars and send their children to European boarding schools—defend their diminished privileges with a melancholy and nostalgic zeal. Satrapi presents their efforts to preserve the privileges of class without question or critique. The class-ridden nostalgia of exilic literature is unaltered by the medium.

Persepolis was deployed in another political arena when it was chosen in 2009 as the book read in the citywide "One Book, One Philadelphia" event. The change of audience and political context reshaped the reception and the significance of the book. In Philadelphia, in 2009, the choice of *Persepolis* was an effective (if not completely conscious or willful) endorsement of the effort to construct Iran as a pariah state and of Islam as peculiarly hostile to women. There are parts of Philadelphia that must have wondered why they should feel sorry for the little rich girl. Nevertheless, the choice of *Persepolis* as the book to unite the reading city was another refusal of the clash of civilizations.

Cairo by G. Willow Wilson and M. K. Perker is a different story. Here the class politics is inverted. People on the margins are not the source of a threat, but the site of possibility. Wilson and Perker's work, written in English for a Western audience, places the action in the Muslim world. They are themselves a cooperative against the clash. Wilson is an American, Perker a Turk. Wilson is a Muslim convert and a journalist, Perker a comic book artist and editorial illustrator who has drawn both Turkish comic books and illustrations for the *Wall Street Journal*. The characters in the graphic novel are a hash dealer; an Israeli soldier; his sister, a dancer; her lover, a journalist; an American tourist with naive cosmopolitan sympathies; a Lebanese American with terrorist ambitions; and a djinn.

While Satrapi constructs her narrative as personal rather than political, Wilson and Perker's project is self-consciously Andalusian. It begins in the space outside the city, on the frontier, in the desert. The desert in question is on the border with Israel. It is populated by the liminal: by animals (drugged animals), women, enemies, nomads. This liminal, frontier space gives way to another, to Cairo, *al Qahira*, the *umm al dunya*, Mother of the

World. Cairo, in this portrayal, is between East and West, Muslim and secular, sacred and profane, the past and the present, the prosaic and the magical.

The characters are all people on a frontier, people in a space between. The hash dealer stands between the lawful and the unlawful and is asked to decide whether the Israeli is enemy or ally, danger or endangered, lover or alien. The Israeli is a soldier lost in an enemy desert. First wanting to go home, she comes to question where home is, and the boundaries dividing friend and enemy. The two Americans, out of place and uncertain of their identities, both want to mix it up in places that are not their own. They are shaped in the image of a familiar American interventionist mentality and the "it works anywhere" universalism that belongs to both America and Islam. The willful, naive know-it-all abandons her belief that she can "fix this," and learns to subordinate herself to the hardworking, frustrated Cairene journalist. The would-be suicide bomber is himself killed and reborn, fused with the djinn. The djinn's object is freedom: his freedom and the freedom of others.

The most improbable of the characters and the plot elements (I do not exclude the djinn here) is the Israeli soldier. She points toward the novel's Andalusian objective. She is the enemy who becomes the ally and friend. Locally, she acts as an endorsement of the Israeli politics of *Yesh g'vul*, "there's a limit," that gave voice to refusals to serve in the occupied territories. Her role in the plot insists on the presence of Israel in the Middle East and an affirmation of the potential *sharkiyya*, the Middle Eastern-ness, of an amended Israel.

The novel also, and more profoundly, fields a set of political challenges that suggest the broader political significance of the Andalusian project in our time. The text casts itself against several of the pieties that govern elite responses to the "clash of civilizations." *Cairo* advances a local rather than global cosmopolitanism.[19] Cairo's ancient, non-Western cosmopolitanism stands against the liberal model of prescriptive cosmopolitanism fielded by John Rawls and Martha Nussbaum.

The novel challenges the rule of law as a transcultural panacea; it refuses the divide between sacred and secular that buttresses the "clash of civilizations" thesis. Liberalism's principled refusal of the sacred casts it as an alternative to "Islamic extremism" or "Islam." This is often accompanied, however, by an affirmation of secularism's "Christian roots." We see, once again, a glimpse of liberalism's forked tongue. As Slavoj Žižek's writings indicate, commitment to the Western secular is a ready bridge to an affirmation of Christendom.[20]

Like Dipesh Chakrabarty in *Provincializing Europe*, Wilson and Perker refuse to believe in Weber's now-canonical view that modernity is disenchanted. The djinn-haunted world of Cairo is an enchanted postcolonial space. Cairo is inhabited by djinns and evil magicians and is paralleled by the Under Nile, a space of magic (perhaps of the sacred) linking the Muslim and Pharaonic pasts. This refusal has immediate political significance. It sets aside the scholarly constructions of an inevitable and wholly disenchanted modernity—our "secular age," as Charles Taylor calls it. It acknowledges the continuing force of the sacred. This reaching toward the presence of the enchanted and the divine is visible in Harry Potter and American mega-churches, in the spread of Sufism and the work of A. S. Byatt and Terry Pratchett. Neither Europe nor the Americas are as secular or as disenchanted as scholars believe. Islam is not alone in reaffirming the presence of the sacred in Western life.

The tradition of the comic book also informs Michael Chabon's *Gentlemen of the Road*. This might seem an odd work to place cheek by jowl with graphic novels. It is authored by a Pulitzer Prize–winning, critically acclaimed novelist and in that respect might belong not with *Cairo* and *Persepolis* but with Orhan Pamuk's *Snow* or *My Name Is Red*; Tariq Ali's *Book of Saladin* or *Shadows of the Pomegranate Tree*; or Salman Rushdie's *The Enchantress of Florence*. Like these it is marked as an instance of high rather than popular culture. Like these it gives us a reimagined past. I might as easily have turned to these as instances of the Andalusian imperative. (You should, because they too are very, very good.) I turn to Chabon because Chabon's novel travels to Andalusia by a less predictable route: its central characters are Jews, not Arabs or Muslims, and it takes place on the outskirts of Khazaria.

In *Gentlemen of the Road*, Chabon gives us a reimagined Andalusian past. Chabon's Andalusia is in the Caucasus and in the surrounding plains and valleys, east of the Black Sea. It is semiotically centered on Khazaria, the kingdom of the Jews. Chabon writes in the afterword that he wanted to call this book "Jews with Swords." The publisher's reluctance to accept that title testifies to the challenge Chabon fields. Imagining Jews with swords who live by arms and robbery, as well as wit and commerce, challenges stereotypic views of the relation of Jews and Muslims to violence.

Chabon undoes the stereotype that poses armed (always armed) Muslims against unarmed Jews. *Gentlemen of the Road* gives us Arabic-speaking Jews allying themselves with a Muslim army. Muslims and Jews fight together—and fight other Muslims and Jews. There is a rape victim, but that victim is a Muslim, and on her way to political power. Chabon advances a refusal of historical victimhood as definitive and a refusal of violence as the site of division.

Chabon's geography also alters—and clarifies—the idea of Europe. He gives us a different, forgotten Europe: a more Eastern Europe; a Europe inhabited by Jews and Muslims; a Europe ruled by Jews and Muslims. This is a real Europe, and in the present as well as the past. Chabon's reminder of European history comes in the context of controversies over the presence of Muslims in Western Europe—controversies that insist upon the novelty of the Muslim presence and the ancient and enduring Christianity of Europe. The geographic placement of *Gentlemen of the Road* reminds us of the depth and historic resonance of the case to be made for Turkey's membership in Europe, if not in the European Union.

Chabon's reimagination of the European past is an undoing of what Gil Anidjar calls "the Jew, the Arab" as the other of Europe.[21] It challenges the construction of Jew as victim and the insistence on the primordial enmity between Jew and Muslim, or Jew and Arab. For all his literary eminence, Chabon has more history at his back than Huntington does.

The Local Team

These are fictional worlds, and though they bring new music and new practices into the world, though they revive lost memories of older worlds, they are still a little distant from the worlds we inhabit. Yet it is on the streets, in workplaces, and at sporting events that we see conviviality most vividly. It is in this commitment to the everyday that history (or what passes for it) can be overcome. Conviviality can be built out of the most unpromising material: old enmities.

French-speaking Belgians may have welcomed Muslim immigrants because many of the newcomers spoke French and the rest were happy to learn it. In a country where newly confident Flemings were facing off against French-speaking Walloons, the arrival of immigrants seemed to swell the numbers of the underdog side. A beleaguered Belgium, faced with the prospect of Flemish secession, might look to recent immigrants to defend it. This old enmity has produced, especially in Brussels, a climate in which Muslims and non-Muslim live easily together.

Older and less potent enmities could also serve as the grounds for conviviality. At the opening of the World Cup in 2010, Rangers defender Madjid Bougherra told a reporter that the Scottish fans were rooting for his Algerian homeland. "Everywhere I go in Glasgow people stop me and tell me to beat England," Bougherra told the reporter. He was confident, the report continued, that the Glasgow Rangers' Tartan Army would be cheering for Algeria.[22] He was right. A YouTube video shows Glasgow fans, dressed in their Rangers gear, wearing Algerian football scarves and handing them to Bougherra to be autographed. The "one two three viva Algérie" chant can be heard in the background.[23]

Bougherra had been embraced with enthusiasm by his new team and country. Another YouTube video shows a balding, middle-aged Glaswegian enthusiastically singing the verse added to celebrate Bougherra's arrival:

"He's six foot three and has a tan / He does not eat on Ramadan / Madjid! Madjid!"[24] Madjid's Muslim faith presented no obstacles for the Rangers fans. Bougherra, for his part, praised the openness of his new team and country. Scotland, he declared in an interview, was a vastly better place to play than France.

"I don't know why I would change clubs because I have everything in Glasgow," Bougherra said after the Rangers took the title in 2009. "Not just the Champions League, but the sort of football and atmosphere that can bring out the best in me. The people are passionate about the game; they are like Algerians." An article chronicling "a title celebration like no other" in the *Sunday Scotsman* detailed Bougherra's strict Islamic faith: "In observing his faith he does not drink alcohol, prays five times a day and each year follows Ramadan, a month-long period of fasting wherein food does not pass the lips from sun up to sun down." The land of Knox and Rutherford can, it seems, still recognize the value of religious discipline. Islam, the reporter wrote, gave Bougherra "humility" and "values." He concluded, "Bougherra's presence in Scotland doesn't just make Rangers' backline better. It makes Planet Old Firm appear a better place."[25]

Scotland was already a better place, in Bougherra's view. He confided in another interview: "Leaving France has saved my career. You would have to be in my shoes to understand it. If you had a name like Madjid, Mohamed or Mamadou you always had to work harder than others to gain respect. Thankfully fate decreed that I'm now in a country where there is a different and more flexible mindset." The reporter—conscious, as the most responsible so often are, of the failings of his team and country—wrote, "Given the religious hatred that surrounds the Old Firm, most Scots will be stunned to hear our nation being praised for the way its people respect the faiths of others."[26] Protestant or Catholic Scots might remember the inscriptions on the streets of St. Andrews that mark places where people were burned for their religious faith. Recent immigrants are more impressed by the tolerant present than the intolerant past. The Scots did well, in Bougherra's estimation, when they were measured against the practices of other European nations. Bougherra laid the case out forcefully, detailing instances of discrimination at Dijon, and saying: "France is an increasingly difficult place to live in. People should be more open-minded, the way they are here." His French coach had tried to stop him from fasting on Ramadan. In Scotland, his fast just gave them another verse for a football song. The Scots could see their own success at making Planet Old Firm a better place mirrored in Bougherra's praise.

America's most famous Muslim athlete had a harder road to acceptance, a more complex and prolonged struggle. Muhammad Ali would carry the torch for his country at the 1996 Olympics, but the road to that moment was a long one. In the beginning, the conversion of Cassius Clay seemed to mark a profound rejection of that nation. It was bound up with the fighter's refusal of the war in Vietnam, with his denunciation of white supremacy and the American racial order, with the civil rights movement and the threat of prison. In the end, the result was much the same: acceptance and honor for the athlete, humility and happiness for those who saw their country become a better place.

Manolete, perhaps the greatest Spanish bullfighter, began his early career with a touring group of toreadors called "Los Califas." From this side of the Atlantic, the idea of a bullfighting caliph seems to belong to Dalí and surrealism. In Spain, the name is a commonplace for sports clubs of all kinds. Cordoba has the Plaza de Toros de los Califas. There is the Club Atletismo de los Califas (a running club for men and women) and Orientación Califas, an orienteering group, and, of course, the Los Califas football club. There are the Los Califas cat-breeders (specializing in Cornish Rex, Maine Coon, and Siamese). Nearly anything from Cordoba can bear the name of the caliphs: nursery schools, mountain-bikers, a band, a guild in the World of Warcraft, or groups of men who get together to hunt or fish. Cordoba remains Ciudad de los Califas, the city of the caliphs, and its people still dress themselves in the name and glory of the Umayyads. There are echoes here of the American practice of naming teams "Indians" or "Braves" or "Redskins." The name honors an old enemy. The greater the strength of the defeated, the greater the victory. That enemy has become no longer alien, no longer an enemy, but one's own.

Writing on the Body

The most controversial of the texts on Western Islam is not Huntington's or any of the works discussed above. It is the text dress writes on the woman's body. While legislators, philosophers, and public intellectuals inveigh against the veil and its role in furthering an anti-Western Islam, women walk about my city in a wide variety of Muslim dress, from headscarves to *niqabs*, without drawing a second glance. The Muslims of my city are not, for the most part, the spectacular characters of *The Taqwacores*. They are ordinary people, going about their lives.

On any given day, I can drive to school and see a woman in a headscarf jogging on Kelly Drive and another in full *niqab* pushing a stroller. I can see the same when I walk through the campus. I have never had a woman in a *niqab* in my class, but I have had many *muhajibat*, women in headscarves, in seminars and lectures and as advisees. I have veiled colleagues. I see them all occasionally on campus, along with men whose clothing marks their adherence to Islam. If I buy food from one of the food trucks on campus, I may be in line with one. If I stop at the Whole Foods grocery on Callowhill, I might end up in the line with the veiled checker. If I park in the wrong place, I might get a ticket from a veiled parking enforcer. They are woven with me into the life of my city.

There are other items of dress, derived from the Arab and the Muslim, that lack the metonymic significance ascribed to the headscarf and *niqab*. The presence and use of these testifies to the many adoptions and fusions that are now ordinary to us. Henna, once exotic, can now be found in any grocery or drug store. The fez, that Turkish signifier of modernity, appears and disappears: sometimes a foreign and antique headgear, sometimes worn by Western soldiers and presidents. (I recently saw a green fez worn by a reveler on St. Patrick's Day. Apparently some bar was giving them out.) The once-dignified headgear of elite modernity is transformed into the uniform of Western soldiers and Shriners, and then, at the apex of kitsch, to the pet fez and the nipple fez. The kaffiyeh, which served in the sixties and seventies as a signifier of anticolonial solidarity, becomes an object whose political salience is itself contested. As the kaffiyeh reemerges as a sign of solidarity with Palestine, it prompts the not altogether unexpected response of the Zionist kaffiyeh: woven in blue and white in a pattern of Magen Davids. More revealingly, perhaps, the kaffiyeh has become so common an object of fashion that its political significance can be lost for a moment. Rachael Ray, filming a Dunkin' Donuts commercial, wore a scarf whose kaffiyeh-like appearance went unnoticed by the advertising executives and the film crew, only to be challenged vociferously later.

Juan Williams, a commentator on Fox and NPR, ignited a firestorm when he told Bill O'Reilly, "When I get on the plane, I got to tell you, if I see people who are in Muslim garb and I think, you know, they are identifying themselves first and foremost as Muslims, I get worried. I get nervous." Williams insisted, "I'm not a bigot."[27]

The most interesting response to Williams was one that made the fundamental silliness of the debate visible. A website invited Muslims to post photographs of themselves "wearing things." They did. The website exploded with photos of Muslims wearing all sorts of things. They wore uniforms: a woman, Wafa Dabbagh, in her uniform as a lieutenant commander in the Royal Canadian Navy; a much-decorated marine; American army reservist Shareda Hosein. A picture of a stern bearded man in a suit, with the American flag behind him, read, "This is Ahmed Bedier. He likes to wear little Muslim lapel pins." The "little Muslim lapel pin" was an American flag. There were photographs of Muslims in lab coats and basketball uniforms (professional and pick-up); of Muslim athletes in hijabs; of Muslims in short (very short) shorts, in sundresses, burkas, jeans, designer clothes, and "traveling rock band garb." Khalil Ismail posted a photo of himself "wearing the traditional preppy Muslim garb of his native Baltimore, Maryland."

Many people had a little fun with Williams and those who shared his fears. One photo showed two basketball players in the heat of the game "Marko Keselj made an ignorant comment about Semih Erden's Muslim garb, and Semih got a little bit upset." Another showed Sarah Cheikh "wearing a heathered purple vest over a white button-down blouse. Oh, and she's also wearing a really big snake. I might have to agree with Juan Williams on this one—I would be scared of her Muslim garb if she were sitting next to me on a plane!"

Andrew Sullivan took Williams more seriously. Williams, Sullivan wrote, "says that Muslims wearing Muslim garb are somehow more scary to him than Muslims not wearing such garb." Given the garb of (for example) the 9/11 attackers, who took care not to "look Muslim," this is, as Sullivan notes, deeply irrational. "It also sends a signal to Muslim-Americans that there are appropriate ways to dress publicly if you are not to provoke fear. . . . Would someone say that Jews should not wear yarmulkes in public, because it presents them 'first and foremost' as Jewish? Or that gays should never appear effeminate? Or that African-Americans should always wear suits and ties—because a different appearance can legitimately provoke nervousness or discomfort?"[28] The same set of concerns had troubled *Newsweek* during the fuss over Rachael Ray's "kaffiyeh." "It's doubtful the ad would have been pulled if a handful of critics found Ray's garb too Hispanic or too African-American." That, they concluded, would have been seen as "bigoted or insane"[29]

Both qualities are on full display in a video posted by Pamela Geller. Geller, with a diamond "love" pendant hanging ironically in her rather weathered cleavage, points out that "what you won't see in the Israel Day parade is a kaffiyeh." This clearly required some explanation. Geller, stooping to meet the gaze of the video camera, says, "The kaffiyeh is the symbol of Islamic jihad," and compares it to the robes of the Ku Klux Klan, and the swastika. Geller's ranting does not speak for Jews. Her video got a sharp response from commentator "Lion of Judah," who wrote that he and "many of my fellow Marines" had worn the kaffiyeh in Afghanistan.[30]

Andrew Sullivan asked, "Where does this stop?" The answer from "Muslims wearing things" was "It already has." Juan Williams, the photos showed, probably saw Muslims every day and never thought to fear them. They were not alien; they were familiar. They were welcome in the White House. A picture of a White House gathering was captioned "Imam Talal Eid is pictured here attending a dinner in the state dining room of the White House, in 2005. As a Harvard doctorate alum, Talal's crimson accents were clearly a diss to George Bush's pedestrian Yale degree."[31] The imam went to Harvard. Even at Samuel Huntington's own institution, the clash of civilizations falls before the evidence of people making a common life together.

Eating Together

Food enables us to express our opinions as it nourishes our bodies. The question of what one takes within one's boundaries—the boundaries if not of the body politic, of the body political—is full of significance. Consuming halal or kosher food is a means of governing the body. More pedestrian practices—the placement of food on the grocery shelves, for example—also provide political texts. As once suspect or alien populations become familiar, their food ceases to be "ethnic food" and becomes simply "food": moved off the "ethnic food" shelves. This process marks an often-neglected aspect of ethnic politics: as the formerly alien becomes familiar and one's own, the receiving people are altered. They alter their tastes and practices.

In the midst of deportations, ethnic profiling, and the continuous and vituperative Islamophobia of right-wing talk radio in the United States, the signs in the grocery store tell of daily acceptance. There is more and more hummus, more and more tabouleh, more falafel, more couscous, more once-alien food that has become our own. Middle Eastern food has become American. Pita chips, couscous, and tabouleh are on every grocery shelf; hummus, baba ghanoush, cacik, and kefir in every refrigerator case. Tastes change. The flavors of cardamom, cumin, and cinnamon, za'atar, harissa, and ras al hanout have a new familiarity for what we call "white-bread Americans." At the same time, the space of authenticity shifts. One of my students, offering me some baklava, declared, "It's real—it's from Dearborn."

Restaurants and shops are halalizing: buying and selling, serving, and (most importantly) advertising halal meat. In Philadelphia, halal meat can be found not only at the Makkah Market, but in Amish farmer's markets, not only in the Kabobeesh restaurant, but in the neighborhood pizza shop. The marking of food as halal is uncontroversial. What remains difficult in the American context is any suggestion of support for Palestine or the Palestinians. This, not the clash of civilizations, fuels the struggles in the grocery. Zionists market alternative versions of "Jerusalem salad" and other foods cleansed of their ethnic and Muslim associations, while the Boycott

Divestment Sanctions movement calls for the removal of "blood hummus." Yet this small intense politics is answered by the larger politics of conviviality. For most people most of the time, the choices have become neutral ones: between cinnamon sugar and Tuscan flavored pita chips, or roasted red pepper or basil or horseradish hummus, or between hummus and guacamole.

Mapping Islam in the Heartland

Islam has an older presence in the American heartland. The place we call the heartland, or the Midwest, was once called the "Great American Desert." It is punctuated with recollections of other desert lands in an all-too-Western East. There is Medinah, Illinois; Morocco and Algiers, Indiana; and Cairo, Illinois. There are more. There is Damascus (Virginia, Maryland, Ohio, and Oregon), Mecca (California, Indiana, and Tennessee), and Tangier Island in the Chesapeake Bay, where people still speak an archaic form of English. Were these cities named in a rosy hazy of Orientalism? Perhaps so. America is full of artifacts testifying to the appeal of the lands of *A Thousand and One Nights*. Early twentieth-century West Hollywood, California, had the Garden of Allah apartment complex, and almost every town has buildings from the twenties and thirties ornamented with Arab and Muslim motifs. The construction of the Arabo-Muslim Middle East as an object of desire testifies to the limits of "the clash of civilizations."

Not all these towns and cities are artifacts of an Orientalist imaginary. Elkader, Iowa, has more political origins. The city's historical society posts the following account of the city's founding. "Timothy Davis, John Thompson and Chester Sage laid out a plan for their community which was officially platted on June 22, 1846. They named the new village Elkader after Abd el-Kader, a young Algerian hero who led his people in a resistance to French colonialism between 1830 and 1847."[32] Elkader, Iowa, is an artifact of an earlier, largely forgotten, history of anticolonial solidarity.

News, Politics, and Power

Newspapers have largely accepted and enhanced the idea of the "clash of civilizations." Some endorse it explicitly. Others stand back from endorsing it but accept its divisions. These endorsements do not survive a careful reading of the paper. On August 20, 2010, in the midst of the debates over "the mosque at Ground Zero" that was not a mosque and not at Ground Zero, the *New York Times* published several in a series of articles that reinforced the "clash of civilizations." They varied the theme by including a report on differences within the Muslim community over the proper response to the media frenzy over the building.

Buried in the inner pages of the newspaper, in the local news, was a more telling story. In an article on the murder of a woman in Teaneck, New Jersey, the *Times* inadvertently showed that, away from media-fueled civilizational theatrics, the habits and practices of local government had already changed to a capacious conviviality—and that under the most difficult circumstances. Away from the ruckus over the mosque that claimed pride of place on the front page, the paper showed us how a difficult, eccentric WASP, a Muslim mayor, and a Jewish councilman had worked together in governing a town. The article quoted the mayor, Mohammed Hameeduddin. The woman, Joan Davis, was identified by the *Times* as a "local gadfly." Mayor Hameeduddin said, "I don't know if it was a matter of people liking her or not liking her. But she always had a wide array of points she wanted to make. She had some personal issues, but everyone in town felt the need to listen to her, engage her even if they didn't agree with her views." Elie Katz, a councilman, "said he used to drive Ms. Davis to and from council meetings."[33] While the clash of civilizations raged on the front page, the back pages testified to the ability of Ms. Davis, Councilman Katz, and Mayor Hameeduddin to build a town together. The conviviality Teaneck achieved—almost without notice—shows us how close conviviality is to democracy. The question, as Councilman Katz and Mayor Hameeduddin recognize, is not whether people agree, but whether they speak and are heard; not whether you like your neighbors' opinions—or your neighbors—but whether you have the strength and generosity to make a life with them.

The election of Teaneck's mayor had made the news earlier. ABC News ran a story about Hameeduddin's election, noting that he had been voted in with an Orthodox Jewish deputy. The story noted that Hameeduddin was a practicing Muslim and characterized his deputy as "devout." The city is diverse, with significant African American as well as South Asian and Orthodox Jewish populations. The election, Hameeduddin said, was not about diversity: "In Teaneck, it's about policy." The mayor was faced with the problem of keeping the city from bankruptcy in a time of recession. "In New Jersey right now, we have trying times and tough choices to make economically," said Hameeduddin, "and economics cross all barriers." But the mayor did put in a good word for his constituents. "'No where else is this possible,' said Mohammed Hameeduddin, Teaneck's first Muslim mayor."[34]

The mayor was wrong. Muslim mayors are more common than the press coverage would lead you to believe. Despite the sound and fury of the controversy over the veil, France has had Muslim mayors. The Netherlands has had a Muslim mayor. Canada has a Muslim mayor in a great and powerful city.

Calgary elected its first Muslim mayor in 2010. Calgary is in the heart of Alberta, a Canadian province generally considered conservative, and proud of it. The election of Naheed Nenshi was, the new mayor and his fellow citizens insisted, not about Islam. The president of the rival Progressive Conservative Party said that Nenshi identified "key priorities that mattered to Calgarians."[35] A local imam said, "He is a Muslim. So what? What's the big deal?"[36] The triumph of the Muslim mayor was less about the clash of civilizations than about the clash of Canadas. Toronto's conservative (and eastern) *Globe and Mail* wrote that "Mr. Nenshi was a rallying point for progressive Alberta—young and old, white and non-white, eager to debunk their city's conservative Cowtown image."[37] The Canadian—and American—media seized on Nenshi's election as a sign that the world had turned upside down. Calgarians hoped that "now maybe Torontonians will stop thinking of us as Neanderthals." Columnist Licia Corbella had doubts: "Regardless of the many sexist and racist laws and taboos westerners have knocked down against the wishes of 'easterners' the unfair stereotype sticks like bullpoop on Alberta boots."[38] The stereotype, as powerful in the United States as it is in Canada, cast enlightened eastern elites (Volvo-driving, Birkenstock-wearing liberals) against the redneck cowboy bigots (truck-driving, Carhartt-wearing conservatives) of the high mountains and the open plains. The clash, as the Canadian case suggests, is not between civilizations but within them. Geert Wilders contends with Job Cohen and the women of al Nisa, Anders Breivik with the Socialist camp at Utøya; Tariq Ramadan contends with Caroline Fourest and Paul Berman; and I contend with Debbie Schlussel, Berman, and their like.

Perhaps the clash of civilizations may be stronger in the Old World than in the New. Where people still claim the titles of *comte* and *graf*, one might expect a little less commitment to the idea "that all men are created equal," and, perhaps, less willingness to take a Muslim as one's representative. Where nations still retain established (Christian) churches and Christian Democrats participate in the party system, one might not be surprised to find Muslims effectively excluded from the electoral system. But Europe, despite the success of far-right parties, despite the spectacular antics of Geert Wilders and Odile Bonnivard, has also elected Muslims. There are Muslim deputies in virtually all of Europe's parliamentary assemblies. There are Muslim ministers, Muslim mayors, and Muslim local officials. Perhaps more importantly, people campaign with vigor: as Muslim candidates and for Muslim candidates.

I once visited Copenhagen shortly after elections. The national results had not been especially congenial to Copenhagen's Muslim citizens. Yet in neighborhoods regarded as Muslim (they look mixed to an outsider) there were campaign posters for many local candidates. The candidates were drawn from the Muslim community.

They were appealing to a heavily immigrant constituency. But they ran like Danes, campaigned like Danes, and at least one of them won. Even as conservative Danish politician Pia Kjærsgaard inveighed against the hostility of Islam to democracy and the impossibility of integration, Muslims were showing themselves to be willing democrats, working on integrating themselves into the nation's government.

There may be (there probably are) more Muslim politicians than we know. Like the Marranos of the Reconquista, some Muslim politicians have thought it best to keep their faith a private matter. Daniel Streich—a Swiss politician and member of the Swiss People's Party (SVP), best known abroad for its campaign against minarets—was one such quiet convert to Islam. Streich held local office but had not been active in the campaign against minarets. That campaign, he found, made his position difficult. He left his party but remains a conservative. As *Tikkun* observed, anti-Muslim sentiments may be strongest on the political right, but "conservatives can become opponents of Islamophobia," and "Western converts to Islam seem to come from all parts of the political spectrum, not just from the Left."[39]

A Muslim presence in politics, whether in Europe or North America, will not remove all controversies or usher in an era of uninterrupted peace. Politics is not a quiet, uncontroversial business, especially when it is democratic. In city, state, provincial, and national politics, Muslims will fight with Muslims—and with Christians, Hindus, Jews, and the rest—over all the issues that roil cities around the world. There will be demagogues and gadflies. There will be inflammatory rhetoric and civilizational theatrics. There will be pettiness and bigotry.

In local elections, however, snow removal and garbage collection, pensions, policemen, and property taxes overwhelm concerns with the clash of civilizations. Perhaps we can strive for more of that practical wisdom on the national level.

Stakes

Reading Elkader on the American map, and veils on the American street, suggests that Ramadan may be more right than he knew: we are already on Andalusian territory. The "clash of civilizations" has given way to conviviality in popular practice. The opposition of "us vs. them" has given way to the complex demands and possibilities of ordinary life together.

If the "the clash of civilizations" is not a fact, but a polemic, it is one that we need to analyze as well as reject. This is a construction, after all, that has found eager adherents well beyond the foreign policy conservatives of Huntington's circle. John Rawls could imagine a hierarchical state only by making it Muslim and by situating it outside the "society of liberal peoples."[40] Derrida wrote of "Islam, the Other of Democracy."[41] Žižek wrote, "We usually speak of the Jewish-Christian civilization—perhaps, the time has come, especially with regard to the Middle East conflict, to talk about the *Jewish-Muslim civilization* as an axis opposed to Christianity."[42] These are honorable men, who have, elsewhere in their work, borne witness to injustice. Yet they have fallen prey to prejudice. This must be overcome, for there is much at stake.

There are still our *Muselmänner*, the prisoners at Guantánamo, Bagram, and places whose names we do not know. There are the continuing wars in Iraq and

Afghanistan, with drone strikes on civilians in Yemen and beyond. There are continuing deportations, prosecutions, and instances of harassment. There is a steady stream of incitement fielded by politicians and pundits: Charles Krauthammer, Michele Bachmann, Peter King, Bernard-Henri Lévy, Elisabeth Badinter, Angela Merkel, Jack Straw, and David Cameron. In the first instance, we need to disavow and disable the doctrines of a scholarship that fosters a false enmity. This has immediate and imperative importance. But it is not all that is at stake.

The discourse of the "clash of civilizations" has consequences for democracy and for the commons.

In the academy, this may be most visible in Derrida's repudiation of the rioting *shebab* of the *banlieues*, and the democratically endorsed Front Islamique du Salut in Algeria. It is visible when Rawls denies the presence and structuring power of hierarchy in the West. It is visible in Cixous's choice of enmity with Islam over class solidarity in "Mon Algériance."[43]

Outside the academy, the use of enmity as an excuse for the refusal of economic demands can be heard (and read) throughout the Western media, where the exploitation of the many by the few takes second place to the dangers of Islam. As in the writings of Susan Okin, Caroline Fourest, and Ayaan Hirsi Ali, a reading of the popular press reveals that the "clash of civilizations" is also deployed to deflect critical engagement with sex, sexuality, and sexual hierarchies in the West.

The enemy who would "take our freedom," who "hates our way of life," is made the excuse for giving up our freedoms and abandoning our way of life. People defend their freedom by lining up like cattle in airport security lines and thanking the officers; by voting greater powers of surveillance to an already intrusive government. We are told to defend our way of life by buying larger SUVs and paying vast amounts of public money to dubious "security consultants" and "terrorism experts."

Knowing these things, I see the Muslim question as the Jewish question of our time: standing at the site where politics and ethics, philosophy and theology meet. This is the knot where the politics of class, sex, and sexuality, of culture, race, and ethnicity are entangled; the site where structures of hierarchy and subordination are anchored. It is here, on this terrain, that the question of the democratic—its resurgence or further repression—is being fought out.

Acknowledgments

This small book comes from a long period of research. I was obliged to stop, change my plans, and think again many times. Much of my past work has been spent in the past. For this work, I had to learn to talk with the living. I am grateful to those who guided me, and particularly aware of the distance that remains (in some cases) between my views and theirs. No one but me should be held responsible for what I have written here.

I owe a particular debt to Paul Gilroy, who explained his idea of conviviality over tea in London, and gave me a word for what I saw in place of the clash of civilizations. Jesper Vind Jensen, Klaus Wivel and Margarethe Wivel, Frederik Stjernfelt, Yngve Georg Lithman, Gunnar Skirbekk, and Anders Berg-Sørensen opened their contacts, their homes, their work, and their countries to me. In Thorvald Sirnes I have found a guide, a fierce critic of injustice and an intellectual ally. Joost Taverner and Simon Richter enabled me to see Amsterdam's past in its present. Veit Bader helped me solve the problem of the hidden mosque. Patrick Weil debated the French laws on veiling. He and Arun Kapil have helped keep me informed on events in France. Ellen Kennedy and Peter Funke have given me the benefit of their thoughtful, learned, and often divergent understandings of Germany.

So did Jane Caplan, who showed me the *Stolpersteine*. Talal Asad, Joseph Massad, Emran Qureishi, Tariq Modood, Barry Cooper, Nubar Hovsepian, Andrew March, Amaney Jamal, and Marwan Kraidy each greatly advanced my thinking concerning terror, sexuality, speech, war, and the West. Aristide Zolberg, a great scholar of immigration, a man always open to the new in the world, has given me the benefit of his learning and an affection for Belgium.

My sister, Vanessa Norton Sullivan, accompanied me on some of my research trips. Her clarity of vision and discerning comments on what she saw around her were, and remain, a valued resource.

For many years I have taught Muslim political philosophy to undergraduates. Lately I have also explored with them the convivial matrix of popular culture. A number of them are cited in these pages. I owe all of them a debt for their openness, their love of learning, and the willingness with which they seize the once alien as their own.

Murad Idris, Begum Adalet, Osman Balkan, Jurgen Reinhoudt, Piotr Szpunar, Samah Elhajibrahim, Christian Jurlando, and Jon Argaman, graduate students and colleagues, have read and argued with me, and helped me over and over again, with translations of words and practices. They are crafting a new, more demanding, and more honorable academy.

My research was funded in part by the University Research Fund of the University of Pennsylvania, by the Edmund and Louise Kahn Term Chair, and by a fellowship from Princeton's University Center for Human Values. My work was greatly advanced by the intellectual richness of these universities.

This book took longer than I expected in part because I felt the expressions of enmity and hatred that haunt the Internet were insurmountable. I could overcome this because of enduring friendships, the acceptance and neighborliness I saw in the streets around me, and incidents, large and small, that gave me a sense of solidarity. Listening to Jacques Rancière and Étienne Balibar discuss the Algerian war for independence and the France of the present gave me, as their work has always done, a sense of the way forward and of a France that remains committed to liberty, equality, and fraternity. Roxanne Euben, Amy Kaplan, Wendy Brown, Judith Butler, Rogers Smith, Eve Troutt-Powell, Timothy Powell, Rogers Smith, Robert Vitalis, and Deborah Harrold make, in their scholarship and their friendship, my America. Deborah Harrold told me to go out into the world, and, when in doubt, to go to the front door. That door opened to the generosity of many people, of all faiths and none. Joan Scott gave me first her brilliant work on the veil and, later, her advice and her strength.

Ruth O'Brien, Brigitta van Rheinberg, and Rob Tempio constantly cross the boundary between editing and scholarship. They work to make intellectual life whole.

I remember the late Fazlur Rahman, whose learning and generosity made generations of students at home in the texts of Islam, as we together made that learning at home in the West.

I thank the people of my city. Though it is famously cranky, cross-grained, and parochial, divided into close-held neighborhoods suspicious of strangers, it is still, as in the time of the Revolution, a place that can make the world new. The streets testify that it is still the city of brotherly love.

Philadelphia, April 2012

Notes

Introduction

1. Karl Marx, "On the Jewish Question," in *Karl Marx: Selected Writings*, ed. David McClellan (Oxford: Oxford University Press, 2005), 46–64. Benedict Spinoza, *Theological-Political Treatise*, ed. Jonathan Israel, trans. Jonathan Israel and Michael Silverthorne (Cambridge: Cambridge University Press, 2007); Giorgio Agamben, *Homo Sacer*, trans. Daniel Heller-Roazen (Stanford, CA: Stanford University Press, 1998); Antonio Negri, *The Labor of Job*, trans. Matteo Mandarini (Durham, NC: Duke University Press, 2009). The Holocaust is at the heart not only of Continental philosophy as it endeavors to overcome its past, but also of the work of Anglo-American philosophers like Michael Walzer. The refugees Hannah Arendt, Leo Strauss, Emil Fackenheim, and others made the concern central to the American academy of the second half of the twentieth century.
2. Slavoj Žižek, "Defenders of the Faith," *New York Times* editorial, March 12, 2006.
3. Leo Strauss, *Persecution and the Art of Writing* (Chicago: University of Chicago Press, 1988).
4. Jacques Derrida, *Rogues: Two Essays on Reason*, trans. Michael Naas and Pascale-Anne Brault (Stanford, CA: Stanford University Press, 2005).

Chapter 1
Freedom of Speech

1. Ken Connor, "Tough Questions about Islam and Democracy," *Baptist Press*, posted September 26, 2006, www.bpnews

.net/bpcolumn.asp?ID=2396; later reposted on http://www.human events.com/2006/09/22/why-did-popes-speech-spur-violence/.
2. http://www.netanyahu.org, posted February 7, 2003.
3. Keith Porteous Wood, quoted in César G. Soriano, "Europe Struggles to Balance Free Speech, Limits on Expression," *USA Today*, February 27, 2006.
4. Talal Asad, "Multiculturalism and British Identity in the Wake of the Rushdie Affair," *Politics and Society* 18 (1990): 455, 456.
5. Andrew Anthony, "Amsterdamned, Part One," *Guardian*, December 5, 2004.
6. Ian Buruma, *Murder in Amsterdam: Liberal Europe, Islam, and the Limits of Tolerance* (New York: Penguin Books, 2006), 9, 88.
7. *Luger* (1981). See also Buruma, *Murder in Amsterdam*, 89. A still of the scene with the cats is posted on the van Gogh website, http://www.theovangogh.nl.
8. Anthony, "Amsterdamned, Part One."
9. Buruma, *Murder in Amsterdam*, 90, 91.
10. Peter van der Veer, "Pim Fortuyn, Theo van Gogh, and the Politics of Tolerance in the Netherlands," *Public Culture* 18, no. 1 (2006): 111.
11. *Naar Nederland*, www.thiememeulenhoff.nl.
12. Jörg Lau, "Allah und der Humor," *Die Zeit*, February 1, 2006. English translation at "Who's Afraid of Muhammad?" www.signandsight.com, February 2, 2006. The translation from German to English comes with a curious change of title in which God gives way to Muhammad and humor to fear. Either "Who's Afraid of God?" or "Muhammad und der Humor" would give a more accurate account of the issues.
13. Or so he claimed. As Jytte Klausen notes, Bluitgen has not been willing or able to identify the illustrators who turned him down. Klausen, *The Cartoons That Shook the World* (New Haven, CT: Yale University Press, 2009), 18.
14. Lau, "Allah und der Humor."
15. "Dyb angst for kritik af islam," *Politiken*, September 17, 2005.
16. "Muhammeds ansigt," *Jyllands-Posten*, September 30, 2005.

17. Flemming Rose, "Why I Published Those Cartoons," *Washington Post*, February 19, 2006.

18. "Those Danish Cartoons" (lead editorial), *New York Times*, February 7, 2006.

19. Daniel Howden, David Hardaker, and Stephen Castle, "How a Meeting of Leaders in Mecca Set Off the Cartoon Wars around the World," *The Independent*, February 10, 2006.

20. I am indebted to Piotr Szpunar for pointing out the distorting effects of the Nigerian case and directing me to a closer examination of these figures.

21. Klausen tells us that the figures are "estimates based on local newspaper reports" (*The Cartoons That Shook the World*, 107). These numbers are themselves unreliable. My own brief check of local newspapers suggested smaller figures with a death count of 16 rather than 45 for the February 18 riot.

22. http://news.bbc.co.uk/2/hi/8468456.stm.

23. http://news.bbc.co.uk/2/hi/africa/4726204.stm.

24. http://www.nytimes.com/2006/05/30/world/asia/30afghan.html.

25. "Who's Afraid of Muhammad?"

26. Here and throughout, I am indebted to Jeppe van Platz for translations from the Danish.

27. Martin Asser, "What the Muhammad Cartoons Portray," BBC News, February 9, 2006.

28. The text is more commonly translated as "*Jyllands-Posten*'s journalists are a bunch of reactionary provocateurs." My translator argues that "right-wing" or "rightist" is more accurate.

29. Tariq Ramadan, "Free Speech and Civic Responsibility," *International Herald Tribune*, February 5, 2006.

30. Emran Qureishi, "The Islam the Riots Obscured" (op-ed), *New York Times*, February 12, 2006.

31. Andrew Walsh, "To Print or Not to Print," *Religion in the News* 9, no. 1 (Summer 2006).

32. Dyab Abou Jahjah, "Walking the Thin Line," January 31, 2006, http://www.arabeuropean.org.

33. Paul Belien, "Muslim Radical Defends Freedom of Speech, Deplores Europe's Hypocrisy," *Brussels Journal: The Voice of Conservatism in Europe*, February 3, 2006.

34. "Europe's Blasphemy Laws," Deutsche Welle, February 7, 2006, www.dw-world.de.
35. Mark Trevelyan, "UK Seeks Way to Stop Militant Grooming on the Web," January 17, 2008, Reuters.com.
36. Preston Grall, "Internet Insider," January 18, 2008, http://blogs.computerworld.com.

Chapter 2
Sex and Sexuality

1. Some of the essays gathered in the volume—notably those by Bonnie Honig and Azizah al Hibri—dispute Okin's claim quite effectively, but it is her view that is dominant.
2. Slavoj Žižek, "A Glance into the Archives of Islam," originally published as a *New York Times* editorial, revised and republished on lacan.com.
3. David Cameron, speech to the Munich Security Conference, February 25, 2011, quoted on http://www.newstatesman.com/blogs/the-staggers/2011/02/terrorism-islam-ideology.
4. Geert Wilders, speech to the Magna Carta Foundation, March 25, 2011, quoted on jihadwatch.com.
5. The film is available on YouTube and at a variety of other sites.
6. See Joan Wallach Scott, *The Politics of the Veil* (Princeton, NJ: Princeton University Press, 2007), 151–74.
7. Ayaan Hirsi Ali, *Infidel* (New York: Free Press, 2008), 31–34. As Hirsi Ali notes, "Female genital mutilation predates Islam" and is not coincident with it.
8. Ibid., 351.
9. Ibid., 256–57, 235, 261.
10. These quotations appear in the publicity front matter to the 2008 Free Press paperback edition of *Infidel*. They tell us not only what was said but what the publishers want readers to see in the book.
11. Ibid., 237.
12. The website http://www.theovangogh.nl/ preserves De Gezonde Roker as a memorial.
13. Van der Veer, "Pim Fortuyn, Theo van Gogh, and the Politics of Tolerance in the Netherlands."

14. The editorial was entitled "Tolerance or Death!" with the tag line "European culture leaders should smack down fanatical Islamists. Instead, they're bending over for them." It was published in *Reason* magazine, November 30, 2005.

15. Afsaneh Najmabadi, *Women with Mustaches and Men without Beards: Gender and Sexual Anxieties of Iranian Modernity* (Berkeley: University of California Press, 2005).

16. Joseph Massad, "Re-orienting Desire: The Gay International and the Arab World," *Public Culture* 14, no. 2 (Spring 2002): 361–85, 362.

17. Scott, *The Politics of the Veil*, 179, 176.

18. Alain Badiou, "The Law on the Islamic Headscarf," in *Polemics*, trans. Steve Corcoran (New York: Verso, 2006), 102–3.

Chapter 3
Women and War

1. *Words of Women from the Egyptian Revolution*, posted by Leila Zahra on youtube.com. There are several episodes.

2. February 16, 2011, www.debbieschlussel.com. Schlussel's comments appalled commentators on left and right, but she was not reproached, much less penalized by her regular employers, Fox News, the *New York Post*, and the *Jerusalem Post*.

3. Michelle Malkin, *USA Today*, August 20, 2004. Also available on michellemalkin.com.

4. Ellen Goodman, "The Myth of 'Security Moms,' " *Boston Globe*, October 7, 2004. I am indebted to Inderpal Grewal's analysis of the figure of the security mom in " 'Security Moms' in the Early Twentieth-Century [*sic*] United States: The Gender of Security in Neoliberalism," *Women's Studies Quarterly* 34, nos. 1/2 (Spring–Summer 2006): 25–39.

5. Joe Klein, "How Soccer Moms Became Security Moms," *Time*, February 10, 2003.

6. Susan Sontag, "Regarding the Torture of Others," *New York Times*, May 23, 2004.

7. Ted Olson, "More Christian Organizations Respond to Abu Ghraib Scandal," *Christianity Today*, http://www.christianitytoday.com/ct/2004/mayweb-only/5-10-42.0.html.

Christianity Today condemned the Abu Ghraib abuses as torture early on, as did Fr. Richard Neuhaus of *First Things*, and the Vatican.

8. Sontag, "Regarding the Torture of Others."
9. Evan Thomas, "Explaining Lynndie England," *Newsweek* May 15, 2004, http://www.newsweek.com/id/105054.
10. Janis Karpinski, *One Woman's Army: The Commanding General of Abu Ghraib Tells Her Story* (New York: Miramax, 2006).
11. Seymour M. Hersh, *New Yorker*, May 24, 2004.
12. Ibid.
13. "The Women of Guantánamo," *New York Times*, July 21, 2005.

Chapter 4
Terror

1. Paul Berman, *The Flight of the Intellectuals* (New York: Melville House, 2010), 256.
2. Faisal Devji, *Landscapes of the Jihad: Militance, Morality, Modernity* (Ithaca, NY: Cornell University Press, 2005). See also Ellis Goldberg, "Smashing Idols and the State: The Protestant Ethic and Egyptian Sunni Radicalism," *Comparative Studies in Society and History* 33, no. 1 (1991): 3–35. Ali Eteraz wrote a September 28, 2007, opinion piece for the *Guardian* in which he noted the "plethora of writing calling for an Islamic Reformation" and arguing that it had already occurred (read Abdul Wahhab as Luther).
3. Richard Curtis, "Arab Americans React Cautiously to Barak Victory but Jewish American Peace Activists More Optimistic," *Washington Report on Middle East Affairs*, July/August 1999, 50.

Chapter 5
Equality

1. John Rawls, *The Law of Peoples* (Cambridge, MA: Harvard University Press, 1999), vi.

2. Homi Bhabha, "Of Mimicry and Man," in *The Location of Culture* (London: Routledge, 2008), 122. There are also liberals for whom Rawls is not liberal enough. These liberal critics of *The Law of Peoples* include Kok-Chor Tan, "Liberal Toleration in Rawls' Law of Peoples," *Ethics* 108 (1998): 276–95.
3. Rawls, *The Law of Peoples*, 35.
4. Ibid., 5.
5. Arif Jamal, "Moving Out of Kazanistan: Liberal Theory and Muslim Contexts," in *Muslim Societies and the Challenge of Secularization*, ed. Gabriele Marranci (London: Springer, 2010).
6. Rawls, *The Law of Peoples*, 75, 76, 78.
7. David Reidy, "Rawls on International Justice: A Defense," *Political Theory* 32 (2004): 315.
8. John Tasioulas, "From Utopia to Kazanistan: John Rawls and the Law of Peoples," *Oxford Journal of Legal Studies* 22, no. 2 (2002): 383. Tasioulas does **not** appear to know that head-to-toe covering is not required for Muslim women, or that modest dress is required for Muslim men. He is also mistaken in suggesting that denying university education or professional occupations to women is Islamic.
9. Neil Beers, "Reconstructing Rawls: On the Nature of a Truly Decent Hierarchical Society," http://www.sewanee.edu/philosophy/Journal/Archives/2002/Beers.htm.
10. Jamal, "Moving Out," 83.
11. Ibid., 85.
12. Michael Gross, "Doctors in the Decent Society: Torture, Ill-treatment and Civic Duty," *Bioethics*18, no. 2 (2004): 181–203. See especially 184–85, 200. Gross's account is well intentioned and aimed primarily at interrogating the practice of torture in Israel. It is, however, riddled with facile misconstructions of Islam and simple errors, including the mistranslation of *hudud (*limit) as "acts against God."
13. Uday Mehta, *Liberalism and Empire* (Chicago: University of Chicago Press, 1999).
14. *New York Times*, January 21, 2011.
15. Rawls, *The Law of Peoples*, 67.
16. *Zakat* is usually translated as "charity." Like charity, it is provision made to those in need. Qutb insists, however, that

zakat is not charity but a right, and that providing *zakat* is a moral and political obligation.

17. Franklin Delano Roosevelt, Fireside Chat 16, Miller Center Presidential Archive,

18. Sayyid Qutb, *Social Justice and Islam*, trans. John B. Hardie (Washington, DC: American Council of Learned Societies, 1953), 73, 76, 77.

19. Ibid., 99–100.

20. Ibid., 47–49.

21. Thomas Paine, *Common Sense, the Rights of Man and other Essential Writings* (New York: Penguin 2003), 233.

22. Roxanne Euben's book *The Enemy in the Mirror* explores, more extensively than I do here, the extent to which Qutb offers a critical reflection on Western principles and practices, including those of liberal theory. Euben, *The Enemy in the Mirror* (Princeton, NJ: Princeton University Press, 1999). Andrew March offers a reading of Sayyid Qutb that reveals the affinities between the liberal approach and that of Sayyid Qutb. March, "Taking People as They Are: Islam as a 'Realistic Utopia' in the Political Theory of Sayyid Qutb," *American Political Science Review* 104, no. 1 (February 2010): 189–207.

23. Qutb, *Social Justice and Islam*, 161.

24. Ibid., 141.

25. George Kateb, *Human Dignity* (Cambridge, MA: Harvard University Press, 2011).

26. Qutb, *Social Justice and Islam*, 150.

27. John DiIulio, *Godly Republic* (Berkeley: University of California Press, 2007).

Chapter 6
Democracy

1. Derrida, *Rogues*, 28–29.

2. Ibid., 30.

3. Ibid., 31.

4. Derrida acknowledges this on 35 but casts it as a structural inevitability, a process without agents or the possibility of escape.

5. Wendy Brown, "Sovereign Hesitations," in *Derrida and the Time of the Political*, ed. Pheng Cheah and Suzanne Guerlac (Durham, NC: Duke University Press, 2009), 123–24.

6. Derrida, *Rogues*, 28–29.

7. Ibid., 35; Jacques Rancière, *Hatred of Democracy*, trans. Steve Corcoran (New York: Verso, 2009). I cannot praise this honorable book enough.

8. Derrida's third lesson on democracy also deals with the conflict between democracy and sovereignty understood as single and incarnate. I will not take this question up here. Wendy Brown and I both discuss the limits imposed by Derrida's reliance on Schmitt's understanding of an incarnate sovereign in Cheah and Guerlac, *Derrida and the Time of the Political*.

9. Derrida, *Rogues*, 28.

10. Derrida, "Faith and Knowledge," in *Acts of Religion*, ed. Gil Anidjar (New York: Routledge, 2002), 46. The "right to literature" alluded to is connected by Derrida to Khomeini's fatwa against Salman Rushdie.

11. Ibn Khaldûn, *Muqaddimah*, trans. Franz Rosenthal (Princeton, NJ: Princeton University Press, 1967). Ibn Khaldun called the quality that binds people together *asabiyya*, solidarity.

12. Derrida, *Rogues*, 64, 65, 66.

13. Jacques Derrida, *The Politics of Friendship*, trans. George Collins (London: Verso, 1997), 232.

14. Al Farabi, "The Political Regime," trans. Fauzi Najjar, in *Medieval Political Philosophy*, ed. Ralph Lerner and Muhsin Mahdi (New York: Collier Macmillan, 1963), 51.

15. Plato, *Republic*, trans. Allan Bloom (New York: Basic Books, 1968), bk. 8.

16. Derrida, *Rogues*, 64.

Chapter 7
Where Is Europe?

1. Terry Karl, *The Paradox of Plenty* (Berkeley: University of California Press, 1997).

2. For a more extensive account see Mehta, *Liberalism and Empire*.

3. Denis de Rougemont, *The Idea of Europe* (New York: Macmillan, 1966), 74.
4. Isaiah Berlin, *Russian Thinkers* (London: Penguin, 1978), 150–238. Rougemont, *The Idea of Europe*, 298, 301, 311.
5. Carl Schmitt, *Roman Catholicism and Political Form*, trans. G. L. Ulmen (Westport, CT: Greenwood Press, 1996), 38.
6. Rougemont, *The Idea of Europe*, 307.
7. Miguel de Unamuno, *Vérités arbitraries: Espagne contre Europe*, trans. Francis de Miomandre (Paris: Editions du Sagittaire, 1925).
8. Yirmiyahu Yovel, *Spinoza and Other Heretics*, vol. 1, *The Marrano of Reason* (Princeton, NJ: Princeton University Press, 1992).
9. Arno Widmann, "No Europe without Muslims: Conference with Jürgen Habermas and Tariq Ramadan," trans. Katy Derbyshire (originally published in *Frankfurter Rundschau*, June 24, 2008), http://www.qantara.de/webcom/show_article.php/_c-478/_nr-781/i.html.
10. Craig Smith, "Granada Journal; Where the Moors Held Sway, Allah Is Praised Again," *New York Times*, October 21, 2003.

Chapter 8
The Burden of the Holocaust

1. Paul Berman, *Terror and Liberalism* (New York: W.W. Norton, 2003), 3–6.
2. Ibid., 23.
3. Israel Gershoni and James Jankowski, *Confronting Fascism in Egypt* (Stanford, CA: Stanford University Press, 2010), 75. The English book is an abridged presentation of the enormous body of evidence Gershoni and Jankowski have edited and published in Hebrew. They continue to work on their documentation of antifascism in the Arab Middle East.
4. See Gil Anidjar's superb study *The Jew, the Arab: A History of the Enemy* (Stanford, CA: Stanford University Press, 2003).
5. Caroline Fourest, *Brother Tariq: The Doublespeak of Tariq Ramadan*, trans. Ioana Wieder and John Atherton (New York: Encounter Books, 2008), 3.

6. Ibid., 61.
7. Žižek, "A Glance into the Archives of Islam." The italics are Žižek's.

Chapter 9
In the American Desert

1. May 1, 2011, www.debbieschlussel.com/36592. On Geller, Spencer, and the "gates of Vienna," see Scott Shane, "Killings in Norway Spotlight Anti-Muslim Thought in U.S.," *New York Times*, July 24, 2011.
2. Alexander Hamilton, Federalist 1, in Alexander Hamilton, James Madison, and John Jay, *The Federalist Papers* (New York: New American Library, 1961), 33.
3. See Marie Gottschalk, *The Prison and the Gallows* (Cambridge: Cambridge University Press, 2006).
4. Sontag, "Regarding the Torture of Others."
5. Matt. 25:40. The philosophic and literary corollary may be Negri's account of his own imprisonment, *The Labor of Job*.
6. Susan Sontag notes the use and effects of editorial cropping of the photographs from Abu Ghraib in her essay "Regarding the Torture of Others."
7. Sheldon Wolin, *Democracy Incorporated* (Princeton, NJ: Princeton University Press, 2008).
8. Adam Zagorin and Michael Duffy, "Inside the Interrogation of Detainee 063," *Time*, June 20, 2005, http://www.time.com/time/2006/log/log.pdf. Also quoted, with ellipses, in Jane Mayer, *The Dark Side* (New York: Doubleday, 2008), 182.
9. Alex Danchev, "Like a Dog! Humiliation and Shame in the War on Terror" (paper presented at the Political Theory Workshop, University of Pennsylvania, October, 2006).

Chapter 10
There Is No Clash of Civilizations

1. Samuel Huntington, *The Clash of Civilizations and the Remaking of World Order* (New York: Simon and Schuster, 1998).
2. Paul Gilroy, *After Empire: Melancholia or Convivial Culture?* (London: Routledge 2004).

3. Tariq Ramadan, *Western Muslims and the Future of Islam* (Oxford: Oxford University Press, 2004), 53. This comes in direct refutation of Paul Berman's tendentious conflation of Ramadan and Qaradawi, in the context of Ramadan rejecting Qaradawi's characterization of the position of Muslims in the West.

4. Ramadan, *Western Muslims*, 78–79.

5. Jean Baudrillard, *Simulations* (New York: Semiotext(e), 1983).

6. It ends badly in a larger sense: the climactic narrative failure is a failure in literary and political terms.

7. http://natsumemaya.net/The Taqwacores.html, http://www.guardian.co.uk/commentisfree/2007/mar/19/sexdrugsand prayer,http://www.last.fm/music/The+Kominas,http://www.sepia mutiny.com/sepia/archives/005438.html, http://swedenburg.blog spot.com/2009/09/even-more-on-kominas-pakistani-rock.html, http://www.rollingstone.com/rockdaily/index.php/2007/10/01/muslim-punk-bands-tour-the-us-tales-of-allah-amps-and-anarchy/. *Hawgdawg*, the blog of Prof. Ted Swedenburg, is an invaluable source for commentary on many aspects of Muslim music.

8. Secret Trial Five was founded by Sena Hussain. Her band toured with the Kominas in 2007. "When they all crashed the Islamic Society of North America's annual meeting in Chicago, they caused a riot, with organizers and police on one side and excited hijabi girls rocking out on the other." www.taqwacore.com.

9. Bhabha, *Location of Culture*.

10. Michel Foucault and Sylvère Lotringer, *Foucault Live* (New York: Semiotext(e), 1989).

11. Michael Muhammad Knight, *The Taqwacores* (New York: Soft Skull Press, 2009), 9.

12. http://swedenburg.blogspot.com.

13. Mark LeVine, *Heavy Metal Islam: Rock, Resistance, and the Struggle for the Soul of Islam* (New York: Random House, 2008).

14. I learned this from Doug Moore, a member of my seminar and a metal critic. Levine notes it in *Heavy Metal Islam*, 5–6.

15. Jonathan Curiel, *Al'America: Travels through America's Arab and Islamic Roots* (New York: New Press, 2008), 127. See, more generally, 119–30.

16. Knight plays with this trope in *The Taqwacores*, where Jehangir tells Yusef Ali, "Yeah, *y'akhi*, Khalifornia. There's a group out there, they're trying to establish the Khilafah out there, call themselves fuckin' Khalifornia" (28).

17. In one of the more heterodox of their practices, the Five Percenters refer to male Five Percenters as "Gods," often taking that as a name, e.g., God Sunz, Divine Life Allah, Superstar Quam Allah. Felicia Miyakawa, *Five Percenter Rap: God Hop's Music, Message, and Black Muslim Mission* (Bloomington: Indiana University Press, 2005).

18. Ramadan, *Western Muslims*, 72, 73, and, more generally, 63–77.

19. This is given another form in *Cairo Cosmopolitan: Politics, Culture, and Urban Space in the New Globalized Middle East*, ed. Diane Singerman and Paul Amar (American University in Cairo Press, 2009). See also Farha Ghannam, *Remaking the Modern: Space, Relocation, and the Politics of Identity in a Global Cairo* (Berkeley: University of California Press, 2002).

20. Žižek, "Defenders of the Faith."

21. Gil Anidjar, *The Jew, the Arab: A History of the Enemy* (Stanford, CA: Stanford University Press, 2003).

22. Alex Young, "Algeria and Rangers Defender Madjid Bougherra: Scotland Fans Are Backing Algeria against England," *Sun*, June 1, 2010, http://www.goal.com/en-gb/news/2890/world-cup-2010/2010/06/01/1952847/algeria-and-rangers-defender-madjid-bougherra-scotland-fans.

23. http://www.youtube.com/watch?v=Bsw1CmaVjo4&feature=related.

24. http://www.youtube.com/watch?v=vJQ2FpzRPTg. This would be followed by other songs, several of which are posted on YouTube.

25. Andrew Smith, "Interview: Madjid Bougherra," *Scotland on Sunday*, May 31, 2009, http://scotlandonsunday.scotsman.com/sport/Interview-Madjid-Bougherra-.5319358.jp.

26. Neil Cameron, "Madjid Bougherra Hails Move to Rangers for Saving His Career after French Nightmare," *Daily Record*, February 23, 2010. There is no small irony in the fact that this is being written by a Catholic.

27. David Folkenflik, "NPR Ends Williams' Contract after Muslim Remarks," October 21, 2010, www.npr.org.
28. Andrew Sullivan, "The Daily Dish," in the *Atlantic* online October 22, 2010, www.theatlantic.com/daily-dish/archive/2010/10/muslims-wearing-things/180895/
29. Lorraine Ali, "Not So Sweet," *Newsweek*, May 30, 2008, www.newsweek.com/2008/05/29/not-so-sweet.html#.
30. http://www.youtube.com/watch?v=bEOAulrllls.
31. http://muslimswearingthings.tumblr.com/.
32. www.elkader-iowa.com/history.html.
33. Trymaine Lee, "Killing of a Local Gadfly Leaves a Town Puzzled," *New York Times*, August 20, 2010, A16–17.
34. Devin Dwyer, "N.J. Town Picks Muslim for Mayor, Orthodox Jew as Deputy," July 6, 2010, ABC News.com.
35. Jason Fekete, "Provincial Parties Seek Lesson from Surprise Win," *Calgary Herald*, October 21, 2010, A5.
36. Mario Tonneguzzi, "Common Values Trump Religion," *Calgary Herald*, October 21, 2010, A5.
37. Josh Wingrove, "Naheed Nenshi: Change Calgary Believed In," *Globe and Mail*, October 19, 2010.
38. Licia Corbella, "Corbella: Can Nenshi Slay Our Redneck Image? Don't Bet the Farm," *Calgary Herald*, October 20, 2010, www.calgaryherald.com/Corbella.
39. Jason Van Boom, "Minarets and the Conversion of a Swiss Politician: Separating Facts from Fantasy," *Tikkun Daily Blog*, February 5, 2010, www.tikkun.org/tikkundaily/2010/02/05/minarets-and-the-conversion-of-a-swiss-politician-the-real-story/#more-9900.
40. Rawls, *The Law of Peoples*.
41. Jacques Derrida, *Rogues*.
42. Žižek, "A Glance into the Archives of Islam."
43. Hélène Cixous, "My Algeriance, in Other Words: To Depart Not to Arrive from Algeria," trans. Eric Prenowitz, in *Stigmata* (New York: Routledge, 1998), 153. I have written a longer account of Cixous's tragic refusal of the Algerian in "The Red Shoes: Islam and the Limits of Solidarity in Hélène Cixous," *Theory & Event* 14, no. 1 (2011).

Index

Abdul-Jabbar, Kareem, 202
Abou Jahjah, Dyab, 35–37
Abraham, 2, 124
Abu Ghraib, x, 72–81, 175, 179–88, 194; domestic issues confronted at, 179; and Guantánamo, 189, 190; photographs from, 181–87, 192; use of dogs at, 189, 192, 193; veiled practices of, 184. *See also* prisons
Abu Laban, Ahmad, 25
Adams, Henry, 171
Adams, John, 171
adhan, 125, 202
Afghani, Jamal al Din al, 15, 195, 238n2
Afghanistan, 28, 68, 165, 179, 227
Africa, 151–52
African Americans, 8, 75, 104, 115, 182–83, 192, 193, 201, 202, 222. *See also* civil rights movement
Afrocentrists, 166
Agamben, Giorgio, 128
Age, The, 52
Ahlan wa sahlan, 126–28, 137
airport security, 184, 227
Alabama, 193
Aladdin (film), 59
Al Ahram, 169
Al Andalus, 123, 157, 200
Alberta, 223–24
Aleppo, 136

al Farabi, 9, 10, 121, 133–34, 135
Alfonso X, 156
Algeria, 119–20, 123, 124, 211, 212, 227
Algerian revolution, 205
Algerians, 124–25, 132
al Ghazali, 83
Algiers, 125
Ali, Muhammad (Cassius Clay), 202, 213
Ali, Tariq: *Book of Saladin*, 209; *Shadows of the Pomegranate Tree*, 209
al Jazeera, 147
Al Misri, 169
al Nisa, 160, 224
al Qaeda, 84
Al Thawra Miskeen, 199
Amador, Xavier, 77–78
American Revolution, 108
Amsterdam, 21–22, 147, 159, 160
anarchists, 85, 86, 92
Andalusia, 11, 156–57, 200, 206, 207, 208, 209, 226
Anglicans, 152
Anidjar, Gil, 210
Anthony, Susan B., 85
Antioch, 144
antisemitism. *See* Jews
Arab Americans, 176
Arab European League, 35
Arabia, 144

Arabic, 126, 163, 170
Arabs, 124, 182, 197; and Abu Ghraib, 76, 77–79; and Amador, 77–78; and Chabon, 209; as enemy of Europe, 148; and Guantánamo, 189; and Karpinski, 78; and music, 203; opposition to fascism, 168–70; sexual humiliation of, 78–79
Arab Socialism, 107
Arab Spring, 131
Arendt, Hannah, 115, 130, 142, 178, 233n1
Aristotle, 115, 127, 128, 136; *Politics*, 121
Armbrust, Walter, *Mass Mediations*, 200
Asad, Talal, 18, 19
Ash, Timothy Garton, 83
Asian culture, 197
assistance, duty of, 99
atheism, xi, 7, 8, 9, 141, 174
Athens, 148
Atlanticism, 150–51
Augustine, St., 151
Australia, 167
Austria, 167

Bachmann, Michele, 177, 227
Badinter, Elisabeth, 6, 227
Badiou, Alain, 63, 64–65, 116
Baghdad, 136
Bagram, 226
Bahrain, 118
Banna, Hassan al, 171, 172
Baptist Press, 16
Barak, Ehud, 89
Baru, *Road to America*, 204, 205
Bastille, 180
Baudrillard, Jean, 199
Bawer, Bruce, 57–58
bearing witness, 125, 143
beauty, 58–59
Bedier, Ahmed, 216
Begin, Menachem, 89
Beirut, 155

Belgium, 211
Belien, Paul, 36–37
Benedict XVI (Joseph Ratzinger), x, 141
Berlin, 162
Berlusconi, Silvio, 166
Berman, Paul, x, 82–83, 106, 168, 169, 170, 171, 172, 174, 224, 244n3; *Terror and Liberalism*, 165–66
Bernard, St., 148
Bethlehem, 144
bin Laden, Osama, 69, 176
blasphemy laws, 8, 17, 18, 38
Bluitgen, Kåre, 24–25, 29, 30, 32
Boies, David, 64
Bonnivard, Odile, 35, 224
border fences, 191
Botero, Fernando: *Abu Ghraib 53*, 183; *Abu Ghraib 66*, 183
Bougherra, Madjid, 211–12
Boycott Divestment Sanctions movement, 219–20
Breivik, Anders Behring, 3, 148, 176–77, 224
Brixton, riots in, 18
Broun, Paul, 177
Brown, Wendy, 122, 129
Brussels, Belgium, 160–61, 163, 211
Brussels Journal, 36
Buddhists, 119
Buenos Aires, 155
Bulgaria, 141
burka, 47, 216; in Netherlands, 159, 160; objections to, 90; and *Submission*, 47. *See also* veil/veiling
Burton, Richard, 59
Buruma, Ian, 20–21, 83
Bush, George, 74
Bush administration, 74
Busta Rhymes, 201
Byatt, A. S., 208

Cairo, 136, 206–7, 208; Queen Boat nightclub, 59
Calgary, 223–24

call to prayer, 43, 203, 204
Calvinism, 22
Cameron, David, 46, 227
Canada, 154, 167, 223–24
capital, 155
capitalism, 63, 142, 145, 146–47, 186, 192
caste system, 153
Castiñeira, Hajj Abdulhasib, 157
Catholics/Catholicism, 45, 116, 146, 147, 157
celebrity, 179, 180, 181, 186, 187
censorship, 34, 186
Center for Information and Documentation on Israel, 21
Chabon, Michael, *Gentlemen of the Road*, 96, 209–10
Chadaev, Alexei, 150
Chakrabarty, Dipesh, *Provincializing Europe*, 208
change, 86, 87, 88, 177
charity, 109–10, 113, 115
Charlie Hebdo, 15, 39–40
Cheikh, Sarah, 217
China, 39
Christians/Christianity, xi, 112, 123, 124, 155, 196; and Abu Ghraib, 183; and Africa, 151; and Amsterdam, 22; and aristocratic hierarchies, 144; bigotry against, 182; and Bluitgen, 30; and capitalism, 145, 146–47; and Chabon, 210; and conquest of New World, 145; in constitution of Europe, 4; critiques of, 9; and democracy, 144, 153; Eastern, 144, 148; equality of primitive, 144; and Europe, 141, 142, 143, 144, 152; and fascism, 168; fear of Islam by, 9; forced conversion to, 143; and free speech, 42; and Greece, 144; and Hirsi Ali, 51; Islam as danger to, 3; and liberalism, 208; and missionaries, 143; in Netherlands, 160; and Ottoman Empire, 149; rejection of enmity in, 174–75;

and Scandinavia, 153; and secularism, 8, 146, 208; toleration and dismissal of, 8; and Unamuno, 151, 152; and van Gogh, 21; and West, 8, 144; and Zionism, 183; and Žižek, 174
church, established, 8, 86, 224
citizens/citizenship: and *ahlan wa sahlan*, 126; American, xi, 41; in Denmark, 224; discrimination against Muslim, 101; and equality of Muslims, 104; Europe as shaped by Muslim, 141; French, 10, 108, 125; and Hirsi Ali, 51–52, 53; and Jewish question, 1–2, 142; Muslims as, 3, 125, 160, 224; and Netherlands, 22, 54, 160; and Qutb, 115; and religious charities, 117; and Roosevelt, 105; and Rushdie, 19; silence as essential to, 41
civilization, 101–2, 150; and al Farabi, 136; and Berman, 166; and Christianity, 144; and Empire of Osman, 149; and Europe, 149; and fascism, 164, 167, 168; and Hegel, 5; and Holocaust, 175; Jewish-Muslim, 174, 226. *See also* clash of civilizations
civil rights, xi, 5, 192
civil rights movement, 115, 130, 177, 192, 193. *See also* African Americans
civil unions, 64
Cixous, Hélène, "Mon Algériance," 227
clash of civilizations, 15, 220; and Berman, 167; and Calgary, 223; and *Charlie Hebdo* debates, 39–40; and conviviality, 195, 196; and Danish cartoons, 32, 39–40; as deflecting critical engagement, 227; and democracy, 227; and Earle, 202–3; as fact vs. polemic, 226; and graphic novels, 204; and Juha, 200; and local politics,

clash of civilizations (*continued*) 226; and media, 221, 227; in Old World vs. New World, 224; and "One Book, One Philadelphia" event, 206; and ordinary life together, 226; and Philadelphia groceries, 219; and Rawls, 95; and Russia and Europe, 150; and sex and sexuality, 55; and Teaneck, New Jersey, 222; and Wilson and Perker, 208. *See also* civilization
class, 205, 206, 227, 228
Cohen, Job, 160, 224
Cold War, 107, 119, 149–50, 191
colonialism, 104; and Berman, 169; and Europe, 155; and France, 62; legacy of, 98; and John Stuart Mill, 116; and New World, 144, 145; and Rushdie, 18
Columbus, Christopher, 144, 145
commons, the, 128, 129, 227
communism, 107, 151, 166
companionship, shared need for, 128
compulsory speech acts, 42, 43–44
Concerned Women for America, 73
Confederacy, 183, 193, 194
confessional impulse, 42
Confucius, 119
Connor, Ken, 16
conscience, 41
Constantinople, 123, 136, 144, 154
constitutionalism, 85, 154
Constitution of the United States, 3, 64, 85; Fifth Amendment, 41
constitutions, 86
conviviality, 195, 196, 205, 211, 221, 222, 226
Copenhagen, 224–25
Corbella, Licia, 223
Cordoba, 156, 214
cosmopolitanism, 5, 23, 40, 128, 134, 135; and al Farabi, 136; and capitalism and Christianity, 146; and Danish cartoons, 33; of Derrida, 125; and Europe, 149; and Muslim tradition, 137; and Rushdie, 17, 20; and sex and sexuality, 57; and Wilson and Perker, 208
Coulter, Ann, 37, 177
coyotes, 191
Cromwell, Oliver, 84, 85
Cromwell, Thomas, 85
Crumb, R., 204
Crusades, 84, 144, 145, 148
culture wars, 102
Curiel, Jonathan, *Al'America*, 201
Custine, Astolphe, marquis de, *Russia in 1839*, 150

Dabbagh, Wafa, 216
Dachau, 143
Dale, Dick, "Miserlou," 201
Danchev, Alex, 190
Danish cartoons, x, 6, 15, 16, 24–37, 39–40, 204. *See also* Denmark
Daston, Lorraine, 87
Davis, Joan, 222
Declaration of Independence, 178
de Klerk, F. W., 85
de Man, Paul, 168
democracies, diversity of, 133–34, 135–36
democracy, 86, 118–37; and Abu Ghraib, 183; and al Farabi, 133–34, 135–36; in Algeria, 119–20, 132; as belonging to past and future, 120, 123–24; and capitalism, 192; and Christianity, 143, 144, 153; and clash of civilizations, 227; and conviviality, 222; and courage, 93, 131; and Derrida, 10–11, 118–26, 129, 131–32, 134, 143, 144, 227, 241n8; in Egypt, 130–31; enmity as tamed by, 129–30; and equality, 105; and Europe, 122–23, 141; and freedom of speech, 34, 41, 43; and Greece, 123, 143–44; heritage of, 122–23; and Hirsi Ali, 51; and Iraq war, 179; and Islam, 119–26, 132, 225; and liberalism,

134; and lynchings, 183; and mass media, 186; in Middle East, 118; and Muslim question, 5; and Muslims, 137; and Muslim tradition, 137; and paganism, 141, 153; and Plato, 115, 133, 135; and Ramadan, 173; and revolution, 134; and Roosevelt, 105; and Scandinavia, 153–54; and secularism, 121; tendency to suicide of, 120, 121–22; and Unamuno, 152; and United States, 178; and *voyouterie*, 134

Denmark: and Afghanistan, 28; and Danish cartoons, 33; demand for Muslim adoption of culture of, 177; free speech in, 38; immigrants in, 59–60, 161–62, 225; Muslims in, 3, 59–60, 161–62, 177, 197, 224–25; representations of Muhammad in, 29–30; things as done well in, 59–60, 161–62; and West, 31. *See also* Danish cartoons

deportations, 219, 227

Derrida, Jacques, x, 146, 240n4; and Arab Spring, 131; and democracy, 10–11, 118–26, 131–32, 134, 143, 144, 227, 241n8; "Faith and Knowledge," 124; and Ibn Khaldun, 128; "Islam, the Other of Democracy," 226; *The Politics of Friendship*, 124, 127; *Rogues*, 122, 124, 125, 131–32; and Unamuno's Spain, 152; *Voyous*, 118–26

detention, xi, 3, 192. *See also* Abu Ghraib; Guantánamo; prisons

Devji, Faisal, 83

difference: and al Farabi, 135; and Derrida, 125; in Europe, 4; and Jewish question, 2; and suicide bombers, 90

DiIulio, John, 117

discrimination: in Great Britain, 17; against Muslims, 3, 17; and Rawls, 96, 97, 102; and Rushdie, 16, 18

Disraeli, Benjamin, 113, 142
dissent, 99, 100, 147, 186
domestic partnerships, 64
Doors, the, 201
Dostoevsky, Fyodor, 150
Dover Air Force Base, 184, 185
Dreyfus, Alfred, 166
drones, 194, 227
Du Bois, W.E.B., 7–8

Earle, Steve: *Jerusalem*, 202–3; "John Walker's Blues," 203
East: and Christianity, 144, 148; and Islam, 144
Eastern Europe, 165
economy, 103, 104, 107–10, 114–15
Edward VIII, 167
Egypt, 118, 130–31, 155, 169
Egyptian revolution, 68–69
Einstein, Albert, 142
El Cid, 148
El Fagr, 25
Elkader, Iowa, 220–21, 226
Elle, France, 52
Elshtain, Jean, 6
Empire of Osman. *See* Ottoman Empire
England, 153
England, Lynndie, x, 72, 73, 75–78, 80–81
English Revolution, 84
Enlightenment, ix, 174; and atheism, 7; and democracy and mass media, 186; and freedom of speech, 41; and free speech, 37; Islam as danger to, 3; and Jews, 1, 2, 142; and refugees from Reconquista in Netherlands, 147; rejection of enmity in, 174–75; and United States, 178; and veil, 65–66; and Žižek, 7, 174
environment, and Qutb, 106–7
Episcopalians, 152
equality, 3, 6, 10, 62, 94–117; abandonment of ideal of, 116; and charity, 113; and democracy, 105,

equality (*continued*)
132; in Europe, 4; of gender, 179; in Islam, 104, 153; and Jewish question, 2; in M. Knight, 199; and liberalism, 95; and Norse dominion, 154; and Qutb, 105, 106; and race, 179; and Rawls, 95, 99, 104; and United States, 107–8, 116, 176; and West, 45; and women, 45, 63, 75, 76, 80, 99–100, 106, 173

Erden, Semih, 217

eroticism, 59, 65. *See also* sex and sexuality

Esau, 5

Eteraz, Ali, 238n2

ethics/morality, 179; and Abu Ghraib, 183; and antisemitism, 2, 175; and Derrida, 125; and Muslim question, 2, 228; and poverty, 113, 114

ethnicity, 4, 101, 219

Euben, Roxanne, *The Enemy in the Mirror*, 240n22

Europe, 131; anti-Muslim sentiment in, 26; antisemitism in, 147–48; anxieties of, 23–24; and Arabic, 163; architecture and Islam in, 163; aristocratic hierarchies in, 144; and Berman, 169; and capitalism, 146; caste system of, 153; and Chabon, 210; and children, 64; and Christianity, 4, 141, 142, 143, 144, 146, 152; constitution of, 4, 7; and cosmopolitanism, 149; and Danish cartoons, 35–36; and democracy, 121, 122–23, 144; difference in, 4; as distrusting itself, 155; and Eastern Christians, 144; equality in, 4; and fall of Soviet Union, 165; fascism in, 167, 168, 170; free speech as limited in, 38–39; and Great Britain, 151, 154; Greeks as common heritage of, 132; hazards to free speech in, 41; and hooded prisoner photograph, 181–82; and immigrants, 156; Islam as shaping, 141, 142; Islam as woven into, 163; and Israel, 154–55; and Italy, 154; Jewish contributions to, 142, 148; and Jews, 141, 147–48, 155; Muslim question in, 4; Muslims and identity of, 156; Muslims as elected officials in, 224; Muslims as enemies of, 148; Muslims denied free speech in, 36; Muslims discriminated against in, 3; myths of origin of, 147; and Nazi past, 142–43; and Netherlands, 154; and Ottoman Empire, 154; and paganism, 143; and politics and shame, 141; Protestant, 146; as refuge for Muslim women, 6; religion in, 4; religious diversity of, 141–42; resistance to change in, 177; and Russia, 149–51, 154; and Scandinavia, 154; secularism in, xi, 4, 121, 208–9; sex and sexuality in, 4, 23, 55; and Spain, 154; and tolerance, 155; and Turkey, 154; twentieth-century wars of, 147; unclear boundaries of, 151–55; and United Kingdom, 154; Western, 210; women in, 4

European street, 155–63

European Union, 4, 11, 154, 166

evangelicalism, 183

evil, banality of, 187

extraordinary rendition, 179

Fackenheim, Emil, 233n1

Fallacci, Oriana, 6

family, 4, 45

fascism, 167–70; Arab and Muslim opposition to, 168–70; and Berman, 166; and Christianity, 168; and Derrida, 10; Egyptian opposition to, 169; in Europe, 167, 168, 170

fear, 86–87, 88, 91, 92

female genital cutting, 6, 47, 49, 50, 236n7. *See also* women
feminism, x, xi, 68, 69, 73, 78, 106, 166
Ferdinand and Isabella, 144
fez, 215
Finland, 38
Fitna (film), 40
Five Percenters, 202
Flaubert, Gustave, 59
food, 128, 218–20
Fortuyn, Pim, 54, 55–56, 159
Foucault, Michel, 42, 66
Fourest, Caroline, 6, 62, 171, 174, 224, 227; *Brother Tariq*, 173
France: abandonment of ideal of equality by, 116; antisemitism in, 148; Arabs and Arabic in, 125; and *banlieues d'Islam*, 3, 62, 125, 132, 134, 227; and Baru, 205; and Berman, 169; and Bougherra, 212, 213; and collaborators, 174; and colonialism, 62; defeat of democracy in, 123; and fascism, 167; and imperialism, 98; Islam as alien to, 125; Jews in, 62; *laïcité* in, xi, 3, 10, 43, 121; liberty, equality, and fraternity in, 10, 62, 116; Muslim dress in, 177; Muslim immigration to, 3; Muslim mayors in, 223; Muslims and Islam in, 125; Muslims discriminated against in, 3; neutrality of public sphere in, 3; and the popular, 135; racial hierarchies in, 62; riots in, 3, 132, 134, 227; and terrorism, 85; veil in, 3, 62; Vichy, 167, 174; women in, 177
Franco, Francisco, 168
Franken, Al, 37
fraternity, 3, 10, 62, 116, 117, 197
fraternity hazing, 74
freedom, 10, 117, 197; in Amsterdam, 21–22, 159; and Berman, 166, 167; of consumption, 21–22; and Guantánamo, 189; and Hirsi Ali, 50–51; and Kateb, 110; loss of, 227–28; and John Stuart Mill, 116; of press, 6, 186; of religion, 189; and sex and sexuality, x, 54, 55, 56–57, 62; and United States, 192
freedom of speech, x, 15–44; and Abou Jahjah, 35–37; and Belien, 36–37; and Christians, 42; and civic responsibility and wisdom, 33; constraints on, 42–43; and Danish cartoons, 33–36; and democracy, 34, 41, 43; and Enlightenment, 37, 41; European limits on, 38–39; and Fortuyn, 56; and Jews, 42; and liberalism, 43–44; and Muslims, 6; Muslims as enemies of, 15, 16; Muslims denied, 36; Muslim traditions of, 33–34; and Netherlands, 22, 160; and Qureishi, 33–34; and Ramadan, 33, 173; and right to remain silent, 40–44; and Rose, 25; and secularists, 42; in speaking truth to power, 40, 43; trivialization of, 34, 37; in United States, 38, 41; and unpopular opinions, 43; and West, 15–16; Western limitations on, 37–38, 39
free market, 107
Free World, 151
French Revolution, 84, 108
Freud, Sigmund, 142, 148
Friedan, Betty, *The Feminine Mystique*, 106
Friedman, Milton, 113–14
friendship, 127, 128–29, 132, 199
frontier, 128, 129, 132, 134, 206, 207
frontiersmen, 136–37
Frum, David, 177
fundamentalism, 73, 84
fundamentalist clerics, 73

Gandhi, Mohandas Karamchand, 85
gated communities, 191
Gay International, 60–61

gays, 6, 55, 56, 57–58, 60–61, 63.
   See also homosexuality
Gebali, Tahani el, 68
Geller, Pamela, 177, 217–18
genocide, 166
Géricault, Théodore, 59
Germany, 3, 38, 141, 162, 167. *See also* Holocaust; Nazis/Nazism
Gershoni, Israel, 168–69, 170
Ghostface Killah, 201
Gide, André, 59
Gilroy, Paul, 196
globalatinizing forces, 10, 123, 124, 131, 143–44, 151, 152
globalization, 71, 75, 149
Globe and Mail, 223
Goldberg, Ellis, 238n2
Goodman, Ellen, 70
Granada, 156, 157
Graner, Charles, 76, 77
graphic novels, 204–9
Grateful Dead, "Blues for Allah," 201
Great Britain, 146; and Berman, 169; constitutionalism, republicanism, and self-rule in, 154; and Danish cartoons, 34; discrimination in, 17; and Europe, 151, 154; and fascism, 167, 168; and Greeks and Romans, 154; and imperialism, 146; Muslims in, 197; and Rushdie, 16, 17, 18; South Asians in, 18–19; and United States, 154. *See also* United Kingdom
Greco-Christian forces, 143–44, 152
Greco-Christian tradition, 10, 123, 124, 128, 131
Greco-Muslim world, 123
Greco-Roman tradition, 123
Greece, 151
Greece, ancient: and Berman, 166; common heritage from, 132; and Derrida, 122, 123, 124, 144; and Great Britain, 154; paganism in, 153
grocery stores, 218–19
Gross, Michael, 97, 98, 239n12

Ground Zero, mosque at, 221
Guantánamo, 188–90, 194, 226; domestic issues confronted at, 179; Muslims in, 175; use of dogs at, 189–91, 192; veiled practices of, 184; and women, 78, 79–80, 81. *See also* prisons
guitar, 163
Gulf War, 165
Gyllenhaal, Anders, 34

Habermas, Jürgen, 155
halal food, 218, 219
Hameeduddin, Mohammed, 222–23
happiness, pursuit of, 6, 64
Harrison, Thomas, 84
Hartz, Louis, 4
Har-Zion, Ze'ev, 168
headscarves, 47, 158, 160, 215
Hegel, G.W.F., 2, 5, 115, 149, 197
Heidegger, Martin, 115, 168
Hendrix, Jimi, 201
henna, 215
Hersh, Seymour, 79
Herzl, Theodor, 155
Hessel, Stéphane, 116
Hezbollah, 168
hierarchical society, 117
hierarchical state, 226
hierarchy, 95, 101, 104, 105
hijabs, 43, 62, 68, 160–61. *See also* veil/veiling
Hijazi scales, 201
Hindus, xi, 119, 153
hip-hop, 201, 202
Hiroshima, 191
Hirsi Ali, Ayaan, 6, 83, 160, 227; *Infidel*, 47, 49, 50–52; and Muhammad as pedophile, 56; and Netherlands, 51–52, 53; and religion, 9, 36; and sex, 49–51; story of, 52–53; and *Submission*, 15, 47, 48, 49–50; threats to, 15
Hitchens, Christopher, 8, 52, 116
Hitler, Adolph, 165, 169, 170
Ho, Don, 201

Hobbes, Thomas, 92
Holocaust, 233n1; and bare life, 128; denial of, 143, 164; and free speech, 38; and heritage tours, 155; and late modern philosophy, 2; memory of, 164, 175; and United States, 178; and Western persecutions, 100–101. *See also* Germany; Jews; Nazis/Nazism
Holy Land, 144
homeland security, 71
homosexuality, 22, 73; and Abou Jahjah, 36–37; and Belien, 36–37; and European past, 24; and Fortuyn, 55, 56; and Gay International, 60–61; in Gulf states, 58; and Islam, 57; in Netherlands, 54. *See also* gays; lesbians; sex and sexuality
"honour-killings," 47
hooded prisoner photograph, 181–82, 183
Horkheimer, Max, 142
Hosein, Shareda, 216
hospitality, 127, 143
housing covenants, 191
human dignity, 117; and Kateb, 110; and possessions, 112; and Qutb, 105; sanctity of property rights, 112; and Singer, 110
human rights, 5, 6, 67, 105. *See also* rights
humor, 31
Huntington, Samuel, 119, 195, 196, 200, 202, 210, 214, 218, 226; *Clash of Civilizations*, 101
Hussain, Sena, 244n8
Hussein, Saddam, 57, 69, 165, 179, 180
Husseini, Hajj Amin al, 166
hybridity, 196
hypermasculinity, 6–7
hypersexuality, 23

Ibn Arabi, 156
Ibn Khaldun, 9, 128–29, 134, 136–37

Ibn Rushd, 9, 156
Ibn Sina, 9
Ibn Tufayl, 9
Ibn Warraq, 83
Ice Cube, 201
Iceland, 38
I Dream of Jeannie (TV series), 59
Ignatieff, Michael, 99
imams, and Danish cartoons, 25–26
immigrants, 137, 196; and Baru, 205; in Belgium, 211; in Denmark, 59–60, 161–62, 225; and Europe, 156; and European anxieties, 23–24; exploitation of, 191; and fascist parties, 170; in France, 3; illegal, 70, 71; and Malkin, 70, 71; in Netherlands, 55, 57, 158; restrictive laws concerning, 191; and Rushdie, 16, 18; in Scotland, 213; as suicide bombers, 90, 91
imperialism, 67, 98–99, 146, 183
India, 145, 146, 154
individuals, 55; and democracy, 132; equality for, 104; Friedman on rational, 113–14; and Hegel, 2; and Hirsi Ali, 51; and Ibn Khaldun, 129; and Kateb, 110; money as currency for, 111; moral status of, 117; and poverty, 109; and property as sacred and inviolable, 112; and *Submission*, 53; and terrorists, 89, 91, 92, 93
Ingres, Jean-Auguste-Dominique, 59
Inquisition, 41–42
Internet, 39
invisible hand, 110–11
IRA (Irish Republican Army), 18
Iran, 206
Iraq, 11, 165
Iraq war, 179, 185, 226. *See also* Abu Ghraib
Ireland, 153
Isaac, 4, 122, 124, 179
Ishmael, 5, 122, 123, 124, 126, 179
Islam, 90; and African Americans, 201, 202; as alien to republican

Islam (*continued*)
values, 125; American anxieties about, 181; and Bawer, 57–58; and Berman, 82–83, 165, 166, 167; and Bluitgen, 24–25; and Bougherra, 212, 213; Cameron on, 46; and Cixous, 227; as danger, 2–3; and democracy, 10–11, 119–26, 132, 225; and Derrida, 118, 119–26, 128; and East, 144; equality in, 104, 153; and European anxieties, 23–24; and European architecture, 163; Europe as shaped by, 141, 142; extremist, 3; and female genital mutilation, 236n7; and feminists, 68, 69; and Fortuyn, 57–58; and globalatinizing tradition, 10; and Greco-Christian tradition, 10, 128; and Gross, 98; and hierarchy, 104; and Hindus, 153; and Hirsi Ali, 51; and homosexuality, 57; and Huntington, 119; in Italy, 153; in M. Knight, 197–98, 200; and liberalism, 104, 208; and multiculturalism, 45, 46; and music, 201, 202, 203; and Okin, 45, 46; and queer sexuality, 57; and Qutb, 107; and Rawls, 96, 97–98, 100, 119; reform movement for, 84, 238n2; representation in, 24; and rights, 6; and Satrapi, 206; and secularism, 9, 120, 121; and Spain, 152, 156–57; speech as free only in attacking, 43; and Stjernfelt, 161; in *Submission*, 15, 47–49, 50; toleration and dismissal of, 8; and United States, 220–21; and West, x, 59, 82, 195–97, 204, 209, 214; Wilders on, 46–47; and women, xi, 3, 6–7, 45–53, 68, 100, 161; as woven into Europe, 163; and Žižek, 45–46, 78, 174. *See also* Koran; Muslims

Islamic Salvation Front (Front Islamique du Salut, FIS), 120, 132, 227

Islamists, 205
Islamofascism, x, 165, 166, 168
Islamophobia, 219, 225
Ismail, Khalil, 216
Israel, 11, 42, 154–55, 168, 178, 207
Istanbul, 123
Italy, 27, 153, 154, 167, 168

Jabotinsky, Meir, 168
Jacob, 4
Jamal, Arif, 97–98
Jankowski, James, 168–69, 170
Japanese internment, 177, 178–79
Jefferson Airplane, 201
Jerusalem, 124, 144, 148
Jesus Christ, 20–21, 183
Jewish anarchists, 5
Jewish philosophy, 10
Jewish question, ix, 1–2, 228
Jewish scripture, 124
Jews, xi, 123, 172, 196; and antisemitism, 2, 20, 21, 38, 147–48, 170–71, 175, 178, 182; as before and after state in time, 5; and Chabon, 209–10; and Derrida, 125; Egyptian support for, 169; emancipation of, 1; and Enlightenment, 142; and Europe, 141, 142, 143, 148, 155; fear of Islam by, 9; free speech of, 42; French, 62; and Geller, 218; and Hegel, 2; and heritage tours, 155; inclusion and emancipation of, 142; Islam marked as danger to, 3; isolation and exclusion of, 142; and liberal institutions, 142; and Marx, 1, 2; and Nazi past, 142–43; and Ottoman Empire, 149; and pogroms, 154–55; as political threat, 2; and Rawls, 100–101; and Reconquista, 147; refusal of, 171; and second-class citizenship, 1; and secularism, 8, 9, 142; in Spain, 152, 157; and Spinoza, 2; and Teaneck, New Jersey, 222; and United States, 4, 178; and Valéry, 147, 148; and van

Gogh, 20, 21; as victims, 210. *See also* Holocaust
jihad, 96, 106, 218
Jim Crow, 193
journalists, 184, 185
Judaism: critiques of, 9; and representation of God, 24; and Western civilization, 175; and Žižek, 174
Judeo-Christian tradition, 119, 131
Juha (band), 200–201
Juste, Carsten, 26, 31
justice, 40, 86; and economic order, 103, 104; Plato on, 192–93; and Qutb, 106, 109; and Rawls, 94, 95, 98, 99, 100, 101–2, 103, 104
Jyllands-Posten, 26, 28–29, 33, 35; "Muhammad's ansigt," 25

kaffiyeh, 215–16
Kafka, Franz, 142, 190
Kahan Commission, 168
Kalman, Maira, 96
Kamel, Bothaina, 68
Karpinski, Janis, 77, 78
Kateb, George, 110
Katz, Elie, 222
Kepel, Gilles, 125
Keselj, Marko, 217
Khazaria, 209
Khomeini, Ayatollah Ruholla, 15, 19–20, 84
King, Peter, 177, 227
Kjærsgaard, Pia, 32, 225
Klausen, Jytte, 26–27, 235n21
Klein, Joe, 70
Knight, Michael Muhammad, *The Taqwacores*, 197–200, 203, 214, 245n16
Knight, Robert, 73
Knox, John, 85
Kominas, 199
Koran: and Derrida, 126; and Guantánamo, 189; and Qutb, 106, 114; speech as free only in attacking, 43; and *Submission*, 47, 49, 50; and women, 61. *See also* Islam

kosher food, 218
Krauthammer, Charles, 227
Krueger, Alan, 89
Ku Klux Klan, 182, 218
Kushner, Tony, *Angels in America*, 178
Kuwait, 165

Land, Richard, 73
Larayedh, Ali, 100
Lau, Jörg, "Allah und der Humor," 234n12
law, 51–52, 85, 86, 102, 189, 190, 208
Law of Peoples, 94, 95, 99, 103
Lebanon, 168
Le Pen, Marine, 148, 205
Lerner, Michael, 178
lesbians, 22, 60–61, 166. *See also* homosexuality
Levellers, "Remonstrance," 41
LeVine, Mark, 203; *Heavy Metal Islam*, 200
Lévy, Bernard-Henri, 227
Lewis, Bernard, 96
liberal democracies, 99–100, 102, 103, 104, 150–51
liberal democratic institutions, 142
liberalism, 73, 142; and Berman, 166; and Christianity, 208; and democracy, 134; and equality, 95; and freedom of speech, 34, 43–44; Gladstonian, 94; and hierarchy, 105; and imperialism, 98–99; and Islam, 104, 208; and Jewish question, 2; and poverty, 112–13; and property rights, 112; and Qutb, 108; and racial and ethnic inequality, 101; and Ramadan, 173; and Rawls, 94–95, 96, 98, 105, 239n2; and United States, 178; as universal standard, 94–95
liberal order: defects and injustices in, 98; economic and social inequalities of, 98

liberal states: as decent hierarchical regimes, 101; and religious toleration, 101
Libya, 27–28, 118
Limbaugh, Rush, 37, 74–75, 177
Lindbergh, Charles, 167
Lindh, John Walker, 203
List Pim Fortuyn, 56
Little Rock, Arkansas, 193
Locke, John, 111, 115, 116
Logan, Lara, 69
loyalty oaths, 41, 43
Lukovich, Mike, 182
lute, 163
lynching, 75, 182–83

Machiavelli, Niccolò, 113
Madrid, 156
Madrid subway bombings, 86
Maher, Bill, 116
Mahler, Gustav, 142
Maimonides, 10, 156, 157
Malcolm X, 104
Malkin, Michelle, 69–70, 71
Mandela, Nelson, 85
Manolete, 213–14
March, Andrew, 240n22
Marhaba, 126
Marranos, 225
marriage, 6, 48, 52, 53, 64, 67. *See also* polygamy
martyrdom, 84
Marvell, Andrew, 147
Marx, Karl, 23, 142, 148, 150, 174; "On the Jewish Question," 1, 2
Mary Poppins (film), 85
Massad, Joseph, 60
Mather, Cotton, 85
McCarthyism, 191
media, 227; and capitalism, 186; and clash of civilizations, 221, 227; and democracy, 186; digital, 185
Medicare, 70
Merkel, Angela, 46, 162, 227
Mexico, drug wars of, 71

Meyerowitz, Rick, 96
Middle East, 11, 169, 202, 220
Middle Passage, 191
military, 86; and Derrida, 120; and Rawls, 102; women in, 72, 75–76, 79–80
military adventurism, 7, 67, 119
Mill, James, 98–99, 146
Mill, John Stuart, 98–99, 116, 146
millenarianism, 183
minarets, 225
Minneapolis *Star-Tribune*, 34
minorities: and Fortuyn, 56; and Rawls, 96, 99, 100–101, 102; rights to place in public square, 43
missionaries, 146
Mitford, Unity, 167
modernity: and Cromwell, 84, 85; as disenchanted, 208–9; and Qutb, 106, 114; terror as antithesis of, 83; and terrorists, 85; and Weber, 208; and Žižek, 174
Mohammed, Iman, 68
monarchy, 86, 92
money, 63, 64, 100, 116, 142; and Friedman, 113, 114; and Locke, 111; and Qutb, 107. *See also* capitalism; poor people/poverty
Montesquieu, Charles de Secondat, baron de, 154
Mormon Wars, 192
Moroccans, 54, 56
Mos Def, 201
Mosley, Oswald, 167, 168, 170
muhajibat, 215
Muhammad: characterized as pedophile, 56; and Hirsi Ali, 56; and Qutb, 107, 109; representation of, 24–25, 29–30, 31, 32; and Rushdie, 16–17. *See also* Danish cartoons
Muhammad I, 156
mujahideen, 84
mullahs, x
multiculturalism, 3, 45; as failure, x, 46; and Merkel, 162; Okin's and

Žižek's condemnations of, 46; and Stjernfelt, 161
Muselmänner, 175
music, 163, 200–204, 210
Muslim Brotherhood, 68, 105, 106, 170, 171, 173
Muslim dress, 214–18. *See also* veil/veiling
Muslim empires, 141
Muslim philosophy, 9–10, 132
Muslims, 123, 182, 196; and Abu Ghraib, 181; and Al Farabi, 136; in Algeria, 124; and Amador, 77–78; and Bawer, 58; in Belgium, 211; Berman's condemnation of, 82–83; in Brussels, 160–61; in Calgary, 223–24; caricatures of, 26; and Chabon, 209–10; and Christianity, 144; as citizens, 3, 101, 104, 125, 141, 160, 224; and cosmopolitanism, 137; and democracy, 137; in Denmark, 3, 59–60, 161–62, 177, 197, 224–25; and Derrida, 124, 125, 126, 131, 133; discrimination against, 3, 17, 101; as elected officials in Europe, 224; emancipation of, ix; as enemies of Europe, 148; and ethics, 2, 228; and European identity, 156; European sentiment against, 26; and excessive procreation, 10; fascism opposed by, 168–70; and Fortuyn, 56, 58; in France, 3, 62, 125, 132, 134, 177, 223, 227; and free speech, 6, 15, 16, 33–34, 36, 42, 43; and Gay International, 60–61; in Germany, 162; in Great Britain, 197; and Greek philosophy, 128; in Guantánamo, 175; as hostile to women, 67; and human rights, 6; humiliation of, 31; as hypermasculine, 6–7; as hypersexual, 23; identity of, 181; and immigration, 137; immigration to France, 3; and integration, 137; in M. Knight, 198; in liberal and social democratic states, 3; and liberty, equality, and fraternity, 3; marked as dangerous, 2–3; in Netherlands, 3, 54, 157–58, 160, 177, 197, 223; in politics, 221–26; as providential enemy, 174; and Rawls, 95–106; in realm of religion, custom, and tradition, 15; and Reconquista, 147; refusal of, 170–71; rendered abject, 76; and Rushdie, 16, 17, 18, 19; in Scandinavia, 161; and sex and sexuality, 6–7, 55; sexual humiliation of, 79; sexual slurs about, 22–23; as shaping Europe, 141, 142; in Spain, 152, 156, 157; and state, 5; as suicide bombers, 90, 91; and Teaneck, New Jersey, 222; and United States, xi, 3, 4–5, 6, 176, 179, 197; and van Gogh, 21–22; Western, 28, 197, 198, 203, 204. *See also* Islam
Mussolini, Benito, 169, 170
Mustafa, Farouk, 126
Mutazalites, 83
My Lai massacre, 191

Naar Nederland (website), 159
Najmabadi, Afsaneh, *Women with Mustaches and Men without Beards*, 58–59
Napoléon I, 108
Nas, *I Am*, 201
Nasser, Gamal Abdel, 107
National Secular Society, 16
National Socialism, 143, 164, 165, 166–67. *See also* Nazis/Nazism
Native Americans, 191, 192
natural world, 87–88
Nazis/Nazism, 115, 164, 218; and Berman, 166; and Europe, 142–43; and free speech, 38; and Germany, 167; and Vichy France, 174. *See also* Germany; National Socialism
Nenshi, Naheed, 223–24

neoliberals, 45
neo-Nazis, 167
netanyahu.org, 16
Netherlands, 41, 146; burka in, 160; Christians in, 160; Conservative and Calvinist parties in, 54–55; and Europe, 154; freedom of speech in, 22, 160; and Hirsi Ali, 51–52, 53; immigrants in, 55; mosques in, 157–58; Muslim conservatives in, 54; Muslim dress in, 177; Muslim mayors in, 223; Muslims in, 3, 157–58, 160, 197; refugees from Reconquista in, 147; secularism in, 160; sex and sexuality in, 54–55; socialism in, 160; women in, 158–59, 160, 177
New Model Army, 84
New World, 144–45, 224
New York Times, 25, 34, 52, 221–23
Nick, Saint, 144
Nietzsche, Friedrich, 66, 85; *On the Genealogy of Morals*, 188
Nigeria, 27, 28
niqab, 90, 215. See also veil/veiling
North Africa, 144
Norway, 3, 38
Notting Hill Gate, riots in, 18
Nussbaum, Martha, 208

Occupy Wall Street Movement, 122
Okin, Susan, 6, 227; *Is Multiculturalism Bad for Women?*, 45, 46
Olson, Theodore, 64
Oman, 97
O'Reilly, Bill, 216
Organization of the Islamic Conference, 25–26
Ottoman Empire, 100, 149, 153, 154, 163
oud, 163, 201, 203

paganism, 141, 143, 153
Paine, Thomas, 84, 108
Pakistan, 97, 165
Pakistani Americans, 176
Pakistanis, 28
Palestine, 11, 165, 219
Palestinians, 42, 89
Palmer, Robert, 201
Pamuk, Orhan: *My Name Is Red*, 209; *Snow*, 209
Pape, Robert, 89
parliamentarianism, 85
parochialism, 95
Patai, Raphael, *The Arab Mind*, 79
Patriot Act, 184
P. Diddy, 201–2; *No Way Out*, 202
Pearl, Richard, 177
people of color, 202
Perker, M. K.: *Air*, 204; *Cairo*, 204, 206–8, 209
Phalange, 168
Philadelphia, 205–6
Pipes, Daniel, 177
Pius II, 148
Plant, Robert, 201
Plato, 115, 128, 136; *The Republic*, 133, 192–93
pogroms, 1, 154–55, 166, 175
police, 86, 192, 193
political philosophy, 10
political theology, 8
politics/political action, 53; as founded in enmity, 128; and friendship, 128–29; and friendship vs. enmity, 132; and Hirsi Ali, 50–51; Muslims in, 221–26; and Netherlands, 22; and poverty, 117; and queer sex, 57; and sex and sexuality, 54; and van Gogh, 54
Politiken (Danish journal), 25
polygamy, 6, 7, 47, 67, 68. See also marriage
poor people/poverty, 23, 105, 110; aid by religious people to, 116–17; and Disraeli, 113; and Friedman, 113–14; and Kateb, 110; and Machiavelli, 113; as problem, 112–13, 114; and Qutb, 109, 113, 114–15; and Rawls, 99;

and Satrapi, 205; *shaabi* as, 135; in Spain, 145; thefts from, 112
pornography, 39, 72–74, 75, 179, 180, 181, 186, 187. *See also* sex and sexuality
Portugal, 151, 167, 168
possessions, 111–12. *See also* property
postcolonialism, 104, 208
Postel, Guillaume, *De la République des Turcs*, 149
post-Westphalian order, 5
Pound, Ezra, 167
Pratchett, Terry, 208
prisons, 3, 179, 180–81, 184, 191, 192, 226
property, 38, 64, 107, 108–9, 110–11, 112
prostitution, 21, 54, 80–81
Protestantism, 30, 84–85, 146, 238n2
Protestants, 183
public sphere, 8, 31
public square, 86, 126

Qahtani, Mohammed al, 189–90
Qaradawi, 244n3
Qatar, 147
Qureishi, Emran, 33–34
Qutb, Sayyid, 105–10, 116, 240n22; and economics, 107–10; and environment, 106–7; and poor people, 109, 113, 114–15; *Social Justice and Islam*, 106, 107

race, 38, 54, 62, 101, 179
racism, 172, 193
Rahman, Fazlur, 34
Ramadan, Tariq, 155, 226, 244n3; and al Ghazali, 83; and Berman, 171, 172, 224; and Danish cartoons, 33; and Fourest, 171, 173–74, 224; and integration, 171, 197; and M. Knight, 200; and West as *dar ash-shahada*, 203–4
Rancière, Jacques, 123
randomness, 86, 87
rap, 201, 202

rape, 48, 49, 67, 75
Rawls, John, x, 119, 171, 239n2; and Cairo, 208; and decent hierarchical peoples, 95, 101, 102, 117; and hierarchy, 226, 227; and Kateb, 110; and Kazanistan, x, 95–106; *The Law of Peoples*, 94–105; and liberal peoples, 95, 96, 98, 101, 102, 105, 226
Ray, Rachael, 216, 217
Reconquista, 147, 225
refugees, 82, 147
Reidy, David, 97
religion, 9, 116–17; and communism, 151; established, 38; in Europe, 4; and European anxieties, 23; and Hirsi Ali, 51; and inclusion of Turkey in European Union, 4; and Kateb, 110; Ramadan on laughter at, 33; and Rose, 31; and Scotland, 212–13; in state, 2; in United States, 208; and van Gogh and Hirsi Ali, 47; and Žižek, 174
religious toleration, 101
Rembrandt Harmenszoon van Rijn, 160
Renan, Ernst, 15, 195
republicanism, 125, 154, 178
reservation system, 191, 192
Richard the Lionheart, 148
rights, 193; Cameron on, 46; and Guantánamo, 190, 191; and Islam, 6; Muslims as challenge to, 5–6; to remain silent, 40–44; and United States, 176; and West, 104. *See also* human rights
right-wing talk radio, 219
rinnegati (renegades), 153
Roland, 148
Rolling Stones, 201
Rome, ancient, 122–23, 148; and Africa, 151–52; and cultures of conquered peoples, 151–52; and Eastern Empire, 154; and Great Britain, 154; Republic vs. Empire of, 144; and Unamuno, 151–52

Roosevelt, Franklin, 105
Rose, Flemming, 25, 26, 29, 31
Rougemont, Denis de, 150; *The Idea of Europe*, 148, 149
Roundheads, 84
Rousseau, Jean-Jacques, 83
Rowling, J. K., 208
Rushdie, Salman, 6, 15, 16–20, 39, 83; *The Enchantress of Florence*, 209; *Midnight's Children*, 16, 17; *The Satanic Verses*, 16–18
Russia, 149–51, 154, 155. *See also* Soviet Union
Russian Revolution, 150

Sabra, massacres at, 168
Sacco, Joe: *Footnotes in Gaza*, 204; *Palestine*, 204
Sadat, Anwar, 84
Saint-Just, Louis Antoine Léon de, 84
Salamanca, 145
Salazar, António de Oliveira, 168
San Francisco Chronicle, 52
Sarkozy, Nicolas, 46, 134, 205
Sarrazin, Thilo, 148, 162
Satrapi, Marjane, *Persepolis*, 204, 205–6, 209
Savage, Michael, 37, 177
Scandinavia, 151, 153–54, 161
Schama, Simon, 147
Schlussel, Debbie, 69, 148, 176, 224, 237n2
Schmitt, Carl, 115, 128, 168; *Roman Catholicism and Political Form*, 150
Scotland, 153, 211–13
Scott, Joan, *The Politics of the Veil*, 62
Sebastian, Saint, 183
Secret Trial Five, 199, 244n8
secular humanists, 3
secularism, 7–10, 116, 142, 155; and Bluitgen, 30; and Christianity, 208; and democracy, 121; and Derrida, 120, 121, 124, 131; and Europe, xi, 4, 141, 208–9; and Fortuyn, 56; and free speech, 42; and Jews, 2, 142; in Netherlands, 160; and neutral public sphere, 8; and United States, 208–9; in West, 8; and Wilson and Perker, 208
security, 5, 184, 227
security moms, 70, 71
self-determination, 23, 43
Selma, 193
separation, of church and state, 8, 9
separatism, 183
September 11, 2001, attacks, 42, 70, 86, 178
Seville, 156
sex and sexuality, 45–66; in Amsterdam, 21, 22, 159; and Arabs, 78–79; and clash of civilizations, 55; commodification of female, 63; criticism of Western models of, 67, 68; and Lynndie England, 76; in Europe, 4, 23, 55; and Fortuyn, 54, 55–56; and freedom, x, 54, 55, 56–57, 62; and Gay International, 60–61; and Guantánamo, 78, 79–80; and Hirsi Ali, 49–51, 53; and Islam, 57; Islam marked as danger to, 3; in M. Knight, 199, 200; and laws, 64; Muslim attitudes toward, 6–7, 55; in Netherlands, 54–55, 57; and politics, 54; and self-determination, 23; slurs about Muslim, 22–23; and *Submission*, 48, 49, 50, 53; and torture, 79; and van Gogh, 53–54; and veil, 63, 65, 66; as weaponized, 79–80; and West, 58, 227; women as marked by and reduced to, 80. *See also* homosexuality; pornography
sexual assault, 67
sexual harassment, 63, 106
sexual humiliation, x, 78–79
sexual license, 180
shaab, 134–35
Shabazz, Malik El-, 202
shahada, 125–26, 203
Sharon, Ariel, 168
Shatila, massacres at, 168

shebab, 131, 132, 202, 227
Sheikh, The (film), 59
Shema, 125, 126
Shi'a, 97
shock jocks, 37–38
Singer, Peter, 110, 116
Skokie, Illinois, 38
Skull and Bones fraternity, 74
slavery, 112, 116
slave trade, 191
Smith, Jacqui, 39
social contract, 94
social democrats, 45
socialism, 160, 174
social justice, 106
Social Security, 70
Society of Friends, 106
Society of Peoples, 94, 95
Somalia, 50
Somali tribal society, 49
Sontag, Susan, 72–73, 74, 182–83
South, 193, 194
South Africa, 154
South Asians, 17, 18–19, 222
Southern Baptist Convention, Ethics & Religious Liberty Commission, 73
South Park (television series), 57
Soviet Union, 122, 150, 165, 166, 167. *See also* Russia
Spain, 145, 148, 214; Andalusian past of, 156–57; Catholics in, 157; as Christian, Roman, and African, 152; conversion in, 152; and Europe, 154; fascism in, 151, 167, 168; and Islam, 152, 156–57; Jews in, 152, 157; and Reconquista, 147, 225; Unamuno on, 151, 152
Spencer, Robert, 177
Spinoza, Baruch, 2, 142, 152
Springer, Jerry, 34
Stalin, Joseph, 165
Stalinists, 45
state: and marriage, 64; and Muslims, 5; and Rawls, 96; religion in, 2; violence of, 4

states, 3, 95
states' rights, 193
state system, 5
Stjernfelt, Frederik, 161
Stolpersteine (stumbling stones), 143
Strauss, Leo, 10, 178, 233n1
Straw, Jack, 227
Streich, Daniel, 225
Stuart, Charles, 85
Submission (film), 15, 40, 47–50, 53
subprime mortgages, 191
suffragettes, 85
Sufism, 208
suicide bombers, 82, 89–93. *See also* terrorism; terrorists
Sullivan, Andrew, 217, 218
surf music, 201
surveillance, 3, 86, 184, 191, 228
Sweden, 38
Swedenburg, Ted, *Hawgblawg*, 200
Swiss People's Party (SVP), 225
Syria, 118

Tahrir Square, 118, 122
Taliban, 63, 165
Tasioulas, John, 97, 239n8
Taylor, Charles, 208
Teaneck, New Jersey, 221–23
terrorism, 82–93; altered expectations from, 88–89; and Barak, 89; fear of, 69–72, 86–87, 89, 91; and Islamic reform, 84; and Jewish anarchists, 5; as rational and reasonable, 89; and suicide bombers, 89–93
terrorists: anarchists of nineteenth century as, 85; as enemies of liberalism and modernity, 83; fear of, 82; Muslim, 5; and Qutb, 105
Tertullian, 151
Test Acts, 41
theft, 111, 112
Theresienstadt, 143
Third world, 151
Thousand and One Nights, A, 59
"Tiny Bubbles" (song), 201

Tocqueville, Alexis de, 4, 149, 171
Todorov, Tzvetan, *The Conquest of America*, 191
Toronto, 223
torture, 72–74, 79, 179, 181, 185, 188
totalitarianism, 165, 166, 167
tourism, 181, 187–88
Trail of Tears, 191, 192
tribes, 5
Tunis, 155
Tunisia, 118
Turkey, 4, 121, 144, 154
Turks, 148, 149, 162
tyrannicide, 84
tyrants, 115, 130

Umayyads, 214
Umm Kulthum, 201
Unamuno, Miguel de, 151–52
uncertainty, 87, 88
United Kingdom, 3, 94, 122, 154; constitution of, 85; and Europe, 154; free speech in, 38, 39; and imperialism, 98. *See also* Great Britain
United States, 85, 176–94; and Abu Ghraib, 179–88; as carceral society, 180–81, 191; continental expansion of, 192; corporations in, 64; as country vs. homeland, 70–71; and Danish cartoons, 34; and democracy in Middle East, 11; and Derrida, 118–19; electorate of, 192; as empire, 191; and Enlightenment, 178; and equality, 107–8, 116, 176; experiment of, 177–78; and fall of Soviet Union, 165; and fascism, 167–68; free speech in, 38, 41; and Great Britain, 154; and imperialism, 98, 177, 178; and Islam, 220–21; and Israel, 178; and Jews, 4, 178; and liberalism, 178; mega-churches in, 208; and Muslims, xi, 3, 4–5, 6, 176, 179, 197; property rights in, 38; republic of, 177, 178; and secularism, 208–9; and surveillance, 184; and Tocqueville, 149; and West, 149; West as centered in, 150; white supremacy in, 151; and WikiLeaks, 39
Universal Code of Human Rights, 104
universalism, 95, 146

Valentino, Rudolph, 59
Valéry, Paul, 147, 148
van der Veer, Peter, 21, 56
van Gogh, Theo, 6, 15, 16, 20–22, 39, 40, 158; and *Submission*, 47, 48; website of (De Gezonde Roker), 53–54
Vanneste, Christian, 36
veil/veiling, 6, 59, 61–66, 214, 215, 226; and Abu Ghraib, 184; in Brussels, 160–61; defense of, 7; in France, 3; legislation against, 204; and *Submission*, 47, 48; as text, 61–62, 65; and Žižek, 46. *See also* burka; hijabs; *niqab*; women
Venice, 149
Venner, Fiammetta, 62
violence: at Abu Ghraib, 181, 185, 188; and Bawer, 58; and Chabon, 209, 210; and Danish cartoons, 26, 27–28, 235n21; domestic, 67; at Guantánamo, 188; and Hirsi Ali, 50; Nietzsche on, 188; and Rawls, 96, 98; against South Asians, 19; state, 4; against women, 48, 49, 67
Vitalis, Bob, 200
Voltaire, 33, 149
von Braun, Werner, 168
Vote Hezbollah, 199

Walker, Kara, 204
Wall Street Journal, 34
Walzer, Michael, 98–99, 178, 233n1
war crimes, 74
War on Terror, 179
wealth, 22, 103, 105, 107, 110, 111, 112, 113, 114. *See also* poor people/poverty

Weber, Max, 208
Weizmann, Chaim, 155
West: and aesthetics, 58–59; and Berman, 82–83, 166; and Christianity, 8, 144; claimed superiority of, 79; conventions of, 29, 30; and Denmark, 31; domestic anxiety in, 4; economic justice in, 104; equality in, 80; ethnic and racial difference in, 101; and fall of Soviet Union, 165; fascism in, 167, 170; free speech in, 15–16, 37–38, 39; and Guantánamo, 189; hierarchy in, 227; and Holocaust, 164, 175; and imperialism, 98–99; inequalities in, 45; and Islam, 59, 82, 195–97, 209; and Judaism, 175; marriage in, 64; Marx on, 150; Muslim question in, 4–5, 62; and Muslims, 28; and National Socialism, 167; and Rawls, 94, 98, 100; as realm of enlightenment, 15; and rights of man, 104; and Russia, 149–51; secularism in, 8; and sex and sexuality, 45, 58, 67, 68, 227; survival of, ix; and Unamuno, 151; and United States, 149, 150; veil in, 62; women in, 67, 75, 78, 80, 99–100; and Žižek, 174
Western Europe, 150
white flight, 71–72
white supremacy, 38, 183, 193
Whitman, Walt, 131, 178
WikiLeaks, 39
Wilders, Geert, x, 40, 46–47, 148, 159, 160, 224
Williams, Juan, 216–17, 218
Wilson, G. Willow: *Air*, 204; *Cairo*, 204, 206–8, 209
Wolin, Sheldon, 134, 186
women, 58; at Abu Ghraib, 78, 184, 185; Americans as liberators of, 78; in Brussels, 160–61; Cameron on, 46; commodification of sexuality of, 63; in Denmark, 161–62; education of, 106; and equality, 45, 63, 75, 76, 80, 99–100, 106, 173; equal pay for, 63, 67; in Europe, 4; and European past, 24; and fear of terrorism, 69–72; in France, 177; in government, 100; and Hirsi Ali, 47, 48, 50; and Islam, xi, 3, 6–7, 45–53, 68, 100, 161; and Koran, 61; in liberal democratic regimes, 99–100; as marked by and reduced to sexuality, 80; in military, 72, 75–76, 79–80; Muslim, 6–7, 67, 68, 69, 78; and Najmabadi, 59; in Netherlands, 158–59, 160, 177; oppression of, 67; progressive empowerment of, 78; and Qutb, 106; and Ramadan, 173; and Rawls, 96–97, 99–100, 102; and Satrapi, 206; subjection of, 64–65, 68, 75–76, 80, 100, 102; in *Submission*, 15, 47–49; and *things* and *althings* of Scandinavia, 153; and Turkey, 4; violence against, 48, 49, 67; Wilders on, 46–47; in workplace, 106; and Žižek, 45–46. *See also* female genital cutting; veil/veiling
work, 106, 109, 116
World Cup, 2010, 211–12
World War I, 149
World War II, 149, 150

Xenophon, 130

Yemen, 118, 227
Yovel, Yirmiyahu, 152

Zahra, Leila, *Words of Women from the Egyptian Revolution*, 68–69
zakat, 103
Zangwill, Israel, *The Melting Pot*, 178
Zionism, 9, 154, 168, 219
Žižek, Slavoj, x, 7–8, 45–46, 78, 141, 174, 208, 226; "A Glance into the Archives of Islam," 174

The Public Square Book Series
Princeton University Press

Uncouth Nation: Why Europe Dislikes America
by Andrei S. Markovits

The Politics of the Veil
by Joan Wallach Scott

Hidden in Plain Sight: The Tragedy of Children's Rights from Ben Franklin to Lionel Tate
by Barbara Bennett Woodhouse

The Case for Big Government
by Jeff Madrick

The Posthuman Dada Guide: tzara and lenin play chess
by Andrei Codrescu

Not for Profit: Why Democracy Needs the Humanities
by Martha C. Nussbaum

The Whites of Their Eyes: The Tea Party's Revolution and the Battle over American History
by Jill Lepore

The End of the West: The Once and Future Europe
by David Marquand

The Muslim Question
By Anne Norton

With Thanks to the Donors of the Public Square

President William P. Kelly, the CUNY Graduate Center

Myron S. Glucksman

Caroline Urvater